Rum, Sodomy, and the Lash

Rum, Sodomy, and the Lash

Piracy, Sexuality, and Masculine Identity

Hans Turley

NEW YORK UNIVERSITY PRESS

New York and London

NEW YORK UNIVERSITY PRESS
New York and London

Library of Congress Cataloging-in-Publication Data
Turley, Hans, 1956–
Rum, sodomy, and the lash : piracy, sexuality, and masculine
identity / Hans Turley.
p.   cm.
Includes bibliographical references and index.
ISBN 0-8147-8223-X (cloth : alk. paper)
ISBN 0-8147-8224-8 (pbk. : alk. paper)
1. Pirates—History.   2. Pirates—Sexual behavior.   3. Pirates in
literature.   4. Homosexuality in literature.   I. Title.
G535 .T87 1999
910.4'5—ddc21   98-40141
                        CIP

New York University Press books are printed on acid-free paper,
and their binding materials are chosen for strength and durability.

Manufactured in the United States of America

10 9 8 7 6 5 4 3 2 1

Contents

Preface

As a child I never played pirate. Of course, like many children born in the fifties, I was terrified and fascinated by Captain Hook in Mary Martin's *Peter Pan*. In a sense, then, Cyril Ritchard's over-the-top portrayal of Hook ("What tempo, Captain?" "A Tango!") probably influenced my choice of subject thirty years later. But Christopher Hill's short essay "Radical Pirates?" was the main inspiration for this book. I had been engaged by Daniel Defoe's great pirate novel *Captain Singleton,* and I had been trying to make sense of what seemed to be almost explicit homoerotic desire shown by the title character for his friend and companion, Quaker William. Hill's essay examines radical Christians after the Restoration and imagines that they might have fled England and become buccaneers and pirates. Since Hill looks at pirates as dissenting from a Christian, economic perspective, I wondered if one couldn't look at pirates from a sexual perspective as well. This thought led to the notion that pirates may have been sexually transgressive, but more important, as the historian Robert C. Ritchie suggested to me, they were culturally transgressive as well.

By the time I started to research late-seventeenth- and early-eighteenth-century piracy, I realized that although many pirate histories had been written over the past two and a half centuries, not much use had been made of the primary sources that were written contemporaneously with the emergence of the great pirate figures. So began a long trip into pirate history and mythology and a realization of the pirate's importance as a cultural trope not only in the eighteenth century but in the late twentieth century as well.

This trip could never have been completed without the assistance and support of a number of scholars in eighteenth-century studies. First and foremost I would like to thank Professors Robert Markley and Thomas Lockwood. Bob read and reread the various drafts of this manuscript. Some chapters he can probably recite from memory. His comments and support over the past years have been invaluable and inestimable. Tom, too, read and commented on earlier versions of the book and restrained my tendentious impulses while helping me with my forays into archives. They provided the best kinds of mentoring and criticism.

Professor Lincoln Faller's generosity with his time and willingness to read and comment so fully on the manuscript at a number of stages have helped me enormously. Lincoln's enthusiasm is contagious. Professor Kathleen Wilson's illuminating suggestions likewise have affected the final version of this book. Credit for the title must go to Kate, *pace* Winston Churchill and the Pogues, but I accept responsibility for using it. Professor Joel Baer has shown great support for this project; without his help, I would never have found my way through the Public Record Office in London. Joel's essays about eighteenth-century piracy are impeccably researched and elegantly argued. The essays have been inspirations for my own attempts at pirate historiography.

Professors Henry Abelove's and George Haggerty's advice on earlier versions of this book pushed my thinking about queer theory and gay and lesbian studies. Professor Sara van den Berg gave me valuable comments as a reader on my dissertation committee. Professor Manuel Schonhorn's wit kept my work in perspective over the past several years. J. M. Coetzee and Dorothy Driver asked questions and pushed my thinking in different directions than I would have otherwise gone. In addition, I thank Professors Paul Alkon, Paul Hunter, Jean Marsden, Jerry Phillips, and my colleagues at the University of Connecticut, Kristina Straub, James Thompson, Philip Baruth, as well as my former colleagues at Texas Tech, particularly Ed Check, Sara Gadeken, Leon Higdon, Allen Miller, Cat Moses, Bruce Clarke, John Samson, and Don Rude. All of the friends with whom I discussed this book contributed to the final shape.

I could not have begun my research without the financial support from the University of Washington when I was a doctoral candidate. A predoctoral fellowship enabled me to begin my research at the British Library and the Public Record Office. Uli—librarian extraordinaire at the British Library—deserves special thanks for his suggestions and help with the library's collection. Thanks to Uli, not once did I order a book that was lost in the Blitz.

I have been lucky enough to have had fellowships from several fine libraries throughout the United States and Canada. With grants from the American Society for Eighteenth-Century Studies and the University of Texas at Austin's Harry Ransom Center and ASECS and McMaster University's William Ready Collections, I was able to complete essential research for this project. The staffs at both of these libraries were generous with their time and the collections. I would like to thank the staff of the William

Ready Division of Archives on Research Collections, McMaster University Library, Hamilton, Ontario, Canada in particular for their enthusiasm and for allowing me the use of the illustrations.

I thank the Johns Hopkins University Press for permission to reprint my article "Piracy, Identity, and Desire in *Captain Singleton*" in *Eighteenth Century Studies,* v. 31, no.2 (1997–98): 194–214. Chapter 7 of this book is a slightly revised version of the article.

A Dorothy Collins Brown fellowship and a Mellon Fellowship from the Huntington Library enabled me to use the Huntington's vast pirate collection over two summers, and to comprehend the immense resources available for a scholar of piracy. In particular, Robert C. Ritchie's advice gave me the confidence to carry on my research.

My editors at New York University Press have been wonderful. Tim Bartlett went beyond the call of duty during his last days there. Jennifer Hammer's advice and criticism were of great help. Many thanks, too, go to Despina Papazoglou Gimbel and a wonderful copyeditor, Rosalie Morales Kearns.

A special acknowledgment should go to Manfred Mickleson. Manfred made me see that I was on to something with my book. Although I have never met Manfred—and know I never shall—he is certainly an inspiration for me and many of my colleagues starting out in eighteenth-century studies.

Professors Joel Reed, Kathryn King, William Christmas, and Alexander Pettit have been valuable colleagues. But more important, their friendship helped me hold on to my sanity. Without them this book may have been written, but I would never have had as much fun doing it.

Finally, without Steve Arnold's support, nagging, friendship, companionship, and love, I would never have finished this project. Steve drew the beautiful illustration for the cover. My heart stands still, Steve, and this book is dedicated to you and to my patient, loving parents, Pat and Bill Turley.

Rum, Sodomy, and the Lash

Introduction

A Merry Life and a Short One

They were a queer lot—in their oddities perhaps even more than their abilities lies the secret of their fascination.

—Philip Gosse, *The History of Pirates*

In a famous passage lifted by many other pirate historians, Captain Charles Johnson vividly describes Blackbeard in *A General History of the Robberies and Murders of the Most Notorious Pyrates* (1724):

> [His] Beard was black, which he suffered to grow of an extravagant Length; as to Breadth, it came up to his Eyes, he was accustomed to twist it with Ribbons, in small Tails, after the Manner of our Ramellies Wigs, and turn them about his Ears . . . and [he] stuck a lighted Match . . . on each side [of] his Face, his Eyes naturally looking Fierce and Wild, made him altogether such a Figure, that Imagination cannot form an Idea of a Fury, from Hell, to look more frightful.[1]

Johnson depicts Blackbeard as the archetypical pirate. Like all the mythic pirate antiheroes, Blackbeard is both the same and more than the "typical" pirate who terrorized the seven seas.

The depictions of pirates in the eighteenth century can give us insight into how certain ideas of masculinity came to be understood as appropriate and "normal." *Rum, Sodomy, and the Lash* is not a traditional history of piracy per se; rather, it looks at the ways history and fiction merge in the representation of the pirate in the early eighteenth century and over the past three centuries. We cannot, I believe, recover the "real" pirate. However— and this is how *Rum, Sodomy, and the Lash* differs from other books about piracy—we can uncover the ways the periodical press, pamphlets, trial records, the confessions of the pirates, and other primary resources established the pirate as "*hostis humani generis*, the common enemy against all mankind." We can then determine how these early sources contributed to the pirate's fictional representations and make connections with other representations of masculine desire and individuality. What, in other words, made the pirate *hostis humani generis*? Was it only the threat he posed to the economy? Or did he threaten not only economic stability but also emergent notions of middle-class propriety? How did the pirate—a serious menace to mercantilism and trade in early-modern Britain—become the outrageously masculine antihero familiar to us through novels, movies, plays, and other outlets of popular culture?

The pirate lived outside the boundaries of conventional European society. He was not only a sexual transgressor, as one historian portrays him, or an economic or political transgressor, as other historians portray him.[2] *Rum, Sodomy, and the Lash* looks at the economic, cultural, and sexual deviance explicit and implicit in pirate characterizations through a wide-ranging body of primary material. The pirate's sexual ambiguity is especially intriguing. Depicted as hypermasculine, the pirate is the antithesis of the feminized sodomite. Yet, though he lives in a homosocial world, sexuality is left out of almost all depictions of it.

Rum, Sodomy, and the Lash explores how the pirate's threat to trade became merged with narratives that suggest that the pirate has "unnatural" desires to live in an all-male society, a culture that transgresses English norms in myriad ways. At the same time that this new representation of the pirate emerged, so too emerged a new representation of homoerotic desire. The pirate was an individual defined by his desire; he had an unnatural desire to live and carouse in a violent, transgressive homosocial world and to perform piratical acts. The sodomite was defined by his unnatural desire as well, but the sodomite explicitly desired to perform sexual acts with other men. The pirate threatened society because he embodied all kinds of economic criminal desires *and* cultural transgressions and deviance. Paradoxically, despite his very real criminality, during these same years the pirate came to be seen as the romantic antihero still popular to this day. The sodomite, on the other hand, became criminalized not because of any explicit threat to the economy, but because he posed a threat to sexual propriety.

Were the pirates sodomites because they lived in an all-male, transgressive society? The evidence for piratical sodomy is so sparse as to be almost nonexistent.[3] More significant for a cultural history of masculine desire, the homoerotic implications of the pirate's transgressive homosocial world are either ignored or overdetermined in popular and serious history, literature, and culture. My aim is twofold: to analyze how eighteenth-century writers perceived the pirate and to show how the pirate came to be portrayed as both the criminal and the romanticized antihero *par excellence* in the following centuries.

More broadly, as both a revisionist history of pirates and a critical analysis of the early novel, this book is intended to open up the pirate's fictional and factual representations in eighteenth-century literature to contemporary literary and cultural studies. I will not retell the biographies of the pirates here, nor will I rehash tales of famous pirate adventures. There are enough books that solidly relate this kind of history. Through extensive archival research of primary sources about the pirate as well as a critical look at the early novel, *Rum, Sodomy, and the Lash* is both a history of pirate identity seen through trial records, confessions, and eighteenth-century histories and a narrative of desire and masculinity in the early novel.

Depictions of Blackbeard show how the pirate became mythologized—indeed sexualized—throughout the centuries. Johnson's *General History* is, explicitly from the title, a history of piracy. Its genre, however, is harder to determine because Johnson embellishes his "history"—the "facts" that can be found in all the primary pirate sources—with fanciful anecdotes. The book then is as much "fiction" as it is history. Johnson focuses most of his attention on the "golden-age" pirates who sailed the seas between 1695 and 1725. Although the book is a "history"—and has been treated seriously as such by historians through the centuries—I argue that through his use of fact and fiction, Johnson began the process that turned the pirate into the romanticized antihero twentieth-century readers are familiar with.

For example, in Johnson's description of Blackbeard's physicality, he suggests that Blackbeard deliberately attempts to embody "a Fury from Hell." Blackbeard is not only "naturally . . . Fierce and Wild," but even adds to his "natural" fierceness. He ties long, slow-burning matches, or fuses, to his curls to emphasize his demonic appearance when he boards and plunders a ship.

Johnson's depiction of Blackbeard illustrates the extremes to which authors go to try to demonize the pirate.[4] He heightens the descriptions of Blackbeard's physical appearance, found in trial records and newspapers of the period, in order to emphasize Blackbeard's villainy. However, not all the pirates in the *General History* are simply "demons." The genre of Johnson's book is difficult to pin down because he makes up pirates within the metanarrative of a wholly factual "history." Some, like Blackbeard, are based on fact. Others, such as the aristocratic and idealistic Captain Misson—who started a democratic government on Madagascar—he makes up out of whole cloth as a way to criticize early-eighteenth-century government.

Johnson shows respect for Blackbeard, this most "frightful" of pirates. He depicts him not only as demonic, but as heroic at the same time. The following passage describes Blackbeard's final battle with Lieutenant Maynard of North Carolina:

> They were now closely and warmly engaged, the Lieutenant and twelve Men, against *Black-beard* and fourteen, till the Blood run out of the Scuppers in Streams; *Black-Beard* received a Shot into his Body, from the Pistol that Lieutenant *Maynard* cock'd, yet still stood his Ground and fought with great Fury, till he received sixteen Wounds, and five of them by Shot. . . . Here was an End of that couragious Brute, who might have pass'd in the World for a Heroe, had he been employ'd in a good Cause. (Johnson, 1:96)

A "couragious Brute": the phrase reveals writers' mixed feelings about the pirate; admiration is combined with fear and loathing. Blackbeard then becomes the model for modern perceptions of the romanticized pirate. He may be a "brute," but this brutality allows him to fight with almost super-human spirit. To the people of Charleston and the colonial and British governments in 1718 and 1719, he was a threat to essential trade along the southern Atlantic coast of the colonies. To Johnson, only a few years later, he is a "couragious Brute," whose vile actions are tempered by his dauntless acts-as-pirate, his heroic defense of his piratical world. If Blackbeard is not a "hero," what is he? He is defined by the conflicting depictions of his transgressive position as both a cultural antihero—courageous—and a dangerous criminal—brutish.

This paradoxical representation of pirate identity can illuminate our understanding of the early-eighteenth-century sodomite. Both pirate and sodomite are, in a sense, outlaws. However, the sodomite is a member of society—unlike the pirate, who self-consciously pulls himself *out* of society. The sodomite performs his transgressions in secret, afraid he will be discovered and ruined or, worse, condemned and executed. The sodomite is the feminized, effeminate sexual criminal. Blackbeard, too, is a criminal, but his crimes are explicitly economic. On the surface, Blackbeard's sexuality is depicted as excessively masculine. His hypermasculinity precludes any suspicion that he might indulge in sodomy.

In the *General History*, Blackbeard's outrageous relationship with his men and one of his wives demonstrates the homoeroticism inherent in transgressive homosocial worlds. Johnson repeats the most famous story, which involves his "fourteenth wife": "His behavior in [the married] State, was something extraordinary; . . . it was his Custom to invite five or six of his most brutal Companions to come ashore, and he would force her to prostitute her self to them all, one after another, before his Face." (1:88). This story merges Blackbeard's violence with sexuality; it illustrates that "homosociality suggests a continuum of male-male relations, one capable of being sexualized, though where and how such sexualization occurs cannot be assumed a priori."[5] If relations between men can be sexualized, how can this anecdote reveal a piratical homoerotic? So the anecdote raises a question: What sexually excites Blackbeard? The violence that his companions show toward his wife or the voyeurism explicit in the anecdote? The homosocial world of the pirate cannot be defined as explicitly homoerotic. However, in one of the few instances of eighteenth-century depictions of pirate sexuality, the erotic specter raised here is curiously ambivalent. It is as if Blackbeard's sexuality has to be linked with violence and voyeurism in order to be depicted: in an unconventional world, conventional sex has no place. But neither can depictions of sex be too unconventional. On a continuum of homosocial behavior, violence and voyeurism are more acceptable to readers (and authors) than explicit suggestions of homoeroticism. Besides, pirates are too "masculine" to indulge in consensual sodomy.

Blackbeard—like all the famous pirates—changes from generation to generation. In a mid-nineteenth-century novel entitled *Blackbeard* (1847), the author transforms the same "Fierce and Wild" pirate into a peculiarly sensitive maritime marauder:

> The head of this strange being was covered with a crimson cap, and his countenance, might have been truly termed handsome, had not the lower part of it been enveloped in a mass of long black hair, which gave to its possessor an air of wild and savage ferocity.
>
> "What strange apparition is this," exclaimed the earl involuntarily, as this singular personage stood erect before him.
>
> "I am no apparition, sir," exclaimed the stranger, in a voice so finely modulated, that it might have been easily taken for a woman's, "but a substantial specimen of vigorous life, who kindly bids you welcome to the pirates' palace." (9–10)

In describing Blackbeard, this author uses diction similar to Johnson's: "long black hair" on Blackbeard's face gives him "savage ferocity." However, he also creates homoerotic implications in the pirate's representation. Here Blackbeard *looks* the part, but does not act the role of the "ferocious" pirate of legend. He is indeed "strange" for a pirate, represented in such a way that his villainy—his historical reputation—merges with his deviant femininity—a literary reinterpretation. Although he *sounds* and *appears* deviant or "strange," he calls himself "a substantial specimen of vigorous life." The tension between his appearance (hypermasculine), his voice (feminine), and his self-description makes his sexuality both ambiguous and suggestive. In other words, does this incarnation of Blackbeard have "feminine" or "masculine" sexual desires?

Two hundred and fifty years later, in a "serious" biography written in 1974, Blackbeard is transformed from a voyeuristic villain into a sort of hairy Hugh Hefner: "Few pirates treated women or girls with greater respect than he. . . . He would not let a girl serve him a drink; he preferred to serve the drink to the girl."[6] Here Blackbeard's transformation into a gentleman is absurd, given the pirate's prior depictions and how we imagine the pirate in our mind's eye. If a pirate like Blackbeard can go through such incarnations—brute, effeminate marauder, gentleman with impeccable manners—it is not surprising that an examination of other representations of the pirate figure through the last three centuries demonstrates the tensions in depictions of pirate masculinity and sexuality.

I shall not make claims that the pirate was a sodomite and that pirate ships were rife with buggery. What interests me instead is the way pirates have been eroticized through the past centuries. We can see this process by examining the way pirate tales change through the last three centuries. Almost all pirate histories, popular and academic, focus on piracy's "golden years" and tell the same stories over and over. We are familiar with at least the names, if not the exploits, of larger-than-life personalities such as Blackbeard, Captain Kidd, and Captain Avery. Pirate history is narrowly focused on personalities because there are few records that allow us to reconstruct pirate life. "Parish registers, censuses, and tax lists are of no use in studying a population that existed at the fringes of, or even beyond, settled societies," writes one maritime historian. "As a result, the social history of the pirates remains almost a void."[7] Unfortunately for the cultural historian, this observation is correct. We are left with only one side of the story: eighteenth-century narratives that sensationalize and demonize the pirates. We read and thrill to tales of violence, tales of bloodthirsty, lusty villains who take no quarter, slit throats without compunction, and throw their victims overboard. But with readerly inconsistency we admire the pirates for their individuality, their success, their great wealth. Thus "serious" books retell these stories and embellish them with rumors of buried treasure, cryptic maps, and exaggerated ideas of plunder. I am not sure that the "reality" of the pirates, their day-to-day social existence, is something readers want to know. These larger-than-life figures remain legendary precisely because there is no "truth" that can be determined, as changing representations of Blackbeard show. The legend and the reality are woven into a fabric impossible to unravel. However, the *way* this fabric is woven can be examined.

All the great pirates will make an appearance in the following chapters. No book that focuses on pirates and pirate literature can neglect the famous personalities whose names still resonate three hundred years after the pirate's golden age. In the first chapter, though, we shall look at how life at sea was depicted by early-eighteenth-century writers and perceived by early-eighteenth-century readers. By closely examining the often dangerous life of the ordinary seaman, we can understand why sailors decided to "go on the account," or turn pirate. In chapter 2 I shall carefully define the differences between buccaneers, privateers, and pirates. Then I shall develop the concept of the "piratical subject" as a way to make sense of why the pirate was both feared and admired by eighteenth-century writers. The "piratical subject" is my term for the merging of the legally defined pirate—*hostis humani generis* or homo economicus—and the culturally revered pirate, a hypermasculine, transgressive, desiring subject. Through historical and fictional representations of the pirate, these two depictions merged into the antihero—the piratical subject—beloved by generations of readers.

In chapter 3 I shall examine how the ephemeral press constructed the pirate figure in the early eighteenth century. We shall look closely at the primary sources: the trial records and pirate confessions. I will show that our own perception of the pirate can be traced to these earlier sources. Chapter 4 builds on these analyses and looks at changing depictions of the legendary Captain Avery. Avery captured the public's imagination when he seized the Great Mogul's treasure-laden ship in the 1690s, supposedly kidnapped and married the Great Mogul's granddaughter, and created a pirate republic on the island of Madagascar. Avery's career illustrates the ways the pirate became heroicized despite his very real threat to eighteenth-century merchant shipping.

Chapters 5 and 6 are a close reading and analysis of *A General History of the . . . Pyrates*, the most influential pirate book ever written. Despite its importance to later pirate historians, it has never been given its due as a work of literature in its own right. Daniel Defoe was given attribution as Captain Johnson in the 1930s. In the last ten years, that attribution has been under considerable doubt.[8] However, whether or not Defoe wrote the *Gen-*

eral History is, I believe, beside the point for *Rum, Sodomy, and the Lash*. The fact remains that the *General History*'s importance to pirate history is inestimable and reflects early-eighteenth-century ideas about the pirate.

Coincidentally enough, the age of the pirates coincided with the period in which Defoe was most prolific. However, because there is much doubt that Defoe actually wrote the *General History*, I shall consider it to be Captain Charles Johnson's work. "Captain Johnson" is, of course, simply a name to attach to the book for convenience. This book—so important to pirate and maritime studies—has been ignored as a literary text. But as I here argue, the *General History* gives us significant insight into how the pirate came to be represented as both archcriminal and antihero; the book is also important in helping us understand modern ideas of masculinity, masculine desire, and male identity.

In the last two chapters I shall examine Defoe's *Captain Singleton* (1720) as well as *Robinson Crusoe* and its two sequels (1719–20). As the sheer quantity of Defoe criticism demonstrates, in particular scholarship about *Robinson Crusoe*, it is hard to overstate Defoe's importance to the history of the English novel and his influence on our notions of the "modern" individual. Since *Robinson Crusoe* was published in 1719, the title character has had an iconic status in Anglo-American and European culture. Despite Defoe's prominence in studies that examine the history of the novel, the analysis of his contributions to the novel's origins and perceptions of early-modern identity has been remarkably narrow.

The Defoe novel, critical reasoning goes, begins to work out newly emergent definitions of bourgeois sexual and economic desire that later authors refine and complicate. Although I agree with this general historical claim, I want to suggest an alternative tradition for the novel and for Defoe's place in a cultural history of masculinity. I do this by emphasizing the transgressive nature of economic and sexual desire and their sites within religious and political ideology in both well-known and less-familiar fictional works by Defoe. The pirate figure—the ultimate outsider in early-eighteenth-century culture—is the place where I begin this investigation. In these novels, Defoe pulled together all the contradictory representations of the pirate. Defoe's fictional protagonists—read alongside representations of the "real" pirates discussed in previous chapters—are the key to our conception of the romantic antihero. His heroes are among the early-modern archetypes for our notions of individuality and masculine desire. At the same time, though, these heroes and antiheroes push the boundaries of what counts as nondeviant masculinity. Indeed, Defoe ends *Captain Singleton* as a celebration of the affectionate—and implicitly homoerotic—relationship between two men.

Because of the deviant homosocial world of the pirate, piracy and implicit homoerotic desire go hand in hand. I am not making overdetermined assertions. I am arguing that the literary and historical representations of the pirate are rife with homoerotic imagery, and that imagery infects our conceptions of the pirate. Think of Captain Hook and the Lost Boys, Long John Silver and Jim, ad infinitum, through John Belushi's queer pirate on *Saturday Night Live* and R. Crumb's outrageous fellator Captain Pissgums.

In *Treasure Island,* Jim the narrator suggests the appeal of the pirate: "His stories were what frightened people worst of all. Dreadful stories they were; about hanging, and walking the plank, and storms at sea, and the dry Tortugas, and evil deeds and places in the Spanish Main."[9] Over a century later, the maritime historian Marcus Rediker argues that "Pirates constructed that world in defiant contradistinction to the ways of the world they left behind" (Rediker, 267). "Dreadful stories" and a "constructed" world, violent acts and exotic places: fiction and history—like legend and reality—merge. An analysis of this merger becomes the means to understand how "identity" and notions of subjectivity are much more complex than a simple dichotomy of villain and hero, "heterosexual" and "homosexual." I will examine subjectivity—that enigmatic, impossible-to-define concept—in the early-modern era and show how the complex depiction of the golden-age pirate can make sense of changing notions of self, masculinity, and sexuality.

1

Life on Board an Early-Eighteenth-Century Ship

> I could not forbear Reflecting on the Prudence of those Persons who
> send their Unlucky Children to Sea to Tame and Reform 'em, which,
> I am well satisfied, is like sending a Knave into *Scotland* to learn
> Honesty; a Fool into *Ireland* to learn Wit; or a Clown into *Holland* to
> learn Breeding; by any of which Measures they that send 'em may be
> sure that instead of mending the ill Habits they have contracted, the
> first will return more Wild, the second more Knavish, the third more
> Foolish, and the fourth a greater Booby.
>
> —Edward Ward, *The London-Spy Compleat*

In an infamous case of a captain's brutality, published as *Unparallel'd Cruelty; or the Tryal of Captain Jeane* (1726), an eighteen-year-old cabin boy had the misfortune to sign on Captain Jeane's ship. At his trial for the young man's murder, the captain said that his cabin boy was "very naughty." He had stolen a dram of rum from the captain's quarters.[1] To the horror of the trial's spectators—and the lurid delight of the trial's transcribers and readers—Jeane showed no remorse for the way "That the barbarous Villain, *for no better he ought to be call'd* had whipped this poor Boy several Times in a very cruel Manner." The captain's "punishment" did not stop with the lash:

> after whipping [the boy], [he] pickled him in Brine; that for nine Days and
> Nights he tied him to the main Mast, his Arms and Legs being all the Time
> extended at full Length; that not content with this, he had him unty'd, and
> laid along upon the Gangway, where he trod upon him, and would have had
> the Men done the same, which they refus'd; by which being exasperated as
> thinking, which indeed he might very well do, that they pitied him, he kick'd
> him about as he lay, unable to get up, and stamp'd upon his breast so

violently, that his Excrement came up involuntarily from him; which he took up, and with his own Hands forc'd it several Times down his Throat; that the poor miserable Creature was eighteen Days a dying, being cruelly allowed Food enough to sustain Life, and keep him in Torture all that Time; that he was severely whipp'd every Day, and particularly the Day he died; that when he was in the Agonies of Death, and speechless, his inexorable Master gave him eighteen Lashes; that when he was just expiring, he put his Finger to his Mouth, which was took for a Signal of desiring something to drink, when the Brute, to continue his Inhumanity to the last, went into the Cabbin for a Glass, which he pissed in, and then gave it him for a Cordial; that a little, 'twas believed, went down his Throat; upon which pushing the Glass from him, he that Instant breathed his last; and God in Mercy put an End to his Sufferings, which seemed to cause an Uneasiness to the Captain for not continuing longer. (4–6)

Asked why he punished the cabin boy so severely for stealing a dram of rum, Jeane explained to the court that "he thought himself oblig'd as a Master, to correct a Servant for such an enormous Fault" (25), that is, breaking into his rum cabinet.

Jeane showed no remorse after he was condemned, nor could he see what the fuss was about: "He insisted to the last, that he could not apprehend it criminal in him to punish the Boy; and that his dying under Correction, was the Lad's Misfortune, but not a Crime chargeable upon him" (22). Indeed, before he was executed Jeane blamed his crew for being "rogues" because they turned him in to the authorities.

The captain was punished by a final irony at his execution. He dangled from the end of the rope for eighteen minutes before he died. "This might have mov'd the Compassion of the populace upon other Occasions," the narrator tells us, "but now it only serv'd to put them upon recollecting the disproportion between the time he suffer'd, and the eighteen Days in which he had kept the poor Creature in Torment for whom he suffer'd" (33–34). Indeed, the spectators did nothing to hasten Jeane's death: "He was left to die, as might happen, without that Assistance, from either the People or the Executioner, which is usual; none gave him one friendly Blow to help him out of his Pain, or even so much as pull'd him by his Legs, to hasten his end" (33).

Although sensational and lurid, *Unparallel'd Cruelty* is germane for a couple of reasons. First, in its over-the-top way, the description of the cabin boy's "discipline" shows how a captain could abuse his power on board ship. Even though the pamphlet might be an exaggeration (and Captain Jeane was obviously mentally unbalanced), it still demonstrates the remarkable discipline a crew was forced to put up with.[2] The lash was the usual punishment for sailors. "Pickling"—or rubbing salt in the wounds after the whipping to promote healing—provided an extra layer of discipline. Both whipping and pickling were accepted by crews as part of life on board a ship. But obviously Captain Jeane's punishment of his cabin boy goes beyond mere discipline and the use of the lash. And what did the cabin boy do? Steal a dram of rum.

The anonymous narrator depicts a sadistic captain who derives pleasure from torturing young boys. Furthermore, the description of Jeane's usage of the boy is pornographic in its attention to sadistic details. Traces of homoeroticism intrude into this narrative, albeit a displaced homoeroticism that substitutes violence for sex. Indeed, sodomitical rape seems to be the only violent act that the captain did not perform on the lad. This luridness demonstrates the difference between life at sea for a sailor and life on land for the landlubber. It is doubtful that the landlubber equivalent of a cabin boy—an apprentice—would have the same kind of punishment if he stole a dram of rum from his master. Or at the least, if the apprentice were punished in such a drawn-out, grisly way, someone would have put a stop to the "punishment." Captain Jeane, the final authority on board the ship, went to horrific extremes to "punish" the boy. Captain Jeane's cabin boy underwent his own "tryal"—for eighteen days—and the crew did nothing to stop the boy's torture.

In its hierarchies and its maintenance of discipline, the merchant ship or naval ship represented a microcosm of English society. However, if the restraints of social custom were unfastened, as they were here by a psychotic sea captain, there was little the crew could do. That the crew stood by and watched Jeane torture his cabin boy shows the reality of life at sea. The ship *was* in fact a microcosm of English society. The crew, taught to obey authority, was forced to watch and wait. They did nothing—nor could they, since doing so would go against the status quo—until they reached England and notified the proper authorities.

Captain Jeane's actions demonstrate the power a ship's captain wielded, and the lengths he could go before his crew might begin to think about mutiny. Why did Captain Jeane's men wait until they returned to England before they did anything about the cabin boy's torture and murder? For one thing, their inaction demonstrates the sailors' respect for or fear of power and their acceptance of their status as maritime laborers. More significantly, *Unparallel'd Cruelty* is a volume for nonsailors. Its shock value highlights the landlubber fascination with maritime life, a fascination exemplified by the glorification of the pirate figure over the next three centuries.

In the guise of a moral tale—Captain Jeane was, after all, punished for his crimes—the story conveys details of the cabin boy's torture with gruesome relish. As we shall see, the descriptions of pirate cruelty are recounted in equally delicious ways in the ephemeral literature of the era and by Johnson's *General History*. Captain Jeane's brutality is a microscopic albeit sensational look at the power held by a ship's captain, one aspect of maritime life hinted at but rarely addressed directly in travelogues by privateers like Woodes Rogers, William Dampier, and others. In its appalling, sensational way, *Unparallel'd Cruelty* probably confirmed for the reader the brutal life of the ordinary seaman.

Of course, the pirate's life was even more brutal. Moreover, the pirate's violence is part of his mystique. He lives in a society against the state, to use Clastres's phrase, an anarchic world to outsiders that actually has its own rules and customs.[3] For example, Blackbeard—perhaps the most famous early-eighteenth-century pirate—shoots his first mate Israel Hands in the knee and lames him for life. "Being asked the meaning of this, he only answered, by damning them, that *if he did not now and then kill one of them, they would forget who he was*" (Johnson, 1:99). Readers are not surprised at Blackbeard's unprovoked stunt because Blackbeard acts the way a pirate is supposed to act: with capricious violence.

In another famous anecdote, Blackbeard says to some fellow pirates, *"Come . . . let us make a Hell of our own, and try how long we can bear it"* (Johnson, 1:100). The "Fury from Hell" (1:100) and "two or three others, went down into the Hold, and closing up all the Hatches, fill'd several Pots full of Brimstone, and other combustible Matter" (1:100). Blackbeard sets the pots on fire, and the men stay below to see who can hold out longest in their "Hell": Blackbeard does, of course. Again readers are not surprised because Blackbeard is merely acting out appalling behavior in a piratical way.

When Captain Jeane insanely tortures his cabin boy, his violence repels the readers. Blackbeard the pirate forces his men to stay below, but he stays in the hold with them. He is, to use Captain Johnson's description, a "couragious Brute" (1:88). His violence—or brutality—repels readers but at the same time confirms his courage because he shares his crew's discomfort. Readers expect Blackbeard to be violent. Captain Jeane, on the other hand, is the captain of a legitimate merchant ship. He showed "Barbarity in the most perfect Degree . . . and all without so much as the Shadow of a reason for it" (1). And "reason" would seem to define the difference between the legitimate world of the merchant ships and the brutal, unreasonable world of piracy. If Captain Jeane were a pirate who tortured his cabin boy in such a loathsome way, readers would not be surprised. However, the early-eighteenth-century maritime world was not a society against the state. Indeed, its entire purpose was to support the state economically. It took a sadist like Jeane to expose the possibility for unwarranted violence in the legitimate maritime world.

Most sea captains, of course, were not insane and did not mete out the kind of sadistic punishment that Jeane did. And they were not self-consciously violent criminals like Blackbeard. Besides, harsh discipline was only one aspect of the trying conditions seamen faced on their long voyages. Travelogues—the published journals kept by explorers and privateers—were an enormously popular genre in eighteenth-century England. These books focus on travel and exploration and the novelty of the flora and fauna of the New World. But the books also recount the deprivations suffered by the privateers and their crews during their long voyages, and show that captains sometimes held only a tenuous grip on their crews' loyalties.

William Funnel was a mate on one of Captain Dampier's voyages around the world. The last line of Funnel's account of the trip sums up the perils sailors could face on such a cruise: "And on the 26th of *August*, 1706. after many Dangers both by Sea and Land, we happily arrived in *England*; being but eighteen out of one hundred eighty-three which went out with us. Finis."[4] *One-tenth* of the crew returned home. The rest died from shipboard accidents and drowning, disease and starvation, and violence. The numbers are horrifying.

Massive loss of life—whether by disease caused by bad food and worse sanitation or calamities such as hurricanes and storms—was not at all unusual on these long voyages, as eighteenth-century readers knew. In 1720 Mist's *Weekly-Journal* announced the recent arrival at Cork of a ship from Borneo:

> most of the Men that were on board her are dead, which was occasioned by the Scarcity of Provisions; their Allowance for some Time being less than a whole Biskit a Day a Man; of the rest that lived to come to Ireland, several died by the other Extream, so that there were scarce Hands left to bring her Home.[5]

This story is only one of many like it in the *Weekly-Journal*. On 7 December 1723, the newspaper printed "A list of Vessels thrown on Shore at Antegoa in a Hurricane on the 19th and 20th of Sept. 1723." It is a huge list of ships that were destroyed and the people who were saved. About thirty craft—snows, brigantines, schooners, and sloops—were lost in that hurricane. More than any other newspaper of the 1710s and 1720s, the *Weekly-Journal* focused much of its news on disasters at sea and the hard lot of the sailor. Readers of this popular newspaper were fully aware of the trials suffered by the ordinary mariner.

In *A Cruising Voyage round the World* (1712), the famous privateer Woodes Rogers describes the hardships faced in a voyage that circled the globe.[6] The book is perhaps best remembered because Rogers discovered the marooned Alexander Selkirk, generally accepted as a model for Robinson Crusoe.[7] But Rogers also brings alive the daily threat of accidental death that was matter-of-fact on long cruising voyages.

For example, early in the voyage, a sailor "fell suddenly without any noise from the Main-Top overboard" (24). Another sailor "fell out of the Mizen-Top on the Quarter-Deck, and broke his Skull . . . so that he died, and was buried the next day" (102). Later, the men are at work on shore "but having sultry hot, wet and unhealthful Weather, our Men being fatigued, they became so weak that they could not work very well at this new Imployment" (177). Although death could be sudden for the seaman, it could also be slow and painful, caused by shortages of food and water and the onset of diseases such as scurvy and the "bloody flux," an intestinal illness that caused severe diarrhea and great loss of blood. Rogers's crew is struck by the flux. After he and his two ships have been seven months at sea, Rogers writes, "if we don't get ashore, and a small refreshment, we doubt we shall both lose several Men" (122).

Rogers himself loses his brother to disease (159–60), and many more of his crew die on the long voyage:

> Finding that Punch did preserve my own Health, I prescribed it freely among such of the Ships Company as were well, to preserve theirs. Our Surgeons make heavy Complaints for want of sufficient Medicines, with which till now I thought we abounded, having a regular Physician, an Apothecary, and Surgeons enough, with all sorts of Medicines on board . . . but now we found it otherwise, and had not sufficient Medicines to administer for the Recovery of our sick Men, which so many being sick in both Ships, makes it a melancholy Time with us. (209)

Even Rogers, a seasoned sea captain, is not prepared for the illness that afflicts his crew. In his understated way—the sick men make him "melancholy"—Rogers acknowledges the perils that a long sea voyage entails. Over the next week, at least seven more men died (210–11). He eventually made it back to England, but not before his crew suffered massive losses, despite generous prescriptions of rum "punch." However, he got some reward for his perseverance: his books made him famous, and he was made governor of Jamaica, where he finally subdued the pirates.

Captain George Shelvocke, in a privateering venture a decade later, was not so lucky. In 1719 Shelvocke began a four-year journey that he later described in *A Voyage round the World by the Way of the Great South Sea* (1726).[8] Like Rogers's venture, Shelvocke's was plagued by lack of food and water and the accompanying illnesses and deaths of his men. Out of fresh water, "we constantly drank our urine," Shelvocke writes, "which, though it moisten'd our mouths for a time, excited our thirst the more" (351). Shortly thereafter, the whole crew began to sicken and die, "which was undoubtedly in the greatest measure owing to the quantities of sweetmeats they were continually devouring, and also to our common food, which was puddings made of very coarse flour and sweetmeats, and salt water instead of fresh to moisten them, and dry'd beef, which was partly destroy'd by ants, cockroaches, and other vermin" (434–35). Captain Jeane forced his cabin boy to swallow "excrement" and "piss." Captain Shelvocke and his crew were forced by circumstance to drink urine and eat "vermin." Indeed, drinking urine was not at all unusual when thirst got to be too much for the sailors. When the marooned sailor John Dean and his comrades were trying to reach some kind of civilization on Madagascar, they too had problems finding water and went to startling extremes to quench their thirst. They were forced "to piss in their Mouths . . . which accordingly they did, and then took Leave and set out on their Travel."[9] It is unclear, though, who pissed in whose mouth.

In the most vivid of all the descriptions of a sailor's hard lot, a Dutch seaman—marooned on the Island of Ascension for buggery—describes in a "journal" his pain as he slowly dies of thirst: "At three in the Morning, went out to catch a *Turtle*, and found one, which I kill'd with my Hatchet, and fill'd a Bucket with his Blood: he had likewise a great deal of Water in his Bladder, which I drank all out, and was much better than his blood" (25). This seaman, in one of the very few early-eighteenth-century maritime texts that actually talk about sodomy, begins to hear the voice of his partner in crime (and lust), who had apparently died. At the same time, he runs out of water and begins to see and hear "Apparitions" of the devil. Whether this little book is authentic is doubtful; more significantly, it reemphasizes the horrors that were possible for an early-eighteenth-century sailor. Near the end of the volume, the marooned sodomite is dying from the bloody flux exacerbated by the lack of drinking water. He writes in his journal that he "drank some boil'd piss mixed with Tea; which, tho I was so very nauseous, revived me much. I made a Virtue out of Necessity, and in my deplorable condition thought it was good" (27).

The problems that vexed Rogers's and Shelvocke's voyages or John Dean and his comrades or even the delusional Dutch sailor were by no means unusual. Like sudden death, these disasters were the risks involved in long cruises through the South Seas or around the tip of Africa. Over and over again readers are confronted by a literal version of Swift's excremental vision. The horror for the readers lies not so much in the descriptions of ingesting vermin and piss, but in the recognition that these men *chose* their way of life.

Not only ship's captains but ordinary seamen kept journals as well. Unlike such privateers as Dampier and Woodes Rogers, these men have been forgotten, their journals lost. Edward Barlow is a remarkable exception. He may not be remembered by many readers, but his journal has been preserved by the National Maritime Museum in Greenwich. Barlow's extraordinary autobiography was published—in an expurgated form—in 1934.[10] It is a shame that this volume is out of print because it is an engaging and valuable document. His journal—as the title page says—covers "His Life at Sea in King's Ships, East and West Indiamen and Other Merchantmen from 1659 to 1703." He began his apprenticeship at eighteen on board the *Naseby* (christened, Barlow tells us, by "Crumbwell"), renamed the *Charles* at the Restoration (44).

Barlow had a knack of being at the right place during pivotal historical moments. For example, his second voyage brought Charles II from Holland to England in 1660. Barlow's journal describes his day-to-day life as Jack Tar until he retired at the extraordinary age of sixty-two in 1703. Along the way, Barlow was shipwrecked and marooned, was involved in mutinies, battled the French and Spanish, was taken prisoner by the Dutch, fought Tangier pirates, and had run-ins with Captain Kidd and William Dampier. And he is notably human in his private account of his life at sea. His complaints about food, the unfairness of his employers, or the evils of the press vividly bring to life the sailor's hard lot. For example, on one of his earlier voyages, Barlow describes the Christmas dinner the crew ate: "For we had nothing but a little bit of Irish beef for four men, which had lain in pickle two or three years and was as crusty as the Devil, with a little stinking oil or butter, which was all the colours of the rainbow, many men in England greasing their cartwheels with better" (68).

The bad food is not the only thing on Barlow's mind. He grouses about the unfair way the ship's owners hold back the crew's pay. "But when payday came," he tells us, "our commander said the owners of the ship would stop 3£ from every man out of his wages for goods that had been damnified and spoilt in the ship." The commander tells the sailors that it's their fault "for not storying them better and not taking care enough of them" (89). In the mid-eighteenth century ordinary seamen on board merchant ships were paid around thirty shillings a month. During wartime, pay was higher. The three pounds that Barlow lost was quite a bit of money.[11]

Barlow is particularly explicit in his descriptions of disease. "Several of our men [were] sick of the 'fflukes,' " he tells the reader, "the sea being an uncomfortable and bad place for sick men" (213). Their health is not improved by their rations, "having no other thing to eat and drink . . . unless we can eat a piece of hard biscuit cake, or a piece of old salt beef or pork, and maybe both stinking and rotten, having lain in pickle one year or two and nothing to drink but a little fresh water, many times both stinking and dirty, and yet cannot get half enough of it" (213).

Although the details about general conditions on the ship are vague, a reader can imagine what it must have been like to be ill on board a small vessel sailing around the world. Quarters were tight, and water was for drinking, not bathing, so the men were unwashed. Worse, to have the "fflukes" at sea, to have only a hole to shit in at the head of the ship—and to share it with your fellow crew—suggests just how vile sanitary conditions were on board. Captain Rogers describes how filthy the sailors could get on a long voyage. It was (and still is) tradition to dunk sailors into the ocean who were crossing the equator for the first time. Sailors would be hoisted "above halfway up to the Yard," and then dropped straight into the ocean "having a Stick cross thro their Legs, and well fastened to the Rope, that they might not be surprized and let go their hold." But there were practical reasons for dunking the sailors as well: "This prov'd of great use to our fresh-water Sailors, to recover the Colour of their Skins which were grown very black and nasty" (23). The problem of unwashed bodies was nothing compared to the unspeakable sanitary conditions on board a ship filled with sick sailors. The early eighteenth century was not, of course, a time that privileged hygiene. However, the "fflukes" combined with the awful food and sanitation created conditions that would have been horrifying for an eighteenth-century landlubber, as indeed they are for a twentieth-century reader.

Barlow describes another harrowing voyage, both for himself and some Dutch sailors he met in India in 1697, near the end of his career:

> One of our men died as soon as ever he came aboard, and another the next day, so that we had then lost forty men since our coming from England. But one of the Dutch East India ships that came in while we stayed, fared much worse, who had lost near a hundred men, and as many more sick and weak; for they carry more men out than English ships to supply their need for their ships sailing to and fro in India. (464)

Despite the example of Captain Jeane's crew, men could only put up with so much deprivation and suffering. Mutiny—or at least attempted mutiny—was common on these long voyages, and discipline was harsh if captains heard mutterings of revolt or were challenged by crew members for what seemed to be capricious orders. Barlow, for example, describes an incompetent captain who, he says, had become "so proud and scornful that we could give him no content. . . . some business arose between him and me, and some few words passing, he abused me very much." The captain, Barlow says, "offered to strike me and took a carpenter's adze, offering to cut me over the head" (357). Barlow was "turned out of the ship and put ashore" by the captain (358). Captain Kidd killed one of his crew whom he said at his trial was causing dissent on board his ship. Kidd "took a bucket bound with iron hoops, and struck him on the right side of the head, of which he died the next day."[12] Kidd was tried for both the murder—for which he was convicted—and the piracy for which he has kept his notoriety. Alexander Selkirk, perhaps the most famous disaffected sailor, was marooned by his own choice on one of the Juan Fernandez Islands, about four hundred miles east of Valparaiso, because he argued with his commander. Of course, Selkirk did not know that his ordeal would last for five years, until Woodes Rogers and his party rescued him.[13] Obviously, mutiny was a serious offense because it was a direct assault on the order—and thus the status quo—of a seagoing vessel. Captains had full authority to invoke discipline to keep order and deal with mutineers as they saw fit. The mutineers could be whipped, hanged, keelhauled, or, like Defoe's fictional Captain Singleton, marooned on an island.

Captain Shelvocke wrote his book as an attempt to justify his actions and to complain about his inability to quell his crew's mutinous mutterings. Woodes Rogers, a much stronger captain than Shelvocke, had his share of attempted mutiny:

> Sept. 11. While I was on board the *Swede* yesterday, our Men mutiny'd, the Ringleaders being our Boatswain, and three other inferior Officers. . . . We put ten of the Mutineers in Irons, a Sailor being first soundly whip'd for exciting the rest to join him. Others less guilty I punish'd and discharg'd, but kept the chief Officers all arm'd, fearing what might happen; the Ship's Company seeming too much to favour the Mutineers, made me the easier to forgive. Some beg'd Pardon, and others I was forc'd to wink at. (12)

Rogers was "forc'd to wink at" a mutinous crew on a number of occasions, but as this quote demonstrates, he was a savvy leader, and able to quash the problems.[14]

Shelvocke's voyage, on the other hand, was plagued by mutiny attempts from the start. At the beginning of the voyage Shelvocke's first mate—the second in command for his small fleet of privateers—began to "dispute the command of the ship" (6). Shelvocke's book, in fact, is a defense of his competence in leading a failed venture, written to counteract the charges made by his second in command, William Betagh, who also wrote a book about the experience. Shelvocke writes, "But the time may be near at hand when his villainy will be detected, and meet with its due reward, and my innocence be clear'd" (viii-ix).

Betagh—the unnamed "villain" who blamed Shelvocke for all the voyage's misfortunes—says that his book was "written chiefly to undeceive mankind in the spurious account of a voyage around the world, publish'd by captain *George Shelvocke*: which account is not only injurious to me, but is intirely the most absurd and falst narrative that was ever deliver'd to the publick."[15] In addition to seeing different perspectives of the same voyage, we can also see the tensions generated by long cruises, lack of supplies, and crew illness.

Halfway through the voyage, Shelvocke has his men careen, or scrape and repitch, the bottom of his ship on a deserted island. Shelvocke is shocked to discover that careening the ship is the last thing his crew has in mind. Instead of finding "every one employ'd" at making the ship seaworthy, "caballing and mutinying seem'd to be the only thing they had in view." "[I]t was so agreeable a subject to them to be continually opposing and tyrannizing over their Captain," he complains, "that I really believe for the pleasure of thinking themselves the equal to me, they would have contentedly have lived on this desart, at least, as long as I had lived" (Shelvocke 226).

Betagh implies why Shelvocke's crew held him in contempt and thus "caballed": "Nor is it so much to be wonder'd at, if we consider a commander of a ship in a far distant latitude, with unlimited power, bad views, ill nature and ill principles all concurring—I say, it's not to be wondered at whatever such a Man does, for he is past all restraint" (Betagh, 40). Betagh suggests that power in the hands of an incompetent leader turns into despotism. "Restraint"—keeping the status quo—is all that allows things to run smoothly on board a ship. Restraint is, of course, the one thing that Captain Jeane lacked. To drive home the point, Betagh compares Shelvocke's corrupted "unlimited power" with that of his lurid counterpart:

> A late instance of this kind is captain *Jayne* [*sic*], of *Bristol* who, in a most extraordinary lingering manner, cruelly starved and tortured his cabin boy to death; nor could his whole ship's company hinder it, tho' it was long a doing: however, when ashore the men were freed from that tyrannical power, and were bold enough to speak the truth, which hanged him. (40–41)

Whether or not Betagh is justified in his characterization of Shelvocke's incompetence is impossible to answer. Significantly, Shelvocke's voyage was a rousing failure, and the "gentleman adventurers" who financed the venture lost a considerable fortune. The quarrel between these two seamen demonstrates, however, the tensions that seethe beneath the surface on board a ship, and the problems that can arise if the captain's power seems ill-managed. If the ship is a microcosm of English society and culture, then of course the sailors will internalize the power that a ship's captain wields. On the other hand, ships sailed far away from the boundaries of English social structure. "Restraint" ran both ways. A ship's captain could go only so far before sailors might be tempted to mutiny.

Mutiny was a threat to the status quo, or the power held by the ship's command. However, sailors on merchant ships were also threatened regularly by impressment into the navy. Most historians decry impressment, or "the press," as cruel usage by the British navy, citing the often strident language of eighteenth-century commentators. *The Sailors Advocate* (1728), for example, condemns impressment:

> Yet not only our Trade, but Liberty also is in danger of being subverted, by a custom which is supported under pretence of necessity. This custom is the *pressing of Seamen*, a proceeding authorized by nothing but forced Construc-

tions of laws, or Unwarrantable violence. The *Magna Charta* says, *that no freeman may be taken or imprisoned, or be disseized of his freehold or liberties*[16]

By invoking the Magna Carta, *The Sailors Advocate* recognizes the seaman as a "free-born Englishman." The pamphlet suggests that whether on land or at sea, the sailor has the same rights as any citizen of England.

The anonymous author of *Plunder and Bribery Further Discover'd* (1712) decries corruption among those who do the pressing: some evil pressers may

> find another Man in the room of the Person so desired for private Consider-
> ation to be released; to perform which Condition, they seize upon such other
> Person in the Town or Parish to which they belong, without due Respect to
> legal Circumstances, and force him into the Service, to supply the Place for
> him, who, for Bribery and Corruption, they released.

The author goes on to compare the "wicked Practice" to "buying and selling Her Majesty's Subjects," or a semilegal form of slavery.[17]

In contrast to the narrators of *The Sailors Advocate* and *Plunder and Bribery* (as well as to many twentieth-century scholars), the maritime historian N. A. M. Rodger believes that these pamphlets overstate the evils of the press. He argues that in the early eighteenth century, impressment was looked on by government authorities as the most efficient way to man ships during wartime: "the political reality of eighteenth-century England was that the very forces which made the press so unpopular also made it inevitable."[18]

In other words, notions of "liberty" were so ingrained into the Englishman's consciousness that even during times of war, Parliament—or the central government—had trouble drumming up support for the navy. And because of these notions of liberty (and memories of Cromwell's military dictatorship), a standing navy or army was out of the question since either one was a threat to liberty should the monarch choose to use it against the people. As Rodger points out, the press "bore largely on an inarticulate and politically weak group," that is, ordinary seamen, and was the only means to ensure that the navy had enough sailors.

Nobody asked the ordinary sailors what they thought of the press, of course. Enforcers of the press, says Barlow, "will not believe a poor man when he tells them that he belongs to another ship unless the man whereto he belongs be in sight." To be pressed "causeth many a poor man to lose both his chest and clothes and several months pay . . . which is a very evil custom amongst our English one with another" (95). For Barlow, impressment meant losing the few possessions he had. For others, impressment could mean a lot worse: disease or even death.

Early-eighteenth-century pamphlets such as *The Sailors Advocate* detail the horrific conditions faced by pressed sailors. The narrator describes—in what could be exaggeration—what newly pressed sailors discovered when they were hauled aboard a guard ship to wait for orders:

> And what was still more discouraging, they found seldom less aboard the Guard-ship, than six, seven, or eight hundred at a time in the same condition that they were in, without common conveniences, being all forced to lie between decks, confined as before, and to eat what they could get, having seldom victuals enough dressed, which occasioned distempers, that sometimes six, eight, and ten, died a day; and some were drowned in attempting their escape, by swimming from the Guard-ship; many of whose bodies were seen floating upon the River, and one of them was drove into a Creek at Chelsey. The rest that survived were parcelled out, to be divided to each Ship that was ready to receive them, where they carried the sickness, that spread itself so as to infect our Squadrons, before they sailed on their expedition.[19]

"Free-born" Englishmen were held prisoner by their own government. Their conditions created disease, they drowned within sight of their nautical comrades, and they "infected" the ships before they even began their voyages.

In *The Sailors Advocate*'s sequel, the author makes many more points about the evils of the press. The navy, the "advocate" tells us, keeps "Seamen on board our Men of War for several Years together, by turning them from one Ship to another." Finally, all of this ill-usage was the major cause for sailors to have "turn'd Pyrates, or have gone into the Service of foreign Countries."[20]

Not all commentators were against the press. "Mr. Observator" wrote in 1702, "if we have not Men to Man our Fleet, we had as good have no Fleet: But a Fleet we must have at Sea, and we must get Men as well as we can."[21] Of course, his observations must be weighed against the perhaps overstated account in *The Sailors Advocate*, or Barlow's views on impressment: "His Majesty's ships taking pains to press poor men, but do not take that care to see they have their right which is due" (146).[22]

Worse than being impressed into the navy, however, was being taken as a slave by Sallee or Algerian pirates: "This week a Ship arrived in the River in 5 Weeks from Barcelona, and brings an Account, that the Sallee Rovers have taken an English Ship, having on Board 15 Men, and carry'd her into Sallee, and the Men up into the Country into Slavery; and that their Ship was chased by them, and narrowly escaped being taken. He adds, That the Garrison of Barcelona consists of French, Scotch and Irish."[23] In a fascinating book called *Barbarian Cruelty* (1751), the author describes what happened to the sailors on board a ship that was wrecked off the Moorish coast. Only half of the original crew of almost two hundred survived the wreck. Those who did survive became slaves: "In these our deplorable Circumstances, many of our People were for renouncing their Faith, and embracing the Law of *Mahomet*, in order, at that dear Price, to be eased of their Slavery; accordingly in less than a Month, Twenty-eight though with great Reluctance, resign'd to the Laws of that false Prophet."[24] Some of the crew managed to escape the worst kind of slavery (but not circumcision) if they renounced Christianity. Seventy years earlier, in 1681, the newspaper *Domestick Intelligence* printed several stories about women whose husbands were held as slaves in "Argiers." The wives "have lately made Collections amongst their Neighbours, and have to their no small encouragement found the Liberallity of several disposed Persons to exceed their expectations, Insomuch that it is not doubted but several of those to be deplored Persons will suddainly be ransomed, there being near 4000 *English* under the merciless Tyranny of those Infidels."[25] The sailors could buy their freedom if their families could afford a ransom. However, most of the four thousand Englishmen held were not officers, who had a little more money than ordinary sailors. Since they were unable to pay the ransom, sailors could be held as slaves for years, perhaps decades, before the English government took action. Of course, it worked both ways, and East African pirates could be captured by European ships and sold as slaves as well.

Slavery, disease, sudden death, impressment, high-handed captains: the sailor's lot was unpleasant at best. Yet the lure of the sea, the romance of the sailor's life, is part of Anglo-American popular culture. To understand the realities behind the romance—or at least the reality as men of the sea described it—is to understand why some sailors opted to go on the account, to turn pirate and be their own bosses. Rediker offers many reasons why sailors chose the pirate way of life. Certainly the international political instability of the late seventeenth and early eighteenth centuries can help to explain the attractions that inclined sailors toward "the brethren of the sea."

The waning of Spanish maritime power coupled with the expansion of Dutch, French, and English trade contributed to the upswing of piracy. While Spain still controlled the trading routes, piracy was less of a problem for other European nations than it was for the Spaniards. The buccaneers before the 1690s were more *hostis humani Iberia* than *hostis humani generis*. As Spain's control of the Caribbean waned after England's Charles II was crowned in 1661, the buccaneers were brought under control when they became too much of a threat to other European nations with interests in the

West Indies. By the end of the seventeenth century, piracy became an alternative for sailors who were eager for better living conditions, more money, and a say in their fate.

Outbreaks of piracy, historians tell us, came in waves. The temptation to turn pirate was dependent on the opportunities for employment and profit that warfare offered. When England was at war, there were jobs for sailors, either on privateers or with the navy. But profit was elusive for the ordinary seaman, and sailors had other worries during wartime besides profit, particularly impressment. Sailors on privateer vessels or merchant ships during war made more money than during peacetime.[26] Once the wars ceased, sailors faced either remaining idle or making smaller wages. Or they could turn pirate.

The Treaty of Utrecht, signed on 11 April 1713, ended the War of the Spanish Succession shortly before the death of Queen Anne. Peace between England and France meant that free trade stabilized at least temporarily. The opportunities to get rich through privateering came to an end. Even with this new stability, the sea was still a place of danger. Merchants and the big trading companies lost profit and sailors lost lives because of attacks by pirates.

Privateer ships during wartime provided chances for great profit. And both privateers and pirates signed "articles" that spelled out codes of behavior and how the booty was to be distributed. Captain Shelvocke's crew, for example, forced their commander to draw up new articles at least twice during the voyage around the world (34–43, 222–25). Their animus toward Shelvocke shows the fine line between privateering and piracy. Indeed, the second set of articles Shelvocke signed strongly implies that the sailors were about to choose a new captain, and thus turn pirate. Near the start of the voyage several of the men sent Shelvocke a letter claiming that "*we have very good reason to believe that if what we shall have the fortune to make this voyage should be carried to* London, *we should never receive half thereof*" (31). The letter was signed by the ship's carpenter, a gunner, a boatswain, an ensign, and five mates.

Shelvocke reluctantly signed the new articles because, he says, it was "not in my power to prevent what follow'd, though I us'd all the artifices I was master of, to destroy their project" (37). "Their project," of course, was mutiny. Shelvocke risked either angering the "Gentlemen at home" who funded the voyage or causing a mutiny by his men, who were worried that they would not get what they thought was their due. He put off signing the new articles. "But after some few days murmuring and uneasiness among themselves and no work going on," Shelvocke writes, "the ship's company came all on the quarter-deck to me in a mutinous manner, desiring to know my final resolution, saying, that I knew theirs" (42). Shelvocke—after some resistance—finally agreed to sign the articles, as he "thought it more advi-seable for the general good to sign, rather than suffer them to proceed in such a piratical manner" (43).

Shelvocke includes a copy of the articles, too long to quote in full. But the main point, the "Imprimis," states *"That our part of each prize we take, shall be equally divided, as soon as possible, after the capture thereof, between the ship's company, according to each man's respective shares, as born on the ships books"* (34). The articles that Shelvocke and the crew signed spell out not only the definition of "plunder" but exactly how that plunder will be distributed to the men, to Captain Shelvocke, and to the "Gentlemen" adventurers in London.

Shelvocke's articles only deal with the economics of the voyage. In con-trast, the pirate captain Gow and his men signed a list of articles that focused on rules for behavior without specifying any of the ways the plunder should be shared:

I. THAT every Man shall obey his commander in all Respects, as if the Ship were his own, and, we under Monthly pay.

II. THAT no Man shall give or dispose of the Ship's Provisions, whereby may be given Reason of Suspicion that every one hath not an equal Share.

III. THAT no Man shall open or declare any Person or Persons what we are, or what Design we are upon; the Offender shall be punish'd with Death upon the spot.

IV. THAT no Man shall go on Shore till the Ship is off the Ground, and in readiness to put to Sea.

V. THAT every Man shall keep his Watch Night and Day, and precisely at the Hour of Eight leave off Gaming and Drinking, and every one repair to their respective Stations.

VI. WHOEVER Offends shall be punish'd with Death, or otherwise, as we shall find proper for our interest.[27]

The articles suggest that Gow and his men have an actual society against the state. Even though they pulled themselves outside the status quo by declaring war against all mankind, they signed a list of articles that regulated their behavior, as Rediker has argued.

Regulated behavior is, of course, relative. Ships' crews, whether pirates or Jack Tar, were a wild bunch. The reality of life at sea belies romantic visions of cruising sailing ships or South Pacific islands with happy natives and happier sailors. The reality was that privateers were in it for the money, the navy enforced strict discipline, and pirate ships were crowded, violent places. The reasons for going on the account were many, but not every sailor turned pirate. Those men who did, however, entered a transgressive society and owed allegiance to no "gentleman adventurers" in England, or to a violent or incompetent captain, or to the cat-o'-nine-tails. A pirate was an individual in a homosocial world that made its own discipline and regulations.

2

Hostis Humani Generis
The Common Enemy against All Mankind

It may be said, that privateers in time of War are a Nursery for Pyrates
against a Peace. —Charles Johnson, *General History*

Lastly, the crime of *piracy*, or robbery and depredation upon the high
seas, is an offence against the universal law of society; a pirate being,
according to sir Edward Coke, *hostis humani generis.* As therefore he
has renounced all the benefits of society and government, and has
reduced himself afresh to the same state of nature, by declaring war
against all mankind, all mankind must declare war against him: so that
every community hath a right, by the rule of self-defense, to inflict
that punishment upon him, which every individual would in a state of
nature have been otherwise entitled to do, for any invasion of his
person or personal property.
—William Blackstone, *Commentaries on the Laws of England*

I will not act so disagreeable a part, to my readers as well as myself, as
to dwell any longer upon a subject, the very mention of which is a
disgrace to human nature. It will be more eligible to imitate in this
respect the delicacy of our English law, which treats it, in it's [*sic*] very
indictments, as a crime not fit to be named. —Ibid.

No matter if the sailor were a pirate, an ordinary seaman, a
buccaneer, or a privateer, he still lived in homosocial camaraderie with his
fellow sailors.[1] Unlike the pirate, however, these other seamen were bonded
together within the infrastructure of English society. The maritime world
replicated the values that could be found at home on land. One of the basic
differences between life at sea and life on land, of course, is that there were
few, if any, women on board navy ships, merchant vessels, or privateers.

Indeed, according to British naval regulations, the captain of a ship was "not to carry any Woman . . . to Sea."[2]

Even when women were not aboard, sailors were superstitious about the very idea of women at sea. The privateer captain Hacke regrets even *discussing* women on board ship: "there arose a prodigious Storm, which did continue till the last Day of the Month, driving us into the lat. of 69 deg. and 30 min. South, which is further than ever any Ship hath sailed before South; so that we concluded that discoursing of Women at Sea was very unlucky, and occasioned the Storm."[3]

Because women were absent from shipboard life does not mean that sailors were "homosexually" inclined. On the contrary, the social structure on board these vessels was part of the whole economic enterprise of England, and it would do little good to try to theorize a homoerotic paradigm for nonpirate sailors. If we imagine a piratical subject, however—a merging of the economic criminal and the cultural transgressor who "declares war against all mankind"—we should be able to understand the implicit link between homoeroticism and piracy. Pirates, in other words, were not bound by any social conventions except their own.

To make my meaning clearer, I will need to describe each of these categories of seamen. The buccaneer ceased to be a threat to Spain's colonies by piracy's golden age in the 1690s. The buccaneer differs from the pirate because he was an outlaw-made-nationalist hero. The buccaneer was heroicized because of his daring raids on Spanish colonial soil. Although condemning in its rhetoric, the English government tacitly accepted these raids because they strengthened the English presence by weakening Spain's claims. By the middle of the seventeenth century, the buccaneers were settled into communities in far-reaching outposts of the Spanish empire in the Caribbean.[4] Given their profligate ways, as Charles Leslie suggests, they ran out of money very quickly: "Wine and Women drained their Wealth to such a Degree that in a little time some of them became reduced to Beggary. They have been known to spend 2 or 3000 Pieces of Eight in one Night; and one of them gave a Strumpet 500 to see her naked."[5] As declared enemies to the Spaniards and the pope, but still Englishmen, the buccaneers moved both inside and outside English society. And women were always a part of the buccaneer mythos, as we can see from Leslie's quote, and as Exquemelin makes clear in *Bucaniers of America*.

The privateer—unlike the buccaneer—was a working member of society. A letter of marque issued by the king authorized him to prey on enemy ships during wartime. A privateer like Sir Francis Drake in the sixteenth century was an English national hero—though certainly a pirate to the Spaniards. Privateering was an accepted means of waging war throughout maritime history.[6]

Piracy and privateering were not the same for the ordinary seaman, though at times the dividing line could be very thin. Although Rediker's *Between the Devil and the Deep Blue Sea* focuses on ordinary seamen, he explicitly heroicizes the pirates from a Marxist perspective. He argues that their "experience as free wage laborers and as members of an uncontrolled, freewheeling subculture gave pirates the perspective and occasion to fight back against brutal and unjust authority and to construct a new social order where King Death would not reign supreme" (286). Rediker's purpose is to focus on Jack Tar—the ordinary seaman—and "to study the collective self-activity of maritime workers" (6). Although he celebrates the pirates' "free-wheeling subculture," Rediker's main points in the book make a distinction between "labor history" and "working-class history." Rediker argues that by the eighteenth century, "pirates had worked in the merchant shipping indus-try, and piracy was deeply imbued with the collectivistic tendencies produced by life and labor at sea" (107). He describes a radical displacement of conventional authority. The sailor-turned-pirate embraced "a way of life voluntarily chosen, for the most part, by large numbers of men who directly challenged the ways of the society from which they excepted themselves" (255).

Rediker makes the crucial point that the pirate "excepted" himself from society. The pirate was by definition, then, positioned as "other" both by himself and by his enemies. He is unlike, say, the British privateer with a letter of marque that enabled him to plunder French vessels. The privateer may "accidentally" become a pirate because peace has been effected with France. However, this accidental pirate has not chosen his "way of life voluntarily." But neither is the pirate in any way like the radical Christian buccaneer imagined by Christopher Hill in his essay "Radical Pirates?". Hill argues that the buccaneer's religious dissent enforced his displacement from English society. Unlike the buccaneers and the privateers, the golden-age pirates not only chose to live outside the parameters of social conventions, but as Rediker and Hill both suggest, *embraced* a life that challenged those conventions.

In "Radical Pirates?" Hill puts forward an imaginative and compelling thesis that argues that the disappearance of radicals from England after the Restoration has always been a problem without a solution for historians.[7] He suggests that historians look at the literature about piracy, particularly works by Defoe. These works of popular history and fiction disseminate iconoclastic ideas and depict a radical "reality" in the Marxian terms that Rediker describes. "Some pirates must have seen themselves as egalitarian avengers," says Hill. "How are we to explain the radical element in these pirate yarns or fantasies?" (167). Here, Hill wants to historicize the "real" pirates, yet he wants to include them with "pirate yarns or fantasies." He misses the connection between the pirates themselves—are they real "egalitarian avengers" or imagined fantasies?—and the authors who write about them: men such as Defoe and Captain Johnson, who mythologize the pirates for their own ideological purposes.

Many of the buccaneers in the Caribbean, Hill suggests, were social outcasts, free thinkers, and dissenters fleeing from English religious intolerance (172). Hill argues—correctly—that the authorities' tolerance for the buccaneers in the West Indies lasted only as long as free trade was impossible for the English (174). After the Spaniards lost much of their power in the Caribbean toward the end of the seventeenth century, the buccaneers became a nuisance to the English. The buccaneers no longer assisted in strengthening the English position in the Caribbean because they began to prey on their own countrymen's ships. They became, in other words, unambiguous pirates "at war against all mankind."

In a striking but persuasive movement, Hill thus connects religious dissent and economic transgression. He then examines Defoe's depiction of Madagascar—legendary seat of pirate "government"—and the establishment of Libertalia, a sort of communist society of pirates supposedly organized by the pirate Captain Misson.[8] Hill suggests that an investigation of Defoe's piratical utopian writings may help us "to understand how those on the margins of society adapted themselves to a world which seemed increasingly hostile" (180). In such biographies as "Of Captain Misson" in the *General History*, Defoe—or Captain Johnson—represents heroic pirates who self-consciously construct radical, democratic worlds in direct opposition to the monarchical governments of Europe. Captain Misson, for example, "propos'd a Form of Government . . . a Democratical Form, where the People were themselves the Makers and Judges of their own Laws" (Johnson, II:100). These articulate and passionate men declared themselves "at war against all mankind" because they were dissatisfied with the class distinctions that constituted their lot in life.

I want to emphasize that depictions of the pirate's glamorous life did not appear overnight with the publication of a single book. Although the privateer authors such as Dampier, Betagh, Shelvocke, and others included accounts of pirates in their narratives, the earliest sustained and complete history of the "golden-age" pirate is Charles Johnson's *General History of the . . . Pyrates*, reprinted many times since its initial appearance in 1724.[9] Four decades before the *General History*, however, John [A. O.] Exquemelin wrote *The Bucaniers of America* (1677).[10] The image of the fearless, bloodthirsty sea dog—the piratical "character" that subsequent generations of readers imagine—can be traced to Exquemelin's volume.

Because of the changing European power structures in the Americas, the buccaneer was almost completely wiped out of the Caribbean. By the time the first English translation of Exquemelin's book was published in London in 1684, the buccaneers were integrated to the colonial Americas not controlled by the Spanish.[11] Those buccaneers who were not integrated turned pirate. This "taming" of the buccaneer—and the basic difference between the buccaneer and the pirate—is best exemplified by the English government's legitimation of the violent and notorious buccaneer Henry Morgan, who was knighted and made governor of Jamaica during the 1680s.

Although the buccaneers faded as an important presence in the Caribbean, their disappearance did not mean the end of colorful maritime marauders. Only a few years later, in 1694, the "golden age" of the pirate exploded into popular consciousness with the exploits of Captain Avery. Avery was only the first of many celebrated antiheroes. He was followed by a legion of equally famous pirates such as Blackbeard, Kidd, and Bonnet. This "golden age" ended only thirty years later, around the time of the publication of the first edition and first volume of Johnson's book in 1724.

According to a recent popular historian, "A basic distinction between buccaneer and pirate was that the former carried the war to the Spanish only, whereas the pirate attacked and stole from all, and owed authority to none."[12] While correct as far as it goes, this definition ignores two crucial factors. First, unlike pirates, buccaneers did not necessarily begin as sailors. Second, for the most part buccaneers were northern European settlers who lived originally as hunters or poor planters on the distant borders of the Americas' Spanish empire. They subsequently found more advantage by pillaging the ships that strayed near their settlements. Not satisfied with the loot they plundered from stray ships, the buccaneers began to make incursions on isolated towns in the Spanish colonies. Finally, the buccaneers made more daring—and successful—raids on larger Spanish cities such as Puerto Bello.

The most famous of the buccaneers, acclaimed as heroes by their countrymen in Europe, epitomized the masculine heroic figures who fought the

Spanish with dashing bravery and almost inhuman ferociousness. These men were not the *hostis humani generis* represented by Avery, Blackbeard, and others, nor did they live in strictly homosocial maritime communities. More like sailors in the navy, they would group to battle, and then go back to their settlements and colonies to spend their booty on rum and women.

Exquemelin—who purported to have sailed with some of these renowned buccaneers—vividly recounts their dangerous, exciting exploits. *Bucaniers of America* was written originally in Dutch, and translated into English from Spanish in 1684. Given the unstable relationship between Spain and England, it should come as no surprise that the English translation of *Bucaniers of America* positions the Spanish in much less favorable light than the Spanish edition, entitled *Piratas de la america*.[13]

The printer or editor writes in the preface to an abridgement of the second English edition, also published in 1684,

> these Gentlemen [who were eyewitnesses in the Caribbean] were pleased to correct, purge and reform [the Spanish translation] of many Abuses and Mistakes, wherewith this Account was sullied by Self-interested Pens; so as Reader, you have here the History of the Buccaniers exposed open before you, and in a condition to undergo the most impartial View and Scrutiny.[14]

Here the translator tells the reader that the buccaneer will be represented impartially. This "impartial View and Scrutiny" means, however, that the buccaneer will be shown to be a brave fighter for English justice despite the inherent brutality of his identity as buccaneer. No claims were ever made by historians such as Defoe or Johnson that the pirate is represented through the "impartial View and Scrutiny" of his describer. Any portrayal of the pirate will be "sullied by Self-interested Pens" because the pirate, unlike the buccaneer, is *hostis humani generis*. Contemporaries who wrote about the pirates explicitly assert that they will condemn their subjects, even if the resulting piratical character is more ambiguously heroic than perhaps the authors intended.

Despite their excesses, the buccaneers were allies and countrymen of those Protestant European governments that had a weaker presence in the Caribbean than the Catholic Spaniards. By demoralizing the Spanish settlements, the buccaneers could help these countries gain an economic foothold in the West Indies. "For this is certain," Exquemelin writes, "that the Kings of *Spain*, have upon several occasions, sent, by their Embassadors, unto the Kings of *France* and *England, complaining of the molestations and troubles, those Pirates did often cause upon the coasts of* America; *even in the calm of*

Peace" (1:79). The Spaniards—who do not use the word "buccaneer" to describe these men and would not recognize the difference here in any case—refer to them as *piratas*. The English and French kings answer the Spaniards with a challenge of their own: "*That such men did not commit those acts of hostility and Piracy, as subjects unto their Majesties; and therefore his Catholick Majesty might proceed against them according as he should find fit*" (1:79). The English and French kings disavow any sovereignty over the buccaneers, but paradoxically neither admit nor deny that the buccaneers are English or French. The French and English monarchs do not tell the Spaniards to leave the buccaneers alone. But in direct contrast to their governments' reactions to the pirates of the early eighteenth century—when a "war" against the pirates was declared—they do not offer to assist the Spaniards in ridding the Caribbean of the buccaneers precisely because the buccaneers are weakening the Spanish presence in the West Indies.

Sir Henry Morgan, the most famous of the English buccaneers, was violent, barbaric, and cruel. For example, he burned and sacked Panama (and then tried to sue the first English printer of *Bucaniers of America* for suggesting that he did).[15] Despite Morgan's behavior, there is never a doubt that because he is at war against the Spaniards, and *only* the Spaniards, and because he fights for the same side as the English, he is and should be considered a hero by the English. To the Spaniards, however, Morgan is the enemy, *la pirata*.

Morgan epitomizes the heroic representation of the buccaneer. When he decides to take Puerto Bello, "judged to be the strongest place the King of *Spain* possesseth in all the *West-Indies,*" Morgan gives a stirring little speech to his fellow buccaneers: "If our number is small, our hearts are great. And the fewer persons we are, the more union and better shares we shall have in the spoil" (2:90–91).

Clichéd it may be, but Morgan's speech is reminiscent of Henry V's exhortation to his fellow Englishmen who are about to fight the French. But Exquemelin complicates this nationalistic exhortation: the buccaneers are not exactly in the fight for honor, for the glory of "Harry! England and Saint George!" The honor is secondary to the economic triumph that motivates the buccaneers to win the battle. Indeed, Morgan's buccaneers do more than just sack the city: "This being done, they fell to eating and drinking, after their usual manner; that is to say, committing in both these things all manner of debauchery and excess. These two vices were immediately followed by many insolent actions of Rape and Adultery committed upon many very honest women, as well as married as Virgins" (2:98–99). Despite the excesses perpetrated by Morgan and his men, the old buccaneer ended his career an English hero, about whom ballads were written. He was made governor of Jamaica and charged with rooting out the remaining buccaneers. He forced them to become planters and to resettle as more or less legitimate members of society. Along with such buccaneers as the Dutch Brasiliano and the French Lo'lonaise, he is not the culturally and economically transgressive *hostis humani generis*, but instead a (barely) legitimate *hostis humani Iberia*.

Unlike pirates, buccaneers could be heroicized as individuals precisely because of the economic havoc they wreaked on the common enemy of England. Paradoxically, though, they retained their status as outlaws within the parameters of conventional society, as exemplified by Morgan's speech. Morgan and his fellow buccaneers were fighting a "good" war, a war that directly helped non-Spanish European interests in the Spanish-controlled West Indies and filled their own pockets—at least temporarily. The buccaneer—the buccaneer-hero—is the epitome of the masculine and unambiguously "heterosexual" hero, whose efforts for his own self-aggrandizement helped the merchants of the Caribbean and thus the non-Catholic governments in Europe.[16]

In 1915 a new edition of *Bucaniers of America* was published, "put into popular shape for juvenile readers." A contemporary reviewer of the edition wrote,

> Much of the book is a bald recital of outrages inflicted upon a helpless people who had done nothing to incur the vengeance of the ruffians who tortured and killed them. . . . If boys must read about fighting, let them turn to some of the great wars which have been waged for a principle and forego these tales of coldblooded outlawry.[17]

The "helpless people" were not seen as individuals by Morgan and the other buccaneers. Rather, they were lumped together as Spanish Catholics, hated by late-seventeenth-century English readers leery of "popish plots" in ways unimaginable for this early-twentieth-century critic. Thus the buccaneers are criminalized by this reviewer because of the success they had as "outlaws." Without the historical context that explains the enmity held by the English toward the Spanish, the buccaneer can be seen as similar to the golden-age pirates. But he should not be.

A buccaneer, finally, was a hero precisely because he fought "great wars which have been raised for a principle." One "principle" was an expression of hatred of Catholics in general and outrage against the Spaniards in particular for what they did to the Native Americans. Another "principle" was economic. Northern European governments had imperatives to open up the Indies for all of Europe. By 1915 all these "principles" had become confused with the completely criminal exploits of the "golden-age" pirates.

The buccaneers, then, are a distinct breed of maritime outlaw. Who remembers the most famous buccaneers, Brasiliano or Lo'lonais? Except for Sir Henry Morgan—whose name and romanticized visage grace a brand of spiced rum—the other buccaneers are scarcely remembered today. But the names of the next generation of sea rovers—the pirates of the late seventeenth and early eighteenth centuries—still resound with mythic resonance almost three centuries after their initial fame.

Exquemelin's book was popular throughout the 1800s into the early years of the twentieth century. But the glamour of the most notorious pirates of the early eighteenth century soon outstripped the celebrity of even the most popular buccaneers. *Bucaniers of America*, so influential for Defoe, Johnson, and other historians of the pirate, became forgotten as the centuries wore on.[18] The nationalism that legitimated the buccaneer is overlooked by popular culture, which favors the more romantic pirate.

The term "pirate" signifies the legally defined criminal whose exploits are exemplified by such legendary names as Blackbeard, Kidd, Roberts, and Bonnet. Each of these larger-than-life personalities plays an important role in the *General History*, in the early-eighteenth-century press, and in our own cultural memory. But they are only the most famous pirates. Other, forgotten marauders created as much or more havoc along European maritime trading routes on the high seas. What I call the "piratical subject," however, exemplifies the characteristic representation of Defoe's and other authors' fictional characters that merge them as explicit villains and antiheroes. Distinctions between history and fiction have become blurred in depictions of the pirates. The piratical subject, then, represents the biographies of "real" and fictional notorious pirates who lived or were created during the three decades of piracy's "golden age." It is, in other words, impossible to separate the "real" pirate who preyed on legitimate traders from the romanticized version accepted as the "reality" in the twentieth century. Historical and literary portraits of the traditional pirate figure arose in the context of Spain's weakening hold on the Caribbean. Political divisions constantly shifted between European nations and their competition for the steady flow of riches heading from the South Pacific and the Atlantic toward northern Europe and Spain allowed the flowering of this "golden age."[19]

By the 1690s, buccaneers no longer were able to keep a base in the

Caribbean. They had been brought under control temporarily at least by Henry Morgan and others. The "sea wolves" were forced into constant movement. They followed merchant ships wherever trade went, be it to the coast of colonial North America, on the middle passage between Africa and the Americas, or on the Indian Ocean. This routing of the buccaneers from the Caribbean, coupled with the political stability exemplified by the end of the Spanish War of Succession and the subsequent Treaty of Utrecht between France and Britain in 1713 played havoc on maritime employment for ordinary seamen.[20] Fearful of impressment in times of war, sailors might have trouble finding berths in times of peace. Piracy became an attractive— often the only—alternative, particularly if the harsh discipline of the British navy were to be avoided.[21]

Unlike the pirate, a privateer occupied a semilegal, shady status in the seventeenth- and eighteenth-century maritime world following the Restoration.[22] During times of war in England, entrepreneurs who had the political or financial clout were able to obtain a letter of marque from the king in order to seize and plunder enemy ships. For example, if England were at war with France, then a ship could be outfitted and manned by sailors in order to seek French ships and their allies and take whatever plunder they wanted.[23] "All prizes and Purchase, which shall be taken by said Ships shall be divided," Captain Edward Cooke wrote in his *Voyage to the South Sea* (1712), "*viz.* two third Parts of the clear Profits to the Owners of the said Ships, and the other third Part to the Officers, Sea-men, and Land-men, who shall be at the taking of such Prizes and Purchase."[24]

There were complications, however. Sometimes privateer crews were frustrated by the lack of booty, or they got greedy or were unhappy with the terms. Then they would deliberately perform acts of piracy by plundering ships of England's allies. Sometimes the privateer captain would break down under pressure from the crew and agree to out-and-out piracy. Sometimes the crew would mutiny, and put the captain and his followers on shore or on a deserted island.[25]

Even though the privateer was *legally* entitled to seize an enemy's ship and take all the booty, the moment that peace was attained the letter of marque became worthless, and the privateer became an enemy to his king and to his former sponsors if he continued to plunder ships. In fact, he was a pirate, even if it were accidental, because of communication problems in a world where news travels very slowly. These complications caused by the unreliability of information could be used against the privateer.

In a defense of the earl of Bellomont, who obtained a letter of marque for Captain Kidd, an anonymous pamphlet writer points out the dilemma that faced the privateer: "And therefore as [pirates] must be subdued like Enemies, the Law considers them as such, with this difference, that Pirates are Enemies to all Princes, to all Mankind, whereas [privateers] become Enemies by accident only and continue such but while the War lasts."[26] Much of the controversy surrounding Captain Kidd's career and trial revolved around the mystery of his missing letter of marque. Kidd was arguably the most notorious pirate in early-eighteenth-century England. However, he began his illicit career as a privateer, with a letter of marque sponsored by the earl of Bellomont, then a colonial governor in New England.[27] When he began his association with Bellomont, Kidd offered to sail to Madagascar, the infamous pirate nest. He told Bellomont that he could suppress the attacks that were a serious threat to the East India Company and other merchants along the major trading routes of Africa and India.

Kidd's offer (and Bellomont's acceptance) is an indication of the pirates' great threat to late seventeenth-century trade. A politician who managed to wipe out the pirates would see his stock rise high among the merchants of England. In the process of ridding Madagascar of the pirates, Kidd argued, he would strengthen the power of Bellomont and his "junto," a group of Whigs who tried to wrest control of the government from the Tories in the 1690s. The fractious partisan fighting between Whigs and Tories resulted in the probable betrayal of Kidd by Bellomont and his cronies. Defenders of Kidd believed him innocent of out-and-out piracy. He became the fall guy for Bellomont and his followers when the letter of marque disappeared and Kidd was unable to produce it at his trial.[28] In order to save their own political lives, after reports of Kidd's piracy began to be heard in England, Bellomont and his cronies left Kidd literally to hang in a sensational trial in 1701. At least that is the impression left by pirate historians over the years. Kidd—according to his apologists—was only trying to reassert his legitimate authority as captain. He was guilty of no more than the justifiable killing of a mutinous carpenter, whom he bashed on the head with a bucket.

As one modern historian points out, the distinction between pirate and privateer complicates the political issues behind Kidd's trial and his eventual mythologizing as a pirate archetype (Ritchie, vi). Kidd *was* a dupe of Bellomont, but he also consciously turned pirate. Then, after his capture, Kidd tried to use his position as an underdog to save his skin. For Kidd, though, turning pirate was no accident. The *Adventure Galley*—Kidd's ship—was his "nursery," and the temptation to raid even allied and English ships became too strong. The more powerful forces of Bellomont and his friends prevailed, however, and Kidd was hanged. Kidd was only one of the first "golden-age" pirates to become a legend.

In a way, the pirate replaced the libertine as a cultural icon, a figure of sexual and cultural anarchy. The heyday of the libertine, during the reign of Charles II, was notable for such men as Rochester as well as characters such as Horner, Don John, and other rakes in the plays of Wycherley, Shadwell, and Behn, among others. By the "golden age" of piracy the libertine was no longer the figure that he had been earlier in the seventeenth century. There are notable differences between the libertine and the pirate, of course. For one thing, a libertine like Rochester was an aristocrat, whereas a pirate like Captain Avery or Blackbeard came from the laboring class.[29] Class—in the sense that nobility allows the abuse of power—does not matter in the same way for the pirate as it did for the libertine.

But we can see in contemporary literature how the pirate resembles the libertine. In a pirate trial pamphlet from 1725, "Robert Joyce deposed, that . . . we were attack'd and took off the said Island, by a Pyrate Ship, of 24 Guns, and 86 Men, one Captain *Anstice* Commander."[30] Joyce, an ordinary sailor, explains to the court the actions of the pirates when they attacked his ship:

> On Board which Pyrate Ship, were the two Prisoners at the Bar, who were the only Persons that would hail me and Four more of our Company on Board the Pyrate Ship, and Beat us sadly because we refused, and *William Ingram* said, G—d D—m you for a cowardly Rogue, you shall be hang'd for your honesty, as well as we for our Roguery.

From Joyce's deposition, we see the ways the pirate is being represented as a cultural icon, even in a "factual" account. The pirate Ingram speaks like a pirate. His diction is clever, profane, and frightening.

Five years before this trial, Defoe's fictional Captain Singleton tells the reader that he is "well prepared for all manner of Roguery" as he joins a gang of pirates (139). The difference between pirates and libertines, I would argue, lies in how the pirates revealed their "roguery." For the libertine, "roguery" was sexual conquest, be it sodomitical or "heterosexual." This sexual conquest was a display of power by men who delighted in all kinds of excess. Further, the libertine showed his power through an anarchic refusal to bow to any conventions, sexual or cultural. Because the libertine as represented by Rochester and others came from the aristocracy and thus could circumvent laws and codes of behavior, he could afford to assert his power through excess. The libertine had homosocial relationships, but these relationships reveal a camaraderie based on a like interest in, basically, wine, women, and song. Rochester refers a few times to sodomy, as in his oft-quoted lines from "The Disabled Debauchee": "Nor shall our *Love-fits Cloris* be forgot, / When each the well-look'd *Link-Boy*, strove to enjoy, / And the best kiss, was the deciding *Lot*, / Whether the *Boy* fuck'd you, or I the *Boy*" (37–40). These lines, however, reveal Rochester's power over both the boy and Cloris and not a reciprocal desire. Rochester would be happy fucking either.[31]

In both *Captain Singleton* and *The Whole Tryal*, the pirates obviously do not come from aristocratic backgrounds. Indeed, one could argue that the pirates belong to no class at all, for they "declare war against *all* mankind." Since they have turned their backs on normative society, they are defined as pirates—and *only* pirates—and thus defined by their transgressive cultural *and* economic defiance. Any debauchery takes place at sea away from societal restraints. Their threat to society is criminal because they wreak havoc on maritime trade, yet they are represented in print by their "otherness," their violence, cruelty, and over-the-top masculine performance when they wreak that havoc.

The pirates' well-known delight in the physical is explicitly over-determined by Defoe, Johnson, and even the trial records, as we can see in the extract from Robert Joyce's deposition. Their behavior is characterized by violence, costume, and profanity, as well as a propensity to drink, play, and make merry, all to outlandish excess. With the exception of some articles that Captain Roberts's crew signed—in which *"No boy or woman [is] to be allowed amongst them"* (Johnson, 1:171)—the pirate's sex life remains uncontrolled by any pirate rules, at least in the primary sources.

The pirate's sexual behavior, then, is left out of eighteenth-century pirate accounts. However, other highly transgressive cultural aspects of their all-male society complicate the accounts of homosocial pirate camaraderie that ignore sexuality. Defoe and other writers suggest that the pirate is a kind of libertine of the seven seas. He thumbs his nose at any conventions, economic or cultural, that might link him to the status quo. Early-eighteenth-century authors thus connected the economic menace of the pirates to the libertine excesses of the aristocracy.

The differences, then, between the buccaneer, the privateer, and the pirate point to the complications inherent in any definition of the golden-age pirate. The pirate could and did go back and forth between the navy or merchant sea trade, the less secure trade of the privateer, and finally to the world of the *hostis humani generis*. What fascinated early chroniclers of sea life, and still fascinates readers and historians today, however, is the romantic pirate figure, the man who declared himself "at war against all mankind."

In order to establish how concepts of desire and deviance are encoded within the hypermasculinity of the pirate tradition, I shall return to a discussion of the "piratical subject." This literary representation of male identity complicates dialectical models of identity. Not only is he a masculine alternative to the noncriminal "hero," he is also opposed both to the heroine and the feminized, effeminate sodomitical subject. The piratical subject is a merging of representations of both economic criminal and cultural deviant. I call this complex figure the piratical subject to differentiate him from a purely legal definition as *hostis humani generis*, just as I prefer to distinguish between the sodomite who performs the act of sodomy and the desiring sodomitical subject, defined not only by the act of sodomy but a *desire* for other men.

To use Michel Serres's terminology, both the piratical subject and the sodomitical subject are parasites that destabilize seemingly straightforward dichotomies such as hero and heroine or man and woman.[32] Imagine an upside-down triangle. In a model that places the primary opposition of the masculine hero against the feminine heroine, the feminized, effeminate sodomite—a criminal—is opposed to both the hero and the heroine. In other words, the dichotomy of man and woman or hero and heroine is interrupted by the effeminate sodomite.

Where does the pirate fit into this triangle? Instead of a triangle, imagine a square. The primary opposition is on top of the square: masculine hero and feminine heroine. On the bottom of the square picture the pirate in one corner under the hero and the sodomite in the other corner under the heroine. The pirate is not a "hero" per se but an antihero; as such, he interrupts the straightforward dichotomy of the masculine hero and the feminine heroine. But the sodomite interrupts those same positions since he is neither hero nor heroine. The pirate's homosocialized masculinity, how- ever, complicates this square. The pirate is opposed to *both* the heroine and the sodomite because he is masculine. But he is also opposed to the mascu- line hero because he is an antihero. The pirate is the masculine antihero on the "same" side as the hero. He is the "criminal," because he is not the hero, but he is not portrayed as *sexually* criminal, which the sodomite is.[33]

Now imagine another square. In one corner on top sits the merchant; in another corner on top sits the pirate. In economic terms and by legal definition, the pirate is a criminal "merchant"—*hostis humani generis*— opposed to the law-abiding seafaring merchant. But in eighteenth-century narratives, the pirate's transgressions were as often heroic as they were criminal. The privateer, a third figure in this model, sits in both corners under the legitimate merchant and the pirate at the bottom of the square. Furthermore, his status is unstable in the legal maritime world. Depending on the political climate and relations between countries, the privateer can move between the positions of the law-abiding seafaring merchant and the pirate. Finally, the pirate can occupy *any* position in the economic square model at any time; he is represented by Johnson, Defoe, and other writers as the not-criminal, not-merchant alternative to the seafaring merchant, the criminal, or at times, the privateer.

In other words, although the pirate is not a legitimate merchant, and is therefore a criminal according to English law, he is still paradoxically portrayed at times by Johnson, Defoe, and others as *not only* a criminal but a hero, and thus opposes himself. The pirate's refusal to be pinned down into *any* dichotomous position in either the economic or the sexual model highlights the instability of sexual and gendered identity, and the instability of dichotomies represented by gender, sexual desire, masculinity, and capital. If we acknowledge both the economic and sexual ambiguities of the pirate, the revealing tensions between and within the various subject positions and the two squares suggest that the pirate can be, in fact, a heroic criminal, sexually and economically embodied in a transgressive way. If the piratical subject is, then, a hypermasculine hero but sexually ambiguous, what does this say about representations of sexuality in the "normal" world?

The pirate in eighteenth-century narratives neither explicitly nor implicitly outlaws deviant sexual behavior in his pirate world. Instead the absence of explicit sexuality in these accounts suggests the piratical subject as an alternative paradigm of masculine identity. This alternative identity, then, can authorize homoerotic desire since there are no explicit prohibitions against this desire in depictions of the pirate's world. It follows that the homoerotically authorized paradigm of the piratical subject resists the censures the sodomite produces within standard boundaries of sexual license.

The difficulty in pinning down the piratical subject lies in the ways all these oppositions are played out not only by Defoe, Captain Johnson, and other eighteenth-century authors, but also by later historians who write about pirates. These authors invariably try to "tame" pirates by damning their economic crimes. Yet these authors are still fascinated by the pirates' extreme individualism. They cannot resist the impulse to heroicize the pirates' economic and cultural outlaw behavior. The pirate is thus able to move between both squares. By looking at the ways historians and eighteenth-century writers and readers perceived the pirates, and further, demonstrating the often contradictory literary representations of the pirate, we can understand the complexity of pirate sexuality. Moreover, the ways the pirate can be perceived as "queer"—as a radical, hypermasculine transgressor who in fact glories in all his transgressions—can help us revise our understanding of homoeroticism in eighteenth-century English literature and culture.

Though I locate sites of homoerotic transgression in pirate narratives, I am not saying that pirates were all queers, buggerers, or sodomites. I am saying that once the hatches to the pirates' holds are opened a crack, "reality" destabilizes, things unsaid may be spoken, and the homoerotic implications of elements in pirate history and fiction can be explored. For example, until recently Defoe critics have always worked from a heterocentric position. Critics who investigate the historical context in Defoe's narratives have not acknowledged the different realities of transgressive individuality that have been silenced by their critical practice. Johnson and Defoe wrote about identities in ways not comfortably suited to conventional sexual and economic depictions of desire. And critical silence means the repression of voices in the heteroglossia that we call the novel or in a narrative of history.

Jonathan Goldberg writes that "To read for sodomy—for sodometries—is to read relationally" (23). Similarly, to read for piracy and for piracies is to read relationally. An exploration of what is repressed in the homosocial discourse surrounding the piratical subject allows a re-vision of pirate history that celebrates rather than represses homoerotic identity. The point is that sexuality and language go hand in hand, and depictions of sexuality are an essential part of any work of literature that is purported to be a "novel" or a cultural history. The sexual difference implicit in representations of the pirate illuminates powerful countertraditions in a history of sexuality.

3

Trial Records, Last Words, and Other Ephemera
The Literary Artifacts of Piracy

A pirate is in a perpetual war with every individual, and every state, christian or infidel. Pirates properly have no country, but by the nature of their guilt, separate themselves, and renounce on this matter, the benefit of all lawful societies.
> — *The Tryal, Examination and Condemnation, of Captain Green*

The French King did it, and the Czar of Muscovy made Alexander, A Carpenter, a Prince, for that Purpose . . . He had seen the Czar of Muscovy through a hole at Sea, lye with Prince Alexander.
> —*An Account of the Proceedings against Capt. Edward Rigby*

Despite the continued popularity of the pirate, demonstrated by the hundreds of books published over the centuries, the literary artifacts of piracy remain little explored. Indeed, until recently a cultural history has not even been attempted.[1] Historians have contented themselves with retelling the same stories over and over—usually based on what has been called a "vulgarization" of *A General History of the . . . Pyrates*.[2] Of course, pirate historicity has not all been a regurgitation of these stories. Some historians have looked at piracy's impact on economics or politics or have examined individual pirates and privateers such as Avery and Dampier. In the past few years there has been a host of books about the "female pyrates."[3]

Despite this attention, little work has been done on the cultural importance of piracy not only to eighteenth-century England but also to twentieth-century readers. Pirates of fiction and fact still fascinate children and adults. Witness Disneyland's pirates of the Caribbean exhibit, the hourly pirate battles at the Treasure Island Hotel in Las Vegas, and such books as Kathy

Acker's *Pussy, Queen of the Pirates* and Zap Comics' Captain Pissgums. A cursory search of *Books in Print* reveals several dozen pirate books aimed at all kinds of readers.

Our own fascination with pirates is nothing new, of course. A huge body of pirate ephemera was published in the late seventeenth and early eighteenth centuries. But left out of any modern discussions of the pirate—with the notable but problematic exception of B. R. Burg's *Sodomy and the Pirate Tradition*—is his sexuality. There are no records that focus directly on the homoerotic life of the pirate. Some of the travelogues by privateers mention sodomy, for example, Captain Hacke tells his readers that his crew consisted of "all Run-away's, some having merited the Gallows, other Fire and Faggot for Sodomy."[4] Burg has uncovered a few sodomy records in maritime archives. But other kinds of cultural deviance can be found in the ephemeral literature of the period.

Throughout the late seventeenth and early eighteenth centuries the publication of trial transcripts and "dying confessions" was very popular. Such pamphlets were a major source of entertainment for the London reading public.[5] The trials helped to establish the public's impression of the pirate, as did the "dying confessions" written by Paul Lorrain, the ordinary of Newgate. The ordinary wrote these confessions for didactic reasons, of course. But he also wrote them to supplement his income as the prison clergyman who ministered to condemned criminals. Other writers who wanted to cash in on the ordinary's success wrote confessional pamphlets as well. The pamphlets describe the final moments before the pirates' executions, and offer a moral for the readers.[6]

The trials for piracy were overseen by the Court of Admiralty rather than the civil courts. At times during the early eighteenth century the government cracked down on piracy. The Admiralty held mass trials and executed large numbers of pirates at one time in order to set an example to sailors who might think about going on the account. The Admiralty wanted "to remind sailors of the consequences of signing on as a pirate, and to comfort and reassure the merchant community of London" (Ritchie, 1). For example, in 1700, fifty-two pirates were ordered executed in one fell swoop, while another thirty-eight were acquitted (Johnson, 1:321-22, 2d ed.).[7] At the trial of the pirates who sailed with Captain Roberts in 1722, over fifty men were condemned and hanged. If the executions were meant to "comfort" the merchants of London and warn Jack Tar not to go on the account, the publication of these events was meant to inform, enlighten, and entertain the reading public—and make a profit for the book sellers.

Until the turn of the eighteenth century, the trials were almost always held in England because the Admiralty feared that officials in the far-flung outposts of the empire could be bribed. However, there were few convictions in England because of such obstacles as finding and transporting rootless witnesses and criminals across vast distances. The law changed shortly before Captain Kidd's trial in 1701. Piracy trials were allowed to be held anywhere within the English colonies that a Court of Admiralty could be assembled.[8] Moreover, if pirates were captured at sea—if the hunters were defeated by the hunted—the victorious captain had the authority to hang the pirates without benefit of an official trial. A pirate named Thomas Armstrong, for example—one of Captain Roberts' crew—was "executed on board the *Weymouth*" in 1722 (Johnson, 1:322, 2d ed.).

Criminal trials in general—whether current or past—could be useful forms of propaganda for Whigs and Tories. Some of the most notorious trials—such as Castlehaven's sensational trial for sodomy and blasphemy in 1631—might be republished decades later if they could serve a political purpose.[9] Indeed, the popularity of the *Newgate Calendar*, reprinted many times throughout the eighteenth century, testifies to the enduring interest in some of the pirate trials. In the 1795 edition, the editor reprinted the texts of at least half a dozen pirate trials from the first two decades of the century.[10]

During the years of piracy's "golden age," the trials were heard in English and then translated into Latin for the official records, although depositions by witnesses and accused were usually not published and most often were transcribed in English.[11] Both court clerks and freelance transcribers would record the more popular trials, and these trials would be published almost instantly as pamphlets. The reproduction of a trial as a pamphlet suggests an authority and a realism that are actually constructed by the trial's transcriber and the pamphlet's printer. Captain Kidd's trial and subsequent execution, for example, led to numerous competing publications.[12] A trial pamphlet can give only a certain perspective of the trial itself. The reader's experience of the trial is distanced from the original written transcript, unavailable to the public in any case, and in Latin. The pamphlet is already a "frame" removed from the actual event, filtered through the lens of the transcriber.

Published pirate trials generally follow the same pattern. Except for different participants, the prosecutors use the same language in the opening statement, and the accusations with few exceptions are similar.[13] The titles of these pamphlets sensationalize and thus grab the potential buyer's attention. One of the most notorious pirate trials—of Captain Avery's crew—is a good example: *The Tryals of Joseph Dawson, Edward Forseith, William May,*

William Bishop, James Lewis, and John Sparkes for Several Piracies and Rob-
beries by Them Committed, in the Company of Every the Grand Pirate, Near
the Coasts of the East-Indies; and Several Other Places on the Seas. Giving an
Account of Their Villainous Robberies and Barbarities. At the Admiralty Ses-
sions, Begun at the Old-Baily on the 29th of October, 1696. and Ended on the
6th. of November.[14] This pamphlet sells the "Villainous Robberies and Barbarities" of the accused and specifies the pirates by name, in this case linking
them with "Every the Grand Pirate." The actual text of the pamphlet
foregrounds a list of the judges and lawyers who hear the case.[15] Printers
wanted buyers, and buyers wanted sensation. This particular trial dealt with
the most famous pirate of the decade—perhaps of the seventeenth century—
Captain Avery. The printer could be sure that his pamphlet sold well.

The transcriber lists the booty captured by Avery and his crew from "a
certain Ship called the *Gunsway*, with her Tackle, Apparel and Furniture, to
the value of 1000£ and of Goods to the value of 110£ together with 100000
Pieces of Eight, and 100000 Chequins, upon the High Seas, ten Leagues
from the *Cape St. Johns* near *Surat* in the *East-Indies*" (A2r). The transcriber
then notes that, "*Dawson, Forseith, May, Bishop, Lewes,* and *Sparkes,* were
brought to Bar and their Indictment read" (1). The indictment—four pages
long—is printed in full, and the defendants are asked how they plead:
"*Joseph Dawson* confessed that he was Guilty, but the rest pleaded Not
Guilty, and put themselves on their Trials" (4).

When the prosecutors speak, they are quoted verbatim. Notice that the
plea is reported in the third person, and the defendants are effectively
silenced. Only Dawson, who pleads guilty, is named. He is already listed
first on both the title page and in the indictment. The other defendants are
grouped together; thus the accused criminals who plead "not guilty" are
distanced from the reader, and the pirates are robbed of any individuality.

Unlike the defendants, the attorney general is quoted in full as he describes the heinous nature of piracy and presents the state's reasons for "trial
without jury." John Quelch and his cohorts hear the prosecutor characterize
them as something close to monsters. The reader, already several "frames"
removed, reads what the accused heard:

> for Pirates are not Entituled to Law, not so much as the Law of Arms; for
> which Reason 'tis said, if Piracy be commited on the Ocean, and the Pirates
> in the Attempt happen to be overcome, the Captors are not obliged to bring
> them to any Port, but may expos [*sic*] them immediately to Punishment, by
> Hanging them at the Main-Yard: A sign of its being a very different and worse
> Nature than any Crime committed upon the Land; for Robbers and Murder-

ers, and even Traytors themselves mayn't be put to Death without passing a formal Tryal.[16]

The attorney general's remarks demonstrate the extraordinary contrast, in the eyes of the law, between piracy and other crimes. The prosecutor explicitly states that piracy is not an "ordinary" felony—like, say, highway robbery, murder, or even treason—but something of "a very different and worse Nature." It was, in fact, in a pirate's "nature" to be a pirate. The pirate is being constructed as a man whose crimes—his piracy—and his *desire* to pursue those crimes define who he is: a pirate. Furthermore, the law says that pirates, unlike outlaws or murderers, may be executed without trial at sea, away from the legal boundaries of the English government.

This is a remarkable law in a country that prides itself on trial by jury, even if we consider the long list of capital crimes against property in the eighteenth century.[17] As all the felony trial records of the period show, accused criminals were at least allowed a trial, unlike the pirates who could be summarily executed at a sea captain's discretion. In Crusoe's *Farther Adventures*, that is Crusoe's very real fear when he is mistaken for a pirate after he accidentally buys a ship from some real pirates.[18]

The notorious and popular Captain Avery, the "Grand Pirate" who was never captured, was the ringleader of Dawson's group. In the trial, the accused pirate David Creagh gives a deposition that describes Avery's plot to take control of the ship on which he and his conspirators crewed. Creagh says he refused to join the pirates, and was ordered below ship to the cabin. As he was going downstairs, he testifies,

> I met with *W. May*, the Prisoner at the Barr. What do you say here? Says he. I made him no Answer but went down to my Cabin; and he said, God damn you, you deserve to be shot through the Head, and then he held a Pistol to my Head. Then I went to my Cabin, and presently came orders from *Every*, that those that would go ashore, should prepare to be gone. And when the Captain was got out of Bed, who was then very ill of a Feaver, *Every* came and said, I am a Man of Fortune, and must seek my Fortune. (15)

This passage is unusually vivid. Creagh's testimony suggests some of the earliest details about the pirate way of life as twentieth-century readers imagine it: the matter-of-fact violence, the profanity, the nonchalant bravery, and the pirate captain's clever turn of phrase. The tension between the pirate-as-criminal and the pirate-as-antihero in both the economic and culturally transgressive models is apparent in this deposition. In a society in which "fortune" signifies economic aggrandizement and heroic individualism, Avery's bravado illustrates the contradictory depiction of the piratical subject. On the one hand, the pirate is an economic criminal—the reason he, or rather his crew, is being tried in the first place. On the other hand, he is depicted in a highly romanticized way that captures the imaginations of the readers and popular historians of piracy.

Furthermore, a contemporary reader of a trial—particularly one as sensational as the Dawson trial—was influenced not only by what the witness said, but what had been disseminated throughout London about the pirates. Avery, the stories told, plundered the Great Mogul's ship and ravished his granddaughter. These tales swept London coffeehouses like a storm, so that the reading audience was prepared for the trial. The liveliness of the language—"God damn you, you deserve to be shot through the Head" or "I am a Man of Fortune"—conveys the effect that later authors draw from for their fanciful and often fabricated histories and novels about piracy.

Dawson's trial—along with Captain Kidd's—is among the most detailed and most famous of the great pirate trials. But like Kidd, these pirates were already famous before the trial took place and before the transcript was published. The result of the trial as it was reported in the pamphlet was inevitable. The readers already knew that the pirates were convicted. Further, anyone could see the pirates' corpses hanging in chains over the Thames.

As Hunter and Davis would argue, there is a novelty to an individual trial. At the same time, though, the similarity between the trials creates a conventional representation of all the pirates, despite the differences in their individual crimes. A pirate's infamy is based on both the similarity of the trials—the comprehensive familiarity that defines the pirate in general— and the particular "heinousness" of the crime, the individual act of piracy. Conventional pirates as a group are made more reprehensible and dangerous; at the same time, certain individual pirates can be criminalized *and* heroicized. Avery plundered the Great Mogul's ship and was never caught. Dawson and his cohorts were on trial for that crime, and Avery was the absent presence who gives readerly interest to the results. Dawson and his comrades were hanged; Avery would be sung about in ballads and written about in plays and novels. The popularity of Avery's trial in absentia is not an anomaly. In Captain Kidd's case, for example, the political "adventure" that got him a commission as a privateer in the first place is erased by the sensational aspects of his trial for piracy.

Much to the horror and fury of the prosecution and the judges, when the jury returned its first verdict in the Avery/Dawson trial the pirates were exonerated from plundering the Great Mogul's ship. Before the second trial began and a new jury was selected, the judge told the prosecution that the "Verdict was a dishonour to the Justice of the Nation" (8). The verdict may have been a "dishonour" to England, but something about the accused pirates helped them get acquitted. If the jury was not bribed (which is doubtful, given the poverty of the accused pirates), then perhaps the glamour of the crimes—the Mogul's riches and the ravishment of his granddaughter—may have had something to do with the pirates' acquittal. Perhaps because the Great Mogul was the victim accounts for the verdict. The Mogul was not a European, and he was an immensely rich autocratic monarch. That combination made a less sympathetic victim for a jury made up of staunch Englishmen. However, although we shall never know *why* the pirates were exonerated, that they were shows tendencies to humanize, in fact heroicize, these "enemies against all mankind," despite the best efforts and noisiest rhetoric of the state. Dawson and his cronies were finally condemned for the piracy of a much less significant vessel.

Sodomites, unlike pirates, were never humanized, much less heroicized, in the literature and trials of early-eighteenth-century England.[19] In *An Account of the Proceedings against Capt. Edward Rigby*, for example, the narrative begins with a paraphrase of the indictment:

> For that [Rigby], the Seventh day of *November last*, did Solicite, Incite, and as well by words as otherways, endeavour to perswade one *William Minton* (of about the Age of Nineteen Years) to suffer him the said *Rigby*, to commit the Crime of *Sodomy* with him the said *Minton*. And the said *Rigby* did also Endeavour and Attempt, to Commit the Crime of *Sodomy* with him the said *Minton*; and did also do and perpetrate divers other Enormities and abominable things, with an intent to Commit the Crime of *Sodomy* with the said *Minton*.[20]

The phrase "commit the crime of Sodomy" is used three times and is linked with ambiguous "Enormities and abominable things." Additionally, the names of both the accused and the accuser are repeated in ways that confuse who is who.

This trial is not the only one in which the complicated diction confuses the reader. In *The Tryal and Conviction of Several Reputed Sodomites* (1707), we get the following deposition:

> *Thomas Lane*, a Foot Soldier, was Indicted for assaulting Mr. *Richard Hemming*: and Mr. *Samuel Baker* on the 15th of *September* last. The Evidence declar'd, that *Lane* was standing upon *London-Bridge*, and that he came to Mr. *Hemmings*, and pulling out his Nakedness offer'd to put it into his Hand,

and withal unbutton'd the Evidences Breeches, and put his Hand in there, but Mr. *Hemmings* put his Hand away; He the rather bore with the Filthiness of the Action, because Mr. *Baker*, the other Evidence, had told Mr. *Hemmings*, that *Lane* the Prisoner was such a kind of Person, and therefore design'd to apprehend him, which they did.[21]

By the end of both of these indictments, the reader is made to separate the accused sodomite (Rigby or Lane) from the accuser (Minton or Hemmings) and must think carefully about who did what to whom. The crime of sodomy began to join the actor with the act, and the actors with one another, just as pirates embodied their crimes of piracy. The accused sodomite and the accuser and their acts are depicted in ways that suggest that their identities and desires to perform or denounce deviant sex acts are difficult to differentiate.

The pamphlets' detail of the events that led to the trials is striking. For example, in Rigby's trial, the published record is virtually pornographic in its description of the accusation; it uses a kind of detail similar to the description of Captain Jeane's torture and murder of his cabin boy. In a summary of the events that led up to Minton's denunciation of Rigby, the following describes the act that caused the arrest:

> thereupon *Rigby* pulled down *Mintons* Breeches, turn'd away his shirt, put his Finger to *Mintons* Fundament, and applyed his Body close to *Mintons*, who feeling something warm touch his Skin, put his hand behind him, and took hold of *Rigbys* Privy Member and said to *Rigby*, *I have now discovered your base Inclinations, I will expose you to the World, to put a stop to these Crimes.*

The exact description of the attempted seduction leaves nothing to the imagination. The diction of Minton's denunciation of Rigby brings to mind a heroine-in-distress fighting for her virtue. But unlike a heroine, who lacks power to defend herself from "ruin," Minton literally grabs the symbol of his seducer's power—"*Rigbys* Privy Member"—and denounces him publicly for his attempted seduction. Similar to the romans à clef by such late-seventeenth- and early-eighteenth-century authors as Behn and Manley, this sodomy trial's narrative makes the reader a voyeur to the erotic "crime."

Rigby's sodomy trial (indeed, all the sodomy trials I have examined) "novelizes" the depositions and creates a sense of "character" for both the accused and the accusers. Like a novelist, the author of a sodomy trial pamphlet attempts a kind of narrative "realism" that positions the reader as someone who could be *like* the accused and accuser. There is a significant distinction, though, between a pirate's trial and a sodomite's trial. The pirate is an explicitly *economic* criminal, whose crimes are a threat to property but who can still be acquitted of the crime, like Dawson, or made a romantic hero, like Captain Avery. The sodomite, on the other hand, is a criminal who poses no explicit threat to property. In a burgeoning middle-class society, domesticity, private life, and marriage are intertwined with the flow of capital. Marriage is not about patrilineal inheritance of land. Instead the married couple form a relationship based on the exchange of capital. For the wife, the exchange is in the private life of the household: her work in exchange for her support. For the husband, the exchange is in the public life of the worker: his work in exchange for his pay. Since the sodomite is left out of this male-female dichotomy, he is no longer explicitly a part of this domestic economy. His threat to the economic order is implicit.

In one of the most graphic of these sodomy trials the accused, Mr. Blair, presents a defense in which he tells the court it is all a misunderstanding. Nothing about the actual act of buggery is ever mentioned in this trial. The only "evidence" presented by the prosecution is testimony that two men were caught near each other in an alley. The bailiff testifies, "I called out, and said, *In the Name of God, what are you doing? Who or what are you?* They seemed to jostle before they could get from one another; they had both their Breeches down. Upon which I called to my Partner, and told him they were a Couple of Sodomites."

Then the bailiff tells the court, "I asked them what they did there? *Blair* said, he went to ease Nature. *I think*, said I, *It is in a very odd Way. D——n you, Sir,* said he, *if I must tell you, I was at Sh-te.* As he said he went to ease Nature, I ordered a Watchman to take a Lanthorn to see, and I went myself, and there was no such Thing."[22] The argument between Blair and the bailiff boils down to whether or not anything untoward happened between Blair and the other accused sodomite, John Deacon. Nothing is ever proved except that the bailiff was unable to "see it" when he went to look for the evidence that Blair "was at Sh-te."

Blair tells the court that he said to the bailiff, "what I am going to propose is not cleanly or decent, but if you will please to order any Servant to go along with me into a back Place, I will convince them that I put [the Sh-te] into my Breeches." The bailiff refuses to look, and the two accused sodomites are found "guilty." The evidence presented by the prosecution does not establish guilt. The evidence does establish, however, that the possibility of the sodomitical act is enough to convict.

Unlike trials for pirates or sodomites, in which participants are directly quoted, in the cases of the "dying confessions," the pirate's words are conveyed through the voice of the ordinary of Newgate.[23] These pamphlets work to provide some sort of moral closure to pirate misbehavior.[24] Usually the ordinary makes the pirate sound like a penitent, showing remorse for his actions and ready to meet his maker. But once in a while the pirate is able to frustrate the ordinary. Then the reader can see how the ordinary scrambles to make a moral lesson out of an unrepentant pirate's execution.

For example, the ordinary was flummoxed by Captain Kidd, who did not show the proper contrition at Execution Dock. The ordinary writes, "to my unspeakable grief . . . [Kidd] was inflamed with Drink." The ordinary then focuses his attention on a lesser pirate, whom he can represent as being truly repentant. The ordinary writes that the condemned pirate Darby Mullins "confess'd he had been a great Sinner . . . had of late very given himself to Swearing, Cursing, profaning the Sabbath-day, &c. which he now acknowledged had deserv'dly brought this Calamity upon him."[25]

The ordinary's account tries to depict the pirate Mullins as a regular guy, an example for others because the pirate repents not only his piratical acts, but his other "great sins": swearing, cursing, profaning the Sabbath. Mullins, the ordinary suggests, is just like us. Of course Kidd, the star of the event, overwhelms the confession of Darby Mullins, whose self-confessed "crimes" are not too sensational in any case. Nor does Mullins show particular remorse for his acts of piracy.

When the ordinary goes to hear Kidd's dying confession, he writes that Kidd "truly repented of his Sins, and forgave all the World; and I was in good hopes he did so." Between the time that the ordinary spoke to Kidd and Kidd's execution, the ordinary discovers that Kidd is so drunk that liquor "discomposed his Mind, that it was now in a very ill frame and very unfit for the great Work, now or never, to be perform'd by him." The ordinary finds that Kidd in his drunken state "was unwilling to own the Justice of his Condemnation, or so much as the Providence of God, who for his Sins, had deservedly brought him to this untimely End." Luckily, the ordinary is able to salvage the situation:

> But here I must take notice of a remarkable (and I hope most lucky) accident which then did happen which was this. That the Rope with which Capt. *Kid* was ty'd, broke, and so falling to the Ground, he was taken up alive; and by this means had opportunity to consider more of that Eternity, he was launching into. When he was brought up, and ty'd again to the Tree I desired leave to go to him again, which was granted. . . . Now I found him in much better temper than before.

Indeed, Kidd's "better temper"—not surprisingly he is now stone-cold sober—at being hanged a second time makes him repent his sins "with all his Heart."

Another pamphlet that describes Kidd's execution goes into much greater detail about what Kidd said before he was hanged.[26] According to this anonymous author, Kidd acknowledges that he was a pirate and a robber. Kidd says that if he had "kept to his commission" to root out the pirates it would have brought him "more Wealth, than he got by indirect Practices." But Kidd is, in this version, pretty much unrepentant through the end:

> Notwithstanding which he could hardly be brought to a Charitable Reconcil-
> iation with those Persons, who were Evidences against him at his Tryal,
> alledging that they deposed many things that were inconsistent with truth,
> and that much of their Evidence was by hearsay; and in the general part of
> his Discourse seem'd not only to reflect on them, but several others, who
> instead of being his Friends (as they promised,) had traiterously been Instru-
> mental in his Ruin.

Does Kidd's drunkenness work against the moral point of the publication of his "last words"? Was he drunk, as the ordinary stated, or was he sober, since the other author does not mention Kidd's condition? Which pamphlet do we believe? In the ordinary's account, Kidd's actions erase—or at least overwhelm—the significance of the lesser pirate Darby Mullin's confession. *Everyone* may swear, curse, or profane the Sabbath. Sailors, in fact, were expected to curse, as numerous pamphlets and proclamations against profanity of the time make clear. Captain Kidd, though, remains the archpirate, just as Captain Avery, never captured, evolves from a criminal to an ever more romantic figure. Indeed, in proclamations issued by William and Mary that offered pardons to the pirates, Avery and Kidd were both exempted from the offered clemency.

Eighteenth-century readers will bring to both of these confessions the context of the trial, the consistency of the confessions themselves, and their knowledge of piracy and pirates constructed through these pamphlets and newspapers. The ordinary of Newgate wants to make the piratical crimes a lesson for everyone. This is an impossibility, as Foucault has noted.[27] The purpose of ideology is precisely not to work perfectly, to justify continuing efforts to enforce that ideology. Readers know that many of the pirates get away, are acquitted, or are pardoned by the king. From the trials, readers know that the pirate is a legally defined criminal, yet "different" too, "for

Pirates are not Entituled to Law," as Dawson's prosecutor says. And besides, pirates are *hostis humani generis.*

The trials and the confessions work against one another in their characterizations of the pirate. The trials attempt to show that the "nature" of the pirate and his crime is very different from the "nature" of the public or the nonpirate criminal. The ordinary's pamphlets, on the other hand, try to bring the pirate back into society by showing that the pirate can repent and display remorse for his sins. The tension between these two extremes demonstrates that the pirate cannot be made to fit within boundaries of normative society. His outsider status refuses to be pinned down.

In many ways, Kidd's status embodies the evolving "nature" of the pirate, from the "common enemy against all mankind" in late seventeenth- and early-eighteenth-century England to the fascinating antihero in the following centuries. Many books have been written about Kidd's exploits, his supposed buried treasure, and the perfidy of the whiggish junto. Fictional recreations based on his legend are legion.[28] The fabled villainy of Captain Kidd has far outstripped the comparably minor pirate acts he probably committed. Through the stories told about Captain Kidd, we can see how the political "truth" of his crime is erased, and he evolves into a merging of archcriminal and romanticized pirate: the birth of a legend.

According to historical and literary tradition, Kidd was either a victim of political machinations or a notorious pirate. He was, in actuality, both. He took advantage of his status as privateer; relying on his powerful political sponsors, he made a self-conscious decision to turn pirate. When, as Ritchie argues, the Tories began to defeat Bellomont and his political friends in the junto, Bellomont could not ignore Kidd's piracy despite the profit that Bellomont might have seen (Ritchie, vi).

During Kidd's trial and execution, pamphlets, trial records, and at least two ballads were published. The political trade-offs within the English government that resulted in Kidd's conviction and execution were obscured by the dissemination of the Kidd legend throughout London. The tension between the "real" Captain Kidd and the Kidd of legend can be located in ballads about Kidd dating from the onset of his trial in 1701.[29] Kidd is a near-perfect example of the evolution of the pirate—an unambiguous criminal—into the piratical subject. A onetime respectable maritime officer, who in the best middle-class tradition tried to get ahead, is rewritten to become the "arch-Pyrate" after the reasons for his trial and the details of his career have been forgotten. However, the Kidd represented in actual trial transcripts differs greatly from the articulate, romantic Kidd represented in contemporary ballads:

> I made a solemn vow, when I sail'd, when I sail'd
> I made a solemn vow when I sail'd;
> I made a solemn vow, to God I would not bow,
> Nor myself one prayer allow, when I sail'd.
>
> I'd a Bible in my hand, when I sail'd, when I sail'd,
> I'd a Bible in my hand, when I sail'd;
> I'd a Bible in my hand, by my father's great command,
> But I sunk it in the sand, when I sail'd.[30]

Captain Kidd of balladry begins to represent the blasphemous outsider who bows to no one, including God, and who buries his Bible as he buries his treasure. Kidd in ballad and legend turns pirate because piracy is in his nature, to the extent that he makes "a solemn vow, to God [he] would not bow" and proclaims his own individualism.

More than twenty-five years after Kidd's execution, Johnson wrote in the *General History,*

> We are now going to give an Account of one whose Name is better known in *England,* than most of those whose stories we have already related; the Person we mean is Captain *Kid,* whose publick Trial and Execution here, rendered him the Subject of all Conversation, so that his Actions have been chanted about in Ballads. (2:65)

Johnson asserts that he will tell Kidd's story as the trial record details it, without the embellishments provided by the ballads. However, even though Johnson attempts to tell the "true" story, like the ballad his account becomes part of the foundation for the legend. The process that erases the motivations behind Kidd's trial—his involvement with soon-to-be discredited Whig factions in shady entrepreneurial activity—begins in this version of Kidd's life. Johnson excludes the political circumstances surrounding Kidd's trial and his actual motivation to go to sea as a privateer. Instead, he concentrates on the ships that Kidd and his men take, the violence of the men on their voyage, and the booty that is captured. It is, in fact, the ballad that becomes the "truth" through the *General History*'s reinterpretation of the ballad.

Johnson writes that in the first months of the voyage, "It does not appear . . . that [Kidd] had the least design of turning Pyrate" (2:70). However, in the next paragraph he writes, he sail'd to *Bab's Key*, a Place upon a little island at the Entrance of the *Red Sea*; here it was that he first began to open himself to his Ship's Company, and let them understand that he intended to change his Measures; for, happening to talk of the *Moca* Fleet which was to sail that Way, he said, *We have been unsuccessful hitherto, but Courage, my Boys, we'll make our fortunes out of this Fleet.* (2:70)

First Johnson emphasizes the site of Kidd's initial foray into piracy: Bab's Key "at the Entrance of the *Red Sea*." Because it is a well-known pirate rendezvous for Captain Avery, Kidd is immediately associated with that other great pirate.[31] Even more important, the words that Johnson puts into Kidd's mouth make him sound like the romanticized pirate in later fiction and popular history. And that, of course, is the basis for the image that the twentieth-century reader pictures.

The "real" Captain Kidd is replaced by a version of the pirate transformed into a pop-culture antihero who cries, "Courage, my Boys." One pictures an eyepatch, a tricornered hat, and a parrot on Kidd's shoulder. Kidd the criminal becomes Kidd the legendary antihero: the piratical subject. The economic representation and the literary representation of Kidd are merged. Forgotten is the corpse in chains that hung over the Thames to warn others against "going on the account." That corpse signifies the important difference between the criminal who steals property and the antihero who can be heroically embodied through his pirate exploits.

The "real" Captain Kidd, represented by Admiralty Court records, first speaks like a defendant on trial for his life—which he was—then he seems resigned to his fate because he has exhausted all his defense. For example, in the following exchange drawn from the trial record, Kidd pleads to have his trial postponed until he can get his hands on his "passes," or the letter of marque, which he believes will exonerate him. Dr. Oxenden, one of the prosecutors, asks him where the passes are. Kidd replies, "I brought them to my lord Bellamont in New England." The court does not allow Kidd's name dropping to get in the way of his plea. He is told, "you have had reasonable notice, and you knew you must be tried, and therefore you cannot plead you are not ready." Kidd's tone becomes more and more agitated as the prosecutors and judges become more and more annoyed that Kidd refuses to enter a plea:

Kidd. If your lordships permit those papers to be read, they will justify me. I desire my counsel to be heard.

Mr. Coniers. We admit of no counsel for him.

Recorder. There is no issue joined; and therefore there can be no counsel assigned. Mr. Kidd, you must plead.

Kidd. I cannot plead till I have those papers that I insisted upon.

Then Kidd says to the court, "My papers were all seized, and I cannot make my defence without them." The court will not budge, and Kidd says, "It is a hard case when all these things shall be kept from me, and I be forced to plead." The recorder says, "If he will not plead, there must be judgment." Kidd replies, "My lord, would you have me plea, and not to have my vindication by me?" The court, obviously impatient with Kidd, asks him for the last time, "Will you plead to the indictment?" Kidd says, "I would beg that I may have my papers for my vindication." The Court seems to have had enough of Kidd's begging, and moves to another pirate on trial, who immediately asks for clemency.

The Captain Kidd represented by the trial transcript is much different from the Kidd of legend. His desperation is obvious in this trial. He needs the "passes"—the letters of marque given to him by Bellomont. He is a far cry from the Kidd who sings,

> I steer'd from sound to sound, as I sail'd, as I sail'd,
> I steer'd from sound to sound, as I sail'd;
> I steer'd from sound to sound, and many ships I found,
> And most of them I burn'd, as I sail'd.

In the space of 150 years, Captain Kidd's career became embellished and romanticized; the real Kidd—whoever he was—became a piratical subject. His piratical subjectivity is an amalgamation of the stories told in the *General History* and all the histories, plays, and novels about Kidd in particular and pirates in general published in England and the United States. *The Pirates Own Book,* published in 1853, is important because of its great popularity.[32] It went through many editions in the nineteenth century, and an inexpensive facsimile is still in print. Not an original work, it is a redaction of the *General History,* with fanciful interpolations by the attributed author, Charles Elms.

For example, Johnson introduces Kidd by writing, "yet there were scarce any . . . who were acquainted with his Life or Actions, or could account for his turning Pyrate" (2:65). Then Elms interpolates his own analysis of Kidd: "Among the distinguished individuals who lurked about the colonies, was Captain Robert [*sic*] Kidd. . . . he had now become notorious, as a nondescript animal of the ocean. He was somewhat of a trader, something more of a smuggler, but mostly a pirate" (Elms, 172).

Unlike Johnson's version, in which Kidd is first represented as a successful middle-class merchant (which he was), Elms depicts a character whose identity is essentially piratical. I use "essentially" carefully here. Kidd's piratical transgressions—economic and cultural—cannot be removed from any other part of his "nature." From the beginning of Elms's biography, Kidd is a pirate even before he links up with Bellomont. He is not simply tempted by the possibility of riches or the patronage of his politically powerful financers. He is an "animal"—not a human, but a pirate. Even his given name has been changed from William to Robert: his surname is all that is needed to signify who and what he is.

In the middle of the *General History*'s straightforward biography of Kidd, Elms attaches the following paragraph: "Previous to sailing, Capt. Kidd buried his bible on the sea-shore, in Plymouth Sound; its divine precepts being so at variance with his wicked course of life, that he did not choose to keep a book which condemned him in his lawless career" (Johnson, 2:68; Elms, 178). Taking his evidence from the ballads sung about Kidd, Elms elaborates the Kidd legend and adds one more "fact" that will help to construct the "truth" of this "arch-pirate": Kidd buried his Bible, a literal transferal of his identity as criminal to all of his transgressive actions. He may have been an "animal," but as the ballad and Elms suggest, he *chose* to become an "animal."

The rest of the chapter remains the same as Johnson's until the end. Elms repeats the stories of buried treasure, the gold Kidd hid "that set the brains of all the good people along the coast [of New England] in a ferment" (178). From the stories of Kidd and his buried treasure come the tales that help to create the allure of the piratical subject. The fictional characters such as Captain Singleton, Long John Silver, or Captain Hook merge with the biographies of the "real" pirates such as Blackbeard, Avery, and Kidd. It becomes impossible to separate the truth from the fabricated in the histories of the pirates who really existed.

Almost fifty years later, at the turn of the twentieth century, Frank R. Stockton—a prolific and popular author of children's adventure books—published *Buccaneers and Pirates of Our Coasts*.[33] The final chapter of this popular history is entitled "The Real Captain Kidd." Stockton follows the outline of Johnson's biography, but rewrites it in an effort to show the psychology behind Kidd's crimes. For example, Stockton writes that Kidd chose not to attack "a fine English ship" because "his character was not yet sufficiently formed to give him the disloyal audacity which would enable him with his English ship and his English crew, to fall upon another English ship manned by another English crew" (312–13). Stockton writes that "Kidd's conscience had been growing harder and harder every day" (314) and "the shrewd and anxious pirate began to act the part of the watch dog who has been killing sheep" (317). The terms of "reality" for subjective identity in the late nineteenth century allow a psychological biography of Captain Kidd. To put thoughts into Kidd's mind further defines Kidd's pirate behavior as an internalized "truth."

Stockton still uses pirate mythology to tell the "real" story of Captain Kidd. Although the author does not believe in the tales of treasure buried all over the eastern seaboard of North America, he gives credit to the story of "hidden booty" buried on Gardiner's Island. He writes that its hiding place was discovered, the chest was dug up, and subsequently "all given up to the government" (319). While some money was indeed found, dispersed among former colleagues of Kidd, it is a far more attractive story to say that the money came from a burial site on an island—even if Gardiner's Island, New York, has little of the allure of either Crusoe's paradise or Treasure Island. Thus Stockton, in purporting to tell the "real" story of Captain Kidd, perpetuates the mythology of the pirate antihero.

Stockton finishes his chapter on Kidd by suggesting two reasons for his notoriety. First, the partisan nature of his trial "made him a very much talked-of man," although Stockton does not establish exactly how the politics worked against Kidd. Second, according to Stockton, the tales of a buried treasure "made him the object of the most intense interest to hundreds of misguided people" (324). Stockton repeats the stories of buried wealth, but stresses that the treasure has already been found. He both has his pirate legend and dismisses it too.

Stockton's characteristic representation of Kidd creates one more reason for the pirate's reputation. Throughout the chapter, he mixes fiction and fact to create his own version of "reality." The importance of Captain Kidd lies in his embodiment as the "archpirate," despite hopeless efforts to un-cover the truth, the "real" Kidd. What matters is that Kidd represents the piratical subject, the man who, in the words of an anonymous pamphlet writer, cannot be pardoned because "a pardon of Felonies is no pardon of Piracy. The Statute does not Corrupt the Blood."[34] Kidd's blood, perhaps, is already corrupted. I want to argue that Kidd is more than the sum of his crimes. He is now the embodiment of evil, yet sympathetic despite his wickedness. He is criminal, merchant, not-merchant, and not-criminal; hero and antihero; masculine and—as Johnson demonstrates in his *General History* and Defoe demonstrates in his pirate fiction—the masculine alternative to the deviant sodomitical subject. The "real" Captain Kidd makes an engaging subject because his career—as I have indicated—is well documented.

I do not wish to locate piratical origins where none exist, despite my efforts to differentiate on some level between "reality" and "fiction." I believe, however, that by examining the piratical subject we can see the instability of identity exhibited through sexual and economic desire that Defoe deals with in his novels. While the piratical subject is being defined with an identity of his own, the sodomite evolves into the sodomitical subject, defined by homoerotic desire rather than just the sodomitical act. The trials and the "Last Words" of the pirates help to initiate the instability of the pirate character in the first years of the eighteenth century. The literature published in the decades following the "golden age" of the pirate established all the cultural manifestations of the pirate way of life, and begins the implicit eroticization of the pirate.

4

Captain Avery and the Making of an Antihero

Avery's glory could not be dismissed as romance: it was fact that persons claiming to represent him had been received at several European courts and were prepared to negotiate alliances; it was fact that from 1705 to 1709, English and Scottish authorities were tempted to consider seriously the proposals of Madagascar's pirate-diplomats.
—Joel Baer, Introduction, *The King of Pirates*

The literary "career" of Captain John Avery (or Every) demonstrates how the pirate has been mythologized and implicitly eroticized. Like Kidd, Avery was the subject of ballads and pamphlets. But in his day, Avery was more of a folk hero than Kidd and Blackbeard ever were. In 1713 he was turned into the protagonist of a tragicomedy by the popular early-eighteenth-century playwright Charles Johnson (not to be confused with the author of the *General History*). In addition, several "biographies" about Avery appeared between 1700 and 1810, including *The King of Pirates* (1720), attributed to Defoe.[1]

Little is known about Avery's actual biography. What we *do* know, however, is that Avery's life became the fodder for a legend that soon outstripped the actual sensational crime that Avery committed: the plundering of the Great Mogul's treasure-laden ship, an incident that enraged the English government and almost caused catastrophic problems for the East India Company and its trade with the Great Mogul. Avery was accused of all kinds of sensational crimes. None of these exploits is entirely true, although there is a kernel of "truth" behind the stories. Avery was said to have established an empire of pirates in Madagascar. He sent emissaries to European countries in order to establish recognition as a sovereign state. And most notoriously, after he plundered the Great Mogul's ship, Avery either ravished or married or ravished *and* married the Mogul's granddaughter.[2]

By 1720, the year *The King of Pirates* was published, Avery's life had been told and retold, until the myth of the pirate precluded any possibility of uncovering the "truth" about the man. The author writes in the preface,

> It has been enough to Writers of this Man's Life, as they call it, that they could put any Thing together, to make a kind of monstrous unheard of Story, as romantick as the reports that have been spread about him; and the more those Stories appear'd monstrous and incredible, the more suitable they seem'd to be to what the World would have made to expect of Captain Avery.[3]

Defoe recognizes the paradox of the piratical subject. What is "monstrous" to Defoe is the fictional exaggeration of Captain Avery, and by extension the attempts by earlier eighteenth-century writers to sanction piracy politically.

In 1718, just two years before *The King of Pirates* was published, a new generation of pirates terrorized the eastern seaboard of the North American colonies. Now that the pirates once again posed a threat to trade, a new Avery biography was a useful way to offer suggestions that might help to mitigate the situation. According to Defoe, writers romanticized—exaggerated or lied about—a man from a generation earlier whose criminal actions were no better than those of marauders now wreaking havoc like Blackbeard, Bonnet, or the particularly devilish Captain England. A new biography was necessary because Avery's previous biographers "put any Thing together." They claimed to tell the truth, but they distorted the "truth," since it was made up out of hearsay and rumor. These authors heroicized the stories that by implication should be most rejected: illegitimate sovereignty, thievery, and economic havoc to the status quo.

For example, in 1709[?] a sixteen-page "biography" of Avery appeared entitled *The Life and Adventures of Capt. John Avery; the Famous English Pirate, (Rais'd from a Cabbin Boy, to a King) Now in Possession of Madagascar.* The preface credits the book to "one Adrian Van Broeck, a Dutch Gentleman, who, after a very liberal Education at Leyden, apply'd himself, as Men of the best Fashion in Holland do, to the Business of Trade" (1). What follows is a remarkably monarchist biography that turns the title character into a heroic libertine.

In this version of Avery's life, he begins as a young man of "low Birth" (3) who manages through pluck and good nature to become captain of a ship at a very young age. As in a Restoration comedy, all the "discerning" people in the story recognize that Avery is a great man. The author describes Avery as "middle-siz'd, inclinable to be Fat, and of a gay jolly Complexion. . . . His Temper was of a Piece with his Person, daring and good-humour'd, if not provok'd, but insolent, uneasy, and unforgiving to the last Degree, if at any Time impos'd upon" (6). "Provok'd" into a duel, he acquits himself heroically. He makes a bad marriage with a sluttish "Farmer's Daughter" (6) who gives birth to a child six months after they marry. To add insult to injury, Avery is cheated out of his portion by his father-in-law. So Avery decides to turn pirate.

This version of Avery's life is remarkable because it is told in the guise of a "real" biography, yet it becomes an encouragement for monarchical virtues. Avery's life follows a few of the usual paths, but with some differences: he captures the Great Mogul's ship, but refuses to ravish the granddaughter. Instead, the two marry in a ceremony performed by one of the Great Mogul's priests, because "*Avery* was e'en contented to dismiss the scruples of his being mary'd after the Church of *England* Method, out of complaisance to so desireable a Creature" (8). He sets up a pirate government on Madagascar and is elected "their Chief, with such a Power as the Doges or Dukes of *Venice* or *Genoa* are now possess'd of" (11).

Indeed, his "commonwealth" becomes so strong that he has fifteen thousand pirate-soldiers at his command. "Towns were built, Communities establish'd, Fortifications built, and Entrenchments flung up, as render'd his Dominions impregnable and inaccessible by Sea and Land" (11). By now Avery is so powerful that it is no surprise that his second in command, a Frenchman named de Sale, plots against him. De Sale's plot is discovered, however, and all the French pirates are forced to leave Madagascar. By the sleight of a pen, Avery becomes an English hero. The biography ends with a kind of "golden-age" description of Madagascar: "the Soil is extraordinary fruitful, in many places affording all Things necessary for the Life of Man in great Plenty" (15–16). The author then suggests to the reader that it would be "a might Advantage . . . to the Crown of *Great Britain*, if Means could be found out by our Superiors, either to suppress these Pyrates by Force, and so get Possession of this wealthy Island, or by Compliance with such Advances as have been made by their Chief towards his Pardon" (16). This suggestion that it might be a good idea to form some kind of treaty with the pirates in Madagascar is one of several from the eighteenth century's first decade.[4]

This small volume was published around the time Defoe wrote in his *Review* that it might be legal to either give the pirates of Madagascar a pardon or "take what they have by force": "it must be lawful to take it as a Condition of admitting them to come in—And all this, supposing they cannot easily or without Hazard or Blood, be otherwise reduc'd—Let them offer their illgotten Money, then I am clear, it will be well gotten money to us."[5] There are any number of texts from this period that defend an alliance with the Madagascar pirates.[6] No other writer, however, is as starry-eyed as the author of *The Life and Adventures of Capt. John Avery*. By reading *The Successful Pyrate* and *The Life and Adventures of Capt. John Avery* we see how the criminal pirate—*hostis humani generis*—became heroicized into the legendary Captain Avery.

In the tragicomedy *The Successful Pyrate*, the playwright Johnson exploited Avery's notoriety in order to demonstrate the danger of a too-strong monarchy.[7] The play was published when worries about succession were once again on Englishmen's minds since Anne—who had no heir—was very ill, and would die the following year in 1714. Johnson romanticized Avery in precisely the ways that enraged Defoe.

In Johnson's version, the pirate—named Arviragus—sets up a glorious kingdom on Madagascar. But Arviragus realizes that as an Englishman, he cannot be an absolute ruler. Just as in the legend of Captain Avery, Arviragus captures the Great Mogul's granddaughter. There is a twist, however, for she is Arviragus's own illegitimate daughter—unknown of course to him—and he plans to marry her. He finally repents his acts, gives his daughter to his rival, and reveals that he desires to return to England after handing over his kingdom to his new son-in-law and daughter. Through illegal trade, the pirate king has established a monarchy, but renounces his monarchical ways and returns to England a self-made rich man.

In *The King of Pirates*, Defoe wants to set the record straight by writing a first-person narrative in Avery's voice—a voice that sounds a great deal like those of Defoe's other heroes. Defoe claims to tell the "real" truth, to demonstrate the extent of the misrepresentation of Avery's legend. "There is always a great difference," he writes, "between what Men say of themselves, and what others say for them, when they come to write Historically of the Transactions of their Lives" (iv). Defoe dramatizes the moral transgressions of the "real" Captain Avery. Paradoxically—within the set of expectations put forth in *Robinson Crusoe*—Defoe also shows how Avery's moral transgressions result in his economic success.

When eighteenth-century readers picked up *The King of Pirates* their responses to Avery were conditioned by the pirate's depiction over the previous decades as both archcriminal and antihero. In *The King of Pirates*, which is written as if it were an autobiography, Defoe's narrative strategy creates a fiction out of assertions of truth based on the "real" narrator's inside knowledge. Instead of "the extravagant Stories already told," Defoe tells us that these letters are "genuine; and, as [the publishers] verily believe these letters [published as the book's narrative] to be the best truest account of Captain Avery's Piracies," then readers should believe this account. Defoe asserts that the letters are free of the embellishment and lies told in the coffeehouses of London or reported in pamphlets and the periodical press. The difficulty is, of course, that readers and Defoe are influenced by preconceptions that construct all pirates as piratical subjects, even in "the best truest account." They are literary antiheroes, whose cultural transgressions disrupt Defoe's emphasis on the economic crimes.

In the earlier narratives of his life, Avery makes a conscious decision to turn pirate and talks his fellow sailors into mutiny.[8] As a privateer, he occupies the unsure place of the freebooter in seventeenth- and early-eighteenth-century maritime history. Avery has a license from the king of England, and is sanctioned by his government to plunder and steal from enemy ships. However, once he "turns pirate" in the eyes of English law, the legend and the reality take on the mythical force that establishes him as the eighteenth century's first maritime outlaw-hero.

Defoe attempts to control this legend, already blurred by the passage of a quarter century. In Defoe's version, Avery begins his career in the uneasy status of a sailor on a privateer ship, where "we had been a Kind of Pyrates, known and declar'd Enemies to the *Spaniards*" (5). Instead of inciting his fellow sailors to mutiny, however, he is captured by pirates, Defoe tells us, and he willingly turns "real" pirate "at War with all Mankind" (5). But although Avery becomes an "accidental" pirate, one who might not have gone on the account if the circumstances had not allowed it, he is still a pirate whose legal status makes him *hostis humani generis*.

After Avery and his companions are captured by "real" pirates, Avery says, "we found they were a worse Sort of Wanderers than ourselves . . . for [before] we never offer'd to rob any of our other *European* Nations, either *Dutch* or *French*, much less *England*; but now we were lifted into the service of the Devil indeed, and, like him, were at War with all Mankind" (6). Defoe does not erase the transgressive behavior explicit in the homosocial pirate world, the cultural and legal deviations from the conventions of the legitimate maritime world. Indeed, he goes so far as to link Avery with Satan himself. Avery says he and his fellow sailors had been "a kind of Pyrates," acknowledging the potential criminality of the freebooter's vocation. However, it is not until they go to war against "all Mankind" and cross the boundaries (always shifting for the privateer) into out-and-out piracy, that they are themselves criminalized by the legal definitions of their countrymen.

Until Avery makes the move from privateer to pirate, he is still on the edges of the legitimate maritime world, still—to some extent—a part of the economic and sexual social order of conventional England. The moment he is no longer "a kind of Pyrate," but a real, true, undeniable pirate, he leaves the normative order. The ambiguous "nature" of Avery's sexuality is evident in his depiction of his relationship with the princess. The literary pirate, in the "service of the Devil," and the criminal—or legally defined—pirate become the piratical subject, quite different from the libertine "hero" of the 1709 pamphlet.

Avery describes in great detail the booty the pirates take. After one particularly successful battle, Avery says,

> Our Men found in the Ship 6 Brass Guns, 200 Sacks of Meal, some Fruit, and the Value of 160000 Pieces of Eight in Gold of *Chili*, as good as any in the World: It was a glittering Sight, and enough to dazzle the Eyes of those that look'd on it, to see such a Quantity of gold laid all of aheap together, and we began to embrace one another in Congratulations of our good Fortune. (16)

The detail and description of the booty recall Moll Flanders's erotic response to money. In Avery's world, Defoe eroticizes money and material wealth, as he does in *Moll Flanders* and *Roxana*. There is a connection between the ambiguous sexuality of the pirate and the "phallic" sexuality displaced onto jewels and money that we see in *Moll Flanders* and *Roxana*. The ability to make money outside "normal" channels of trade and inheritance—in Moll's case, for example, her life of crime and prostitution—seems to unmoor identity from traditional sexual as well as economic definitions.

Moll has an unconsummated affair with a rich gentleman. Instead of the sexual act, they share their wealth: her gentleman friend

> bade me open a little walnut-tree box he had upon the table, and bring him such a drawer, which I did, in which drawer there was a great deal of money in gold, I believe near two hundred guineas, but I knew not how much. He took the drawer, and taking my hand, made me put it in and take a whole handful. I was backward at that, but he held my hand hard in his hand, and put it into the drawer, and made me take out as many guineas almost as I could take up at once. (121–22)

Defoe's language here makes Moll sound like a young woman about to lose her virginity. Likewise, the riches discovered by the pirates cause them to express their joy physically, to "embrace one another" and to share their happiness over their "good Fortune." The excitement that they show over the wealth is enacted through their transgressive brotherhood, just as Moll puts her hand in her friend's money "drawer" (197).

Avery and his men are so successful at piracy that they become notorious throughout the South Seas, hunted by the government that originally sanctioned their outlaw behavior when their enemies were the Spaniards. They are bound together by their criminality and their love for plunder, though they have no place to go and spend the wealth: "So that upon the whole, we concluded there was no Safety for us but by keeping all together, and going to some Part of the World where we might be strong enough to defend ourselves" (28). Alone in the world, they must stay together, outlaws and criminals forced to unite in a transgressive camaraderie.

In order to save their lives (and their booty), they must find a place to hide, a giant closet to go into until they are able, or willing, to come out in the open again. Unlike sailors who work for lawful gain and are thus free to return home and spend their profit, these men have no "home" to return to. If others like them wish to join their brotherhood, they are welcome. Although they "had no great Need of Company, yet [they] were overjoy'd at meeting" others like them who would show up at their hiding place. To be "like" them means to be a pirate, a criminal. To be "like" them, is to share a subjectivity outside the circle of legitimate sexuality, to be piratical subjects. The sodomite's acts pose a threat to normative sexual—and thus economic—relationships. The pirate performs implicit acts of cultural deviance or "Monstrous unheard of Stories." These acts are not confirmed, and consequently they are too ambiguous to criminalize explicitly. The pirates' illicit wealth is the only authentic means to confirm their deviance as *hostis humani generis.*

The pirates choose to hide, of course, on Madagascar, an island whose fame grew along with that of the pirates, an exotic place that provides anything a pirate would need.[9] As we have seen with the two earlier tales about Avery, on Madagascar literary mythologies of the piratical subject converge with the pirate's real legal status as criminal. The legends tell us that Avery established his great notoriety as the "king of pirates" on Madagascar.[10] Much of the early-eighteenth-century fascination with the Avery character came from English interest in Madagascar, the huge island two hundred miles east of Africa in the Indian Ocean. Madagascar is isolated between Africa and India, between the unknown and the exotic. It is a place where pirates can rest, careen, and carouse. According to the stories in Europe, the settlement that the pirates built evolved into a great city and an empire that controlled trade in the Indian Ocean.[11]

Defoe, in his version of Avery's story, tries to downplay the legend of Avery's piratical colonization of Madagascar. Avery discounts the stories that he had sent emissaries to European governments in an attempt to gain recognition for the "nation" in the eyes of the world:

> they were told at *London*, that we were no less than 5000 Men; that we had built a regular Fortress for our Defence by Land, and that we had 20 Sail of ships; and I have been told that in *France* they have heard the same Thing: But nothing of all this was ever true, any more than it was true that we offer'd ten Millions to the Government of *England* for our Pardon. (63)

Defoe details the imagined strength of the pirates' empire, just as he details the incredible booty of a successful raid. On the one hand, then, Defoe is discrediting a legend that constructs the pirate world and its threat to English trade. On the other hand, he is applauding the very legends that he is trying to contradict. Avery and his men become rich, with "gold enough to dazzle the eyes." Avery denies that "we offer'd ten Millions" to England, but he does not deny that he *could* have offered all that money.

Because the pirates are outlaws, they have no need for recognition by European governments. The legends of wealth and desire for recognition are rewritten by Defoe in a way that asserts Avery's desire to be independent of English societal norms. The pirates, says Avery, are not trying to gain the legitimacy of being a nation; on the contrary, they just want to be left alone with their money on their island. They have no desire to be pardoned because they refuse to be a part of the conventional world.

In *The King of Pirates* Avery admits that he himself made up these stories to seek recognition. His pirate colony will seem to be a formidable power and the pirates will be left alone. This assertion represents the ambiguous status of the piratical subject. Defoe wants to discredit the legends that give credence to their legally defined piratical acts, but at the same time cannot resist glorifying the economic success of his antihero. He creates a figure not bound by conventional restraints—represented by the order imposed by the British government—in order to minimize the effect of a financially success-ful pirate. However, the pirate's unconventional "nature" is precisely what provokes such fascination with the piratical figure. The Avery legend, then, is much more complicated as a cultural sign than simply Defoe's representation of his economic transgressions. Averio homo economicus already has been determined as Averio homo eroticus in the stories told about Avery and the Indian princess in *The Successful Pyrate* and *The Life and Adventures of Capt. John Avery.*

On the one hand, Defoe tells us that Avery was not as rich as the public believed; that Avery exaggerated stories of enormous wealth so that sailors would return to Europe and frighten the governments from attacking him. On the other hand, Avery also brags about the hugely profitable raids on individual ships, as we have seen, and particularly the plundering of the Great Mogul's ship, the most famous incident in the creation of the Avery myth.[12] While trying to demystify this episode, Defoe inadvertently points up how homo eroticus and homo economicus are connected. Defoe exploits this story not for the implicit sexual tensions between Avery and the Mogul princess, but instead for the economic anxiety that the mythic piratical act produces. However, if vast wealth fascinates readers of Avery's history— including Defoe—then Avery's sexual exploits necessarily are mythologized as well because the transgressive individuality of the pirate—exemplified here by the Avery legend—intrudes on the legal definition of piracy.

As they cruise the Indian Ocean, Avery and his crew come upon the ships of the Great Mogul, which they take with little resistance. The ship that holds the princess and the treasure "was the main Prise":

> When my Men had enter'd and master'd the Ship, one of our Lieutenants call'd for me . . . he thought no Body but I ought to go into the great Cabin . . . for that the Lady herself and all her Attendance was there, and he fear'd the Men were so heated they would murder them all, or do worse. (57)

The other pirates may be rabble who would rape an Indian princess, but Avery can find a way to save her honor. Although his gallantry may seem to grant more importance to the fate of the princess than the profit from the treasure, it makes more sense to read the episode as a representation of how Defoe tries to negotiate the tensions within the representation of the piratical subject as both antihero and criminal.

In the more traditional tales of Avery's exploits, both the princess herself and the treasure are the objects of Avery's desire.[13] In Johnson's play, for example, the princess is the prize desired by the hero and his rival. In Defoe's narrative, however, the diamonds are eroticized, not the princess. Avery is accused of raping her, but he insists, "they wrong me, for I never offer'd any Thing of that Kind to her, I assure you; nay, I was so far from being inclin'd to it, that I did not like her" (58). What he "likes," of course, is the booty, and although the legend insists that Avery resorted to sexual violence and even reciprocal desire for the princess, he does not succumb, despite the temptation that should tantalize any pirate, unless his community is homoerotically defined.

Avery revels in the treasure and disdains the princess. When he enters the cabin of the princess, he is struck by

> such a Sight of Glory and Misery [as] was never seen by Buccaneer before; the Queen (for such she was to have been) was all in Gold and Silver, but frighted; and crying, at the Sight of me she appear'd trembling, and just as if she was going to die. She sate on the Side of a kind of a Bed like a Couch . . . she was, in a Manner, cover'd with Diamonds, and I, like a true Pirate, soon let her see that I had more Mind to the Jewels than to the Lady. (57)

Sexual desire in a traditionally gendered form is of little interest to Avery, the piratical subject. He sees the "glorious" jewels, and he sees the princess as a kind of "miserable" display case for the jewels that he wants. Defoe's attempt to define piracy as an economic transgression, however, is constantly undermined by the eroticism that is implicit in any literary history of the pirate. Avery disdains sex with the princess but enjoys the company of his men, with whom he lives on Madagascar, who are excited and "embrace one another" at the sight of a heap of treasure. "Like a true Pirate," he is not interested in the lady. But if he does not desire the princess, neither is he a feminized sodomitical subject. He is, instead, the masculine alternative to the conventional hero. Whatever Avery may desire sexually, his sexual subjectivity cannot be defined by his outward masculinity. Transgressive sexual desire—or sexual desire of any kind—is masked by the desire generated by the treasure.

If this were an instance of racial tension and the masking of desire between the genders, the homoeroticism would not be implicit. However, the legends and Defoe's account contradict one another here. Avery's inclinations have to be read alongside the other tales of his desire for the princess. Most other versions of this legend insist that Avery carried the princess away to Madagascar, and that they married and had children. Defoe's efforts to remake a character whose legendary status as a romantic antihero is too well-known by the public to be totally reinvented as an economic criminal result in a self that can be read through a newly emergent homoeroticism.

Avery, in fact, declares that he and his crew "look like Hell-hounds and Vagabonds; but when we are well dress'd, we expect to look as other men do" (80). He does not define himself as *being* like other men, he only wants to *look like* other men. He is unlike other men, yet at the same time he is unlike the legend, the rapacious, insatiable pirate king. Who is the "real" Captain Avery? No one ever finds out. Defoe suggests that Avery, with a few comrades, leaves his home, and abandons Madagascar and the citizen pirates. One "Particular Friend" asks to join him when he leaves the others.

The book ends in the same way that Defoe's pirate novel *Captain Singleton* does. Avery and his friend are making their way to Europe, where they will live together in seclusion. Defoe's ending differs from other representations of the Avery legend. In most other versions Avery disappears from view—just as Defoe tells the story—but steals his comrades' treasure, and probably died in poverty, unable to spend his wealth for fear of discovery.[14] As the story gets told and retold, Avery's greed becomes the cause of his fall. Not only was he a criminal in the eyes of the law, but the literary representation makes him a criminal against other criminals. In Defoe's version, however, years after the "facts" of Avery's death, the pirate king, the transgressive hero made rich by his crimes, gets away with his jewels and retires with a companion. He is a man who, read through the narratives of homoerotic desire, finds a kind of peace with a companion of his own gender.

The ending of *The King of Pirates* is surprisingly similar to the ending of *Captain Singleton*, in which Avery makes a prominent appearance. Unlike *The King of Pirates*, however, *Captain Singleton* makes no pretense toward "truth" and "history" in the same determined way that Defoe represents Avery. On the contrary, despite the usual title page that asserts the "truth" of *Captain Singleton*'s narrative, the novelistic qualities of the book are paramount, and closer to Defoe's other, more popular novels such as *Crusoe* or *Moll Flanders*. If two decades later Richardson can use the domestic milieu to engender female subjectivity, then Defoe is using the popular literature of the day—pirate stories and seamen's journals—to develop a different kind of subjectivity. Subjectivity—an always unstable notion—can be different from more transparent domestic, or what we now call "heterosexual," desire.

5

Fabricated by the Frail Hand of Man

The *General History* and Fictional Reality

It's a Wooden World, fabricated by the frail Hand of Man, and yet is of a more firm Contexture, than the great One, if we may believe old Sages, who tell us, that this would drop to Pieces, if but one Atom only was wanting; whereas our Wood-Creation holds firm together, when batter'd worse than a Bawdy-house.

—Edward Ward, *The Wooden World Dissected*

No Man can have a greater Contempt for Death, for every Day he constantly shits upon his own Grave, and dreads a Storm no more, than he does a broken Head, when drunk.   —Ibid.

Captain Johnson's *General History of the Robberies and Murders of the Most Notorious Pyrates* vividly recounts the biographies of famous and obscure marauders of the "golden age." In volume 1 Johnson concentrates on the most famous sea rovers, such as Blackbeard, Major Stede Bonnet, and Captain Avery. The stories of these men were well known to the reading public. In the second volume, however, Johnson invents pirates out of whole cloth and includes their stories alongside the tales of "real" pirates such as Captain Kidd. Ironically, because of the *General History*'s influence on pirate history, these fabricated pirates have become "real." Popular historians write about them as if they actually existed. In *The Pirates' Who's Who*, for example, Philip Gosse makes no distinction between those pirates in the *General History* who have historical precedents and those whom Johnson makes up.[1] Johnson, of course, makes no distinction either. The unintentional effect of the *General History* is to show us that history and fiction are interpenetrating discourses.

The significance of the *General History* to eighteenth-century culture has been unacknowledged or underestimated by both historians and literary critics in English studies.[2] But the first volume went through four editions between 1724 and 1726. In 1728 a second volume was published.[3] The *General History* is the primary—at times, only—source for the many popular histories that have appeared in the last two centuries, until the groundbreaking work of a few academic historians. This neglect is particularly noticeable given the work's enormous influence on later generations of popular historians and novelists of piracy.[4] Beyond the limits of Defoe studies, piracy itself is such an important cultural trope in early-eighteenth-century England that it is surprising that this book has almost never been seriously treated, given the ways it constructs and mythologizes the pirates as we know them.[5]

Both "history" and social criticism, the *General History* integrates fiction and "fact." The work's unsure generic status probably accounts for its critical neglect. In the rush to discover the "origins" of the novel, critics have overlooked the *General History*'s own fictional attributes because it is called—explicitly—a "history," and its subjects are "real" pirates.[6] Additionally, pirate fiction is not a reputable genre. Witness the huge number of "penny-dreadful" novels and romances in the 1830s, 1840s, and 1850s, and the notable dearth of critical studies about this genre.[7] These novels are a fascinating site for further research, since the way the piratical figure is romanticized demonstrates how the piratical subject changes depending on the cultural context. The issue of generic "respectability" is particularly significant given the emphasis on a few of Defoe's texts and their relevance to the origins of the novel at the expense of his less familiar works. Defoe's novels that have captured critical attention are *Robinson Crusoe, Moll Flanders, Roxana,* and *A Journal of the Plague Year.* His other novels, while discussed in Defoe scholarship, tend to be ignored by more inclusive studies of the novel. *The Farther Adventures of Robinson Crusoe, The Serious Reflections of Robinson Crusoe, Colonel Jack, Captain Singleton, A New Voyage round the World, Memoirs of a Cavalier,* and *Captain Roberts* all come to mind as "forgotten" or neglected in histories of the novel and even in major studies of Defoe. With the exception of *Memoirs of a Cavalier,* all these novels have piratical elements. The neglect of piracy in criticism of Defoe's canon is baffling because scholars have recently examined other traditionally popular literary genres such as crime literature to contextualize and offer new readings of Defoe's major texts and novels.[8]

I want to rectify the neglect of piracy and argue for its importance as a trope in Defoe studies and, more broadly, gay and lesbian studies and queer theory. The purpose of this chapter is not to make conjectures about sex between pirates, or to argue that a readerly response to the pirate is based only on later novels and histories. As I suggested in chapters 2 and 3, the piratical subject can be connected to the newly emergent sodomitical subject. This connection makes perfect sense if we consider the burgeoning emphasis on domesticity, economy, and sexuality in seventeenth-century pamphlet literature, and the emphasis on private experience exemplified by novels such as Defoe's *Robinson Crusoe, Roxana*, and *Captain Singleton*. In the *General History*, piracy represents an economic transgression. But piracy also represents transgression against middle-class and domestic notions of "reality," since as we have seen, women play little part in eighteenth-century depictions of pirate life.[9] As Jonathan Goldberg asks, "How is gender difference produced if the trajectory of desire is not determined by the gender of its object?" (37).

I shall argue, then, that English society's dialectic of fear and admiration of the pirate indicates a conflict between the pirate's representation as legal or economic criminal and his portrayal as a literary antihero. More broadly, this dialectic is a conflict between normative sexuality—private domesticity— and sexually deviant subjectivity. For example, Johnson wonders why Captain England decided to turn pirate: "It is surprizing that Men of Good Understanding should engage in a course of life that so much debases human nature" (1:114, 2d ed.). For the pirate, this "course of life" is both economically and socially transgressive. In the early eighteenth century, the sodomite already was defined by his "course of life," internalized erotic and transgressive desire for other men.[10]

Plain Reasons for the Growth of Sodomy in England (1720), published only four years before the *General History*, shows this depiction of the "unnatural" sodomitical subject.[11] The anonymous author argues that since the sodomite is "unfit to serve his King, his Country, or his Family, this Man of *Clouts* dwindles into nothing, and leaves a Race as effeminate as himself; who, unable to please the Women, chuse rather to run into unnatural vices with one another, than to attempt what they are but too sensible they can't perform" (9–10). The difference between Captain England and the sodomite represented here lies in the contrast between the literary embodiments of the sodomite and the pirate. The "unnatural vices" make the sodomite an explicitly sexual criminal: his crimes are both his unnatural desire for other men and the sexual acts that follow. His private life—unnatural desire—is here made public. Further, the sodomite is impotent around women, but somehow—to this author's dismay—manages to have sex with other men. Likewise, the pirate is unnatural, but paradoxically, despite the assertion that Captain England "debases human nature," he and his ilk can be set up as antiheroes precisely because they transgress in so many public cultural ways. Any private experience he might have, though, is left unexamined.

The "effeminate" sodomite "debases human nature." Although he is a part of English society, he is an "unnatural" sexual criminal whose desires are in opposition to the "normal" heterosexual man and woman. He "dwindles into nothing," out of sight, out of mind, unless caught in the act, or set upon, as groups of early-eighteenth-century young men did to supposed gangs of mollies.[12] The anonymous author writes, "I scorn to stain my paper with the Mention" of the reprehensible acts that the sodomite performs (23). Not the enactment of desire between two men but homoerotic desire itself is anathema to this author, and nearly impossible to imagine.

The sodomites "chuse" a deviant course of life. The piratical subject chooses a course of life and "debases human nature" as well. The actions of these men suggest the complex matrix of homo eroticus—the legally criminalized sodomite—and homo economicus—the legally criminalized pirate. The historical pirates posed a tangible threat to the economic basis of English society. The economy was a foundation as "natural" as heterosexual desire had become by 1720. Captain England—a literary representation—"debases human nature" despite his "good understanding" that ought to prevent his criminal acts. Johnson writes that Captain England took a ship and tortured the master:

> for the Boatswain immediately called to his Consorts, laid hold of the Captain, and made him fast to the Windless . . . afterwards they whipp'd him about the Deck, till they were weary, then told him, because he was a good Master to his Men, he should have an easy Death, and so shot him thro' the Head, and tumbled him overboard into the Sea. (1:135)

Unlike the author of *Plain Reasons,* who leaves the sexual acts between men to the reader's imagination, Johnson explicitly details the criminal actions England and his brethren perform in order to "debase human nature." The pirate's actions—the acts of piracy—are explicitly economic crimes, enacted against seafaring merchants. In popular history of the piratical subject, however, the crimes are embellished by gruesome detail. The reader is both repelled and thrilled by the pirate's violent actions. The narrative detail that imagines how Captain England behaved not only enriches the psychological embodiment of the piratical subject, it also draws a curtain around certain

B. Cote sculp.

Blackbeard the Pirate.

Blackbeard. In this early engraving, Blackbeard's fierceness is not nearly as pronounced as the description in the text would suggest. From *A General History of the Pyrates,* 2d ed., 1724. Courtesy of the William Ready Division of Archives and Research Collections, McMaster University Library, Hamilton, Ontario.

Captain Teach commonly call'd Black Beard.

Blackbeard. In this engraving twelve years later, Blackbeard's visage begins to take on demonic qualities and details that exaggerate even the description from the text. From *A General History of the Lives and Adventures of the Most Famous Highwaymen, Murderers, Street-Robbers, &c.,* 1734. Courtesy of the William Ready Division of Archives and Research Collections, McMaster University Library, Hamilton, Ontario.

Will'. Tele delin   W.* Pritchard sculp
CAP.* AVERY and his Crew taking one of the GREAT MOGUL'S Ships

Captain Avery and his crew taking one of the Great Mogul's ships. From *A General History of the Lives and Adventures of the Most Famous Highwaymen, Murderers, Street-Robbers, &c.,* 1734. Courtesy of the William Ready Division of Archives and Research Collections, McMaster University Library, Hamilton, Ontario.

A GENERAL

HISTORY

OF THE

PYRATES,

FROM

Their firſt RISE and SETTLEMENT in the Iſland of
Providence, to the preſent Time.

With the remarkable Actions and Adventures of the two Female Pyrates

MARY READ and ANNE BONNY;

Contain'd in the following Chapters,

To which is added.

A ſhort ABSTRACT of the Statute and Civil
Law, in Relation to Pyracy.

The ſecond EDITION, with conſiderable ADDITIONS

By Captain CHARLES JOHNSON.

LONDON:

Printed for, and ſold by *T. Warner,* at the *Black-Boy* in *Pater-Noſter-Row,* 1724.

Title page from *A General History of the Pyrates,* 2d ed., 1724. Courtesy
of the William Ready Division of Archives and Research Collections,
McMaster University Library, Hamilton, Ontario.

The *Snow* getting under Sail to look out for some Booty, *Fulker* and the others desired they might be set at Liberty, but it was denied them for the present, tho' not without a Promise that they should be released the first Vessel they took.

The fifth of *June* they left *Carolina*, and the next Day they spied a Sail, which prov'd the *John* and *Betty*, commanded by Capt. *Gale*, bound from *Barbadoes* to *Guiney*. *Fly* gave Chase, but finding the Ship wronged him, he made a Signal of Distress, hoisting his Jack at the main Top-Mast Head; but this Decoy did not hinder the Ship making the best of her Way. *Fly* continued the Chace all Night, and the Wind slackening, he came within Shot of the Ship, and fir'd several Guns at her under his black Ensign; the Ship being of no Force, and the Pyrates ready to board, the Captain struck; and *Fly* manning his Long-Boat, which carried a Pateraro in the Bow, the Crew being well armed with Pistols and Cutlashes went on Board the Prize, and sent Capt. *Gale*, after having secured his Men, Prisoner on board the *Snow*.

This Prize was of little Value to the Pyrates, who took nothing but some Sail-Cloaths and small Arms, and after two Days let her go, but took away six of his Men, setting on board Capt. *Fulker* and a Passenger (Mr. *Atkinson* was detained) and Capt. *Green*'s Surgeon; they kept this Gentleman, Mr. *Atkinson*, knowing he was a good Artist, and lately Master of the *Boneta* Brigantine, as a Pilot for the Coast of *New England*, which they were satisfied he was well acquainted with.

Upon Mr. *Atkinson*'s desiring to have his Liberty with the others, Captain *Fly* made him the following Speech: *Look ye, Captain* Atkinson, *it is not*

not that we care a T——d for your Company, G——d d——n ye; G——d d——n my Soul, not a T——d by G——d, and that's fair; but G——d d——n ye, and G——d's B——d and W——ds, if you don't act like an honest Man G——d d——n ye, and offer to play us any Rogues Tricks by G——d, and G——d sink me, but I'll blow your Brains out; G——d d——n me, if I don't. Now, Capt. Atkinson, *you may do as you please, you may be a Son of a Whore and pilot us wrong, which, G——d d——n ye, would be a rascally Trick by G--d, because you would betray Men who trust in you; but, by the eternal J——s, you shan't live to see us hang'd. I don't love many Words, G——d d——n ye, if you have a Mind to be well used you shall, G——d's B——d; but if you will be a Villain and betray your Trust, may G——d strike me dead, and may I drink a Bowl of Brimstone and Fire with the D——l, if I don't send you head-long to H——ll, G——d d——n me; and so there needs no more Arguments by G——d, for I've told you my Mind, and here's all the Ships Crew for Witnesses, that if I do blow your Brains out, you may blame no Body but your self, G——d d——n ye.*

Mr. *Atkinson* answered, it was very hard he should be forced to take upon him the Pilotage, when he did not pretend to know the Coast, and that his Life should answer for any Mistake his Ignorance of the Coast might make him guilty of, and therefore begg'd he might be set on board Capt. *Gale*; and that they would trust to their own Knowledge, since he did not doubt there being better Artists on Board. *No, No,* replied *Fly, that won't do by* G——d, *your palavring won't save your Bacon.* Muchas palabras no valen nada, *as the* Spaniards *say; so either discharge your Trust like an honest Man, for go you shan't by* G——d, *or I'll send you with my Service to the D——l; so no more Words,* G——d d——n ye.

There

Ann Bonny *and* Mary Read *convicted of Piracy Novr. 28th 1720 at Court of Vice Admiralty held at* St. Jago de la Vega *in ye Island of Jamaica.*

Anne Bonny and Mary Read. From *A General History of the Pyrates,* 2d ed., 1724. Courtesy of the William Ready Division of Archives and Research Collections, McMaster University Library, Hamilton, Ontario.

Captain Bartho.Roberts *with two Ships, Viz . the* Royal Fortune *and* Ranger, *takes 11 Sail in* Whydah *Road on the Coast of* Guiney, *January 11ᵗʰ 172²⁄₄.*

Captain Bartholomew Roberts. From *The General History of the Pyrates,* vol. 2, 1728. Courtesy of the William Ready Division of Archives and Research Collections, McMaster University Library, Hamilton, Ontario.

THE
LIFE,
ADVENTURES,
AND
PYRACIES,

Of the Famous

Captain SINGLETON:

Containing an ACCOUNT of his being fet on Shore in the Ifland of *Madagafcar*, his Settlement there, with a Defcription of the Place and Inhabitants: Of his Paffage from thence, in a Paraguay, to the main Land of *Africa*, with an Account of the Cuftoms and Manners of the People: His great Deliverances from the barbarous Natives and wild Beafts: Of his meeting with an *Englifhman*, a Citizen of *London*, among the *Indians*, the great Riches he acquired, and his Voyage Home to *England:* As alfo Captain *Singleton*'s Return to Sea, with an Account of his many Adventures and Pyracies with the famous Captain *Avery* and others.

LONDON: Printed for *J. Brotherton,* at the *Black Bull* in *Cornhill, J. Graves* in St. *James's Street, A. Dodd,* at the *Peacock* without *Temple bar,* and *T. Warner,* at the *Black Boy* in *Pater-Nofter-Row.* 1720.

Title page from *Captain Singleton,* 1st ed., 1720. Courtesy of the William Ready Division of Archives and Research Collections, McMaster University Library, Hamilton, Ontario.

Robinson Crusoe's Island of Despair. From *The Serious Reflections of Robinson Crusoe,* 1720. Courtesy of the William Ready Division of Archives and Research Collections, McMaster University Library, Hamilton, Ontario.

Robinson Crusoe meets Friday. "I beckoned to him to come nearer." From *Robinson Crusoe* (Boston, 1884). An engraving from a drawing by George Cruikshank. Courtesy of the William Ready Division of Archives and Research Collections, McMaster University Library, Hamilton, Ontario.

Robinson Crusoe discovers the footprint. From *Robinson Crusoe* (London, 1820). Engraving by Thomas Stothead. Courtesy of the William Ready Division of Archives and Research Collections, McMaster University Library, Hamilton, Ontario.

Robinson Crusoe destroys the pagan idol. From *La vie et les
aventures surprenantes de Robinson Crusoe* (Amsterdam, 1720), the
first French edition. Courtesy of the William Ready Division of
Archives and Research Collections, McMaster University Library,
Hamilton, Ontario.

kinds of behavior between pirates that do not jibe with their hypermasculinity.

The sodomite's private sexual transgressions—like the pirate's public economic transgressions—are criminalized. But unlike the pirate's private identity, the sodomite's private identity as homo eroticus is foregrounded. In a reversal of the pirate's representations, the sodomite's economic crimes are masked. Sodomites do not marry, and even if they do, as the author of *Plain Reasons* argues, they are unable to "perform." These men are thus left out of the heterosexual domestic economy. Armstrong and Foucault have shown us the economic ramifications of "heterosexual" desire and the rise of capitalism. Heterosexual desire occupies a dominant place in an emergent middle-class society. This is a society that, as Armstrong writes, classifies men and women into separate and interlocking spheres of economic subjectivity (59). Armstrong argues that the domestic wife "was supposed to complement [her husband's] role as an earner and producer with hers as a wise spender and tasteful consumer" (59). The desire displayed by the sodomitical subject has no place in this paradigm because he has no economic value in a world centered on desire between the genders. There is then a subtle merging of the sodomite's distinct sexual crimes and his implicit economic transgression against the gendered model of the transmission of capital.

The parallels between the sodomitical subject and the piratical subject would be even stronger in the passage quoted above if the author of *Plain Reasons for the Growth of Sodomy* did not further demonize the sexuality of the sodomite and erase his economic transgression. In not very imaginative poetry, the anonymous author joins the sodomite's identity with his acts:

> By thy *jaws* all lank and thin;
> By that forc'd unmeaning grin:
> Thou appear'st to Humane Eyes,
> Like some Ape of monstrous Size;
> Yet an Ape thou can'st not be,
> Apes are more adroit than thee;
> Thy Odittys so much my Mind perplex;
> I neither can Define thy Kind or Sex. (26–27)

The sodomite's "kind," or his "identity" and his "sex," or his gender, "perplex" the author because the sodomite is a man who acts in a nonmasculine way. "Odd" as the sodomite appears in this doggerel, his appearance is inseparable from his sexual identity and his *non*human action: "Like some Ape of monstrous Size." In a dichotomous world of black and white, men and women, or pirate and legitimate merchant, the feminized sodomite is positioned against *both* the heterosexual man and the heterosexual woman. Since he does not act like a man, and he is not a woman, how can he be "human"? To the author of *Plain Reasons*, the sodomite is closer to an "Ape" or a beast. But even "an Ape" he cannot be.

This triangular situation recalls the ways the pirate is positioned as a deviant criminal beyond his economic transgressions. The monstrous "nature" of the sodomite in this early-eighteenth-century pamphlet reflects the outrageous descriptions of the behavior and physicality of individual pirates in the *General History*. But while the sodomite's sexual transgressions are mostly left to the imagination, the pirate's offenses, diverse and not explicitly sexual, are graphically described.

For example, Captain Low, one of the most violent of the pirates, has an "inhumane temper" (Johnson, 1:293). Johnson writes (with slightly odd syntax) that Low "ty'd lighted Matches between Men's Fingers belonging to a Sloop bound in to *Amboy* . . . till the Flesh was all burnt off" (1:293). Then, after taking two whalers, Low "caused one of the Master's Body to be rip'd up, and his Intrails to be taken out; and cut off the Ears of the other, and made him eat them himself with Pepper and Salt" (1:301). Captain Low's behavior is *in*human, different from the sodomite's behavior whose sexual acts are too "monstrous" to describe and thus not human. Low even observes social niceties: he "made" the sea captain season his own ears before he consumed them, an ironically civilized gesture in a world of uncivilized behavior. Further, despite their despicable actions, England, Low, and their ilk appear "normal" within the terms of masculine embodiment, while the sodomite is monstrously and uncertainly embodied "like some Ape of monstrous Size."

Johnson depicts the "inhumanity" of the pirate's acts, in contrast to the "nonhumanity" of the sodomite's acts *and* appearance portrayed by the author of *Plain Reasons*. The sodomite's acts are "impossible to imagine" since desire between two men makes no sense and goes against "nature." Because he lives in conventional society, then, the sodomite must be "less than an ape" or not human.[13] The pirate, on the other hand, never loses his humanity, violent as it may be, despite his brutality toward followers of the status quo. The violent acts he performs on others are graphically represented. These representations, I would argue, attempt to mask the sexual connotations that can be uncovered in a transgressive homosocial piratical society.

According to Joel Baer, the concept of "*hostis humani generis* suggested the extent to which a pirate was thought beyond the pale of civilized society and hence the lawful prey of any who could destroy him by foul means or fair."[14] He points out that in the early eighteenth century the decisive legal view of piratical acts and their consequences allowed the state extraordinary power. According to early-eighteenth-century legal thinking, the pirates' "total denial of human values disabled them from claiming the protection of any established state and validated the severity of their punishments. As they have willingly denied the social feelings that distinguish men from beasts, so mankind may deny to them the benefits of distinctly human institutions, such as civil law" (Baer, 8). This interpretation of eighteenth-century beliefs about "piracy rights" demonstrates the way the state recognized how beyond the pale the pirates were, because of, as we shall see, the pirates' establishment of their own highly organized social institutions. Baer points to a paradox: on the one hand, pirates are more beast than man; on the other hand, they have rules and regulations that make them more man than beast.

The *General History* deals with this problem: by the terms of English maritime law, the pirates can hardly be distinguished from "beasts," yet at the same time, they create homosocial utopian centers in Madagascar or sites of wild excess in the West Indies. One is a remote outpost on the European trading route, the other smack in the middle of colonial trade.[15] Unlike judicial minds that designate the pirates as *ipso facto* criminals, Johnson complicates matters; he contrasts the "bestial" natures of pirates such as Captain Low to other pirates' heroic attempts to maintain a *different* kind of society, for example, Captain Misson's "utopia" on Madagascar. Johnson vacillates between depicting the pirate as an economic outlaw and portraying him as a political exemplar.

Captain Misson became the democratically elected leader of a utopian society on Madagascar called Libertalia:

> Misson thanked [his comrades] for the Honour they conferr'd upon him, and promised he would use the Power they gave for the publick Good only, and hoped, as they had the Bravery to assert their Liberty, they would be unanimous in the preserving it, and stand by him in what should be found expedient for the Good of all, and should never exert his Power, or think himself other than their Comrade, but when the Necessity of Affairs should oblige him. (2:14)

Baer—who attributes the *General History* to Defoe—argues that "Defoe as well as John Esquemeling, historian of the West Indian Buccaneers, simply highlighted the depravity of criminals already notorious for barbarism" (17). But I suggest that the author of the *General History* does more than "simply highlight" the criminals' barbarity; he emphasizes their radical departure from societal norms in other ways as well. Misson and his men are still *hostis humani generis* because they will plunder any country's ships. However, they self-consciously "assert their Liberty" and create their own society against the state. They individually fight to create better lives for themselves in their own society, apart from the structures of English government and power. The pirates were not necessarily religious dissenters, but as Hill suggests, they did dissent from the status quo of nationalism and class difference that left them alienated and in poverty.[16]

Because Johnson's chapter "Of Captain Misson" is a history, and because Misson is a product of Johnson's imagination, the liberty espoused by Misson is a literary—or fictional—reality. That is, because his life is in a history, Misson and his utopia become "true" or as real as any other pirate depicted with a biography in the *General History*. This "truth" in turn threatens the total demonization of the pirate that the legal reality intends. Who in the *General History* are the "real" pirates? Blackbeard, Avery, Kidd, and Bonnet existed, and hard evidence, much of it available at the Public Record Office in London, reported the threats they posed and the attempts to capture them. Misson, on the other hand, probably did not exist, but within the explicitly "historical" terms of the *General History* he is as real as any of the pirates, and his actions as genuine as Blackbeard's atrocities.

Furthermore, the "liberty" espoused by Misson is a radical idea in early-eighteenth-century England. The early-eighteenth-century concept of liberty itself "came to be a negative one. . . . The Englishman's house is his castle, a 'liberty' in the feudal state from which state power is excluded."[17] Obviously, this idea of liberty is only for those who can afford their own property, their own "castle." Misson and his men are pirates who assert their liberty despite their class and propertied situation. They make a world—build themselves a castle—dependent on *other* people's property (the plunder) on an island far from Great Britain (Madagascar).

Not all the pirates are like Misson, who heroically challenged European class division, or like Captain Avery, who captured the public imagination by staging a spectacular act of plunder against the infidel Great Mogul. The bloodthirsty, ear-roasting Captain Low was emphatically not a hero. Edward Thatch, better known as Blackbeard, was an unredeemable monster who preyed indiscriminately on English citizens in the colonies and treated his own crew with self-conscious brutality. (Of course, even Blackbeard got grudging respect from Johnson—"a couragious Brute"—as we saw in the introduction.)

Like the sodomite, the pirate will "chuse to run into unnatural Vices with one another," that is, piracy. Unlike the sodomite—that "Man of Clouts"—the pirate is portrayed as an individualist. He can most certainly "perform"—exemplified by the havoc he unleashes at sea—because the British government has defined him as "a common enemy against all mankind." Both the pirate and the sodomite share complicated homosocial bonds. Unlike the horror shown toward the sodomite, who could only be demonized and thus remained a criminal, complex reactions that individualize pirates such as Blackbeard, Misson, and England disclose both respect and admiration, along with abhorrence.

Pirate society is an alternative world governed by different kinds of norms not defined by gender difference. Both the pirate and the sodomite are attracted to and gravitate toward other men. For the sodomite, this attraction is explicitly eroticized. For the pirate, this attraction is homosocial, but implicitly eroticized because he is culturally deviant, yet his sexuality is neither questioned nor determined. However, the heightened masculinity of the piratical subject comes to interrupt and complicate bifurcations in depictions of gender and economic representation that leave out notions of sexuality. Moreover, the piratical subject interrupts burgeoning domestic concepts of subjectivity that elevate heterosexuality as the only norm. He shows the fine line that separates transgressive homosocial and homoerotic relationships. The pirate will never "dwindle into nothingness," like the "effeminate race" described by the author of *Plain Reasons for the Growth of Sodomy*. To use Michel Serres's terminology, the pirate is a parasite on the social and cultural norms represented by domesticity. The noise that the pirate makes is too loud. That noise cannot be suppressed because the noisemaker—the piratical subject or here the heroic Captain Misson—is represented as economically and culturally unstable. The piratical subject, unlike the sodomitical subject, will not stay in a fixed position, either as an economic transgressor or as a romanticized hero. You never know what the pirate will do next.

In the opening of the chapter on Major Stede Bonnet, ironically one of the most celebrated pirates of the age despite his supposed incompetence,[18] Johnson writes,

> The Major was a Gentleman of good Reputation . . . and had the Advantage of a liberal Education. He had the least Temptation of any Man to follow such a Course of Life, for his Condition was superior to any Thing that could have been expected from the most fortunate Adventures in the pyratical Way: It was surprizing to every one, to hear of the Major's Enterprize, in the Island where he lived; and as he was generally esteem'd and honoured, before he

broke out into open Acts of Pyracy, so he was afterwards rather pitty'd than condemned, by those that had been acquainted with him, believing that his Humour of going a pyrating, proceeded from a Disorder in his Mind, which had been but too visible in him, some Time before this wicked Undertaking [; and which is said to have been occasioned by some Discomforts he found in a married State]. (1:60, bracketed section from 91, 2d ed.)

I do not wish to be reductive and make overly simplistic connections between piracy and sodomy; however, in this passage one can locate sites that mask the threat of the pirate as a sexualized individual much the same way that the sodomite's threat is trivialized in eighteenth-century literature.[19] Johnson calls Bonnet's deviance a "Humor of going a Pyrating, proceeding from a Disorder in his Mind." Bonnet is "psychologically" warped into a course of piracy, just as we see the sodomite "bent" and defined by his sexuality. Indeed, Johnson (and thus the readers) defines Bonnet by his piratical self. His identity cannot be separated from his acts of piracy. Bonnet's medical disorder helps Johnson explain his surprise that an otherwise upstanding man should turn pirate and "debase human nature."

But Bonnet's story shows the instability of the piratical subject. Because of Bonnet's failure as criminal he is "pitty'd" rather than "condemned," seen as "ill qualify'd for the Business," as Johnson puts it (1:91, 2d ed.). The menace Bonnet poses as a pirate is very real, since he and his crew did commit acts of piracy. Yet Johnson obscures that threat because he emphasizes a dysfunctional marriage over Bonnet's criminal activities.

The bracketed section at the end of this long quotation comes from the second edition of the *General History*. When Johnson revised the text he added the reference to "discomforts of the married state." Johnson interprets a medical illness, a "disorder in the mind," as a gendered domestic problem; the disorder is caused by vague difficulties with his marriage. These "discomforts" could be anything from impotence to arguments with his wife over money, drinking, or housekeeping. Two hundred years later, the pirate historian Philip Gosse explicates the "discomforts" and turns them into explicitly "psychological" problems. Gosse writes that "the Major's mind had become unbalanced owing to the unbridled nagging of Mrs. Bonnet."[20] Other historians even in the late twentieth century pick up Gosse's conjecture. In a 1992 history, Jenifer Marx writes that "Discord with his shrewish wife *may* have spurned [Bonnet] on" (emphasis mine). According to another recent historian, Clinton Black, "[Bonnet's] friends were scandalized at first by his strange behavior, but later sympathized with him when it was discovered that he had gone to sea to escape his wife's unbridled nagging."[21]

Bonnet's history is the perfect example of a pirate story that gets told and retold, changing little by little. The assumption made by Gosse, and perpetuated by anyone who reads his book or uses his unreliable history as a source, is that Bonnet left his wife because she was an impossible nag. However, Bonnet did not leave his wife for another woman; he became a pirate, a man driven by a shrewish wife to live in a transgressive world with other men.

If a writer can devise the transition from "discomforts in the married state" to general nagging, an alternative suggests itself: the "discomforts" are sexual. Middle-class society privileges domestic relations as an explanatory structure. "Discomforts in the married state" can be linked to gendered attraction and sexual performance as much as to a "nagging" wife. "Nor was the Major at all qualified for this Business," Johnson tells the reader, "he not being acquainted with Sea Affairs, but had always lived at Land, in a peaceable and creditable manner" (1:60). Johnson explains that Bonnet bought a ship with the specific intent of going on the account. Bonnet did not have to turn pirate to get away from his wife, presumably because he could have become a legitimate sea merchant despite his inexperience. Johnson and Gosse blame Bonnet's wife, thereby occluding the possibility of homoerotic and economically transgressive desire as an explanation for his choice to turn criminal.

The traces of homoerotic noise suggested by the *General History*'s biography of Bonnet and concealed by Gosse's explication are indicative of the shift from a homosocial economic license at sea for the ordinary seaman or merchant to a transgressively homosocial, and thus potentially homoerotic, identity for the piratical subject. Bonnet's main crime seems to be leaving his "nagging wife" rather than the actual piracy. At the very least, the piracy is a radical departure for a man "with a seeming Sense of Virtue and Religion" (Johnson, 1:60). Bonnet may be rather "pitty'd than condemned" by his friends who are not affected by Bonnet's economic threat. Yet his criminal actions result in a blistering sentencing speech by the judge who presides over Bonnet's trial. The judge—a spokesman for the state—first points out that Bonnet is a gentleman and has had a "liberal education" (Johnson, 1:82). He then tells Bonnet, "but that considering the Course of your Life and Actions, I have just Reason to fear that the Principles of Religion that had been instiled [*sic*] into you by your *Education*, have been at least corrupted, if not entirely defaced, by the *Scepticism* and *Infidelity* of this wicked Age" (1:83). The judge fears that Bonnet's crimes represent the worst aspects of early-eighteenth-century social trends, a denial of all the values that hold society together. Bonnet's "infidelity" has less to do with his actual crimes of piracy—his status as *hostis humani generis*—and more to do with the "crime" of turning his back on his wife and what Crusoe calls the "middle state" (*Robinson Crusoe*, 28). The point that the judge makes about Bonnet's moral violations begins to unravel, displaying the complicated merging of homo economicus and homo eroticus in early-eighteenth-century society. In a domestic ideology, new values in which sexuality became identified with gendered domesticity and capital economy clashed with old values, based on class differences, bloodlines or patrilineal inheritance, and religious beliefs.

In a conventional, middle-class world, the meaning of "infidelity" and "scepticism" is wrapped up not only in notions of religion, class, and sovereignty, but with gendered sexual definitions as well. The state and the married couple are complexly intertwined. Bonnet's "infidelity" is not only against the common good, or property rights, of British society—an economic transgression—but against a domestic ideology, his relations with his wife. Bonnet's embrace of the pirate way of life reverses the judge's logic. Bonnet's "scepticism" causes him to leave his wife. His abandonment of normative society leads to a strengthening of transgressive fraternal and political bonds in the pirate world.[22]

Bonnet has been represented as the least "dangerous" of the legendary pirates. So incompetent was he, according to the *General History* and later sources, that when Blackbeard joined forces with him, he relieved him of his command and let Bonnet keep only his title. But the historical evidence suggests an alternative "truth." Bonnet did pose a great threat to trade along the coast of the Carolinas. Newspapers such as the *Weekly-Journal* gave regular accounts of Bonnet's crimes.[23] Even the judge's speech at Bonnet's trial gives ample evidence for his success: "you *pyratically* took and rifled no less than *thirteen* Vessels, since you sail'd from *North-Carolina*. So that you might have been indicted, and convicted of *eleven* more Acts of *Pyracy*, since you took the King's *Act of Grace*, and pretended to leave that wicked Course of Life" (Johnson, 1:107, 2d ed.). However, the literary insistence on Bonnet's incompetence as a pirate, coupled with the infidelity and skepticism he is accused of by the state, hints at a different kind of sexual desire for the piratical subject, with pirate traditions to authorize deviance and nondeviance.

Bonnet remains an important figure in pirate history to both early-eighteenth-century and modern writers in part because he tried to do something about his "inadequacy" by turning pirate. Like the sodomite in *Plain*

Reasons for the Growth of Sodomy, Bonnet is one of those "antiquated Lechers; who have out-lived the Power of Enjoyment; and so Conscious of their own Insufficiency they dare not look a Woman in the Face" (14). But there is a difference between the sodomite and Bonnet. Bonnet *tried* to indicate his masculinity by turning pirate. He may no longer have desired his wife, but he was not an effeminate, effeminized monster.

Pirates have their own notions of conformity, but "conformity" becomes transgressive camaraderie. Their deviant homosocial brotherhood is reminiscent of the fellowship and camaraderie shown by the libertines. The libertine, exemplified by Rochester, was of course an aristocrat who gloried in sexual anarchy and had sex with both women and boys. The pirates, outside the conventions of English society, do not belong to any class. Most of these men were ordinary seamen turned pirates, though some—like Captain Misson, Johnson's fictional hero—came from noble backgrounds. But the pirates' anarchy was primarily economic. Their sexuality is curiously ambiguous. Yet their individuality is exemplified by their heightened masculinity.

Johnson relates the career of the pirate Captain Vane and his crew, who plundered a ship bound for Providence. He writes that they "went to a small Island and cleaned; where they shared their Booty, and spent some Time in a riotous Manner of Living, as is the Custom of Pyrates" (1:104). The ordinary sailor goes to port after weeks or months of legitimate sailing and finds a woman. The pirate goes to an isolated island to share his booty with his fellow transgressors. What exactly is the "riotous Manner of Living" that is their custom? By the 1720s sexuality is a component of identity nearly impossible to ignore in any "history" of an individual or group. Because sexuality and identity cannot be separated, the dead silence in the space of the pirate's homosocial private life suggests that the transgressive homosocial world of the pirate requires the presence of homoeroticism. Whether or not the pirates sodomize one another is beside the point. Rather, sodomy is tantalizingly implicit and repressed. Despite popular perceptions, women were left out of almost all pirate literature in the eighteenth century. Captain Misson's story is one exception—but the women are "natives" and Johnson's purpose is to legitimize a utopian community, to depict and promote an alternative political world. But because other pirate representations are consistently unstable, the pirates' sexuality is repressed in most of these depictions.

Further, because sexuality becomes a defining trait of identity, to ignore the repression of sexuality is to recognize its existence. When Captain Davis stops a quarrel between some fellow pirates, it is difficult not to hear traces of homoeroticism in his speech: "Hearkee you Cocklin, and La Bouse, I find by strength'ning you, I have put a Rod into your Hands to whip my self, but I'm still able to deal with you both; but since we met in Love, let us part in Love, for I find that three of a Trade can never agree" (Johnson, 1: 156). In a burgeoning domestic ideology, "love" takes on meanings that link capital and domesticity with sexuality.[24] The pirates—enemies to everyone except each other—meet "in love" because they are three of a kind who share through their camaraderie a like identity as piratical subjects. Captain Davis links "love" with his status as a pirate—an illegitimate businessman. Conventional though this use of "love" may be, ordinary merchants probably did not meet or part in love because they were inherently competitive. Nor did they "whip" each other with "rods." Unlike the merchant adventurers who sign contracts with one another, pirates "share their booty . . . as is the Custom of Pyrates." This "Custom" of sharing their spoils is based not on legal contracts, but on their word as pirates. The complication lies in what exactly a pirate's word means. Are they criminals or heroes? Their competitive "nature" is defined against the merchants whom they plunder. Pirates "part in love" because they recognize their likeness as both pirates (or criminals) and piratical subjects in this world without women.

Implied homoeroticism is just one transgressive trait of the pirates that should be emphasized. Norman O. Brown writes that "language is an operational superstructure on an erotic base."[25] If Brown is correct, and language is always erotically driven, then the profanity exhibited by the pirates is a transgressive vocabulary that celebrates the pirates' deviance. In Defoe's *Serious Reflections*, Crusoe says, "Talking Bawdy, the Sodomy of the Tongue has the most of ill Manners, and the least of a Gentleman in it, of any Part of common Discourse" (105). Crusoe's metaphor is a striking denunciation of verbal transgression. The language of the pirate is, in Defoe's words, sodomitical. In the late seventeenth and early eighteenth centuries reformers complained about the profane way the youth spoke. William and Mary and Anne issued many proclamations to stop the populace from cursing.[26] Pirates, not bound by any proclamations and not "gentlemen," glory in the profanity.

Johnson depicts the pirate Captain Fly's dialogue with a prisoner as a series of signifiers that the reader must decipher:

Look ye, Captain *Atkinson*, it is not that we care a T--d for your Company, G-d d--n ye; G-d d--n my Soul, not a T--d by G-d, and that's fair; but G-d D--n ye, and G-d's B---d and W---ds, if you dont act like an honest Man

G-d d--n ye, and offer to play us any Rogues Tricks by G-d, and G-d sink
me, but I'll blow your Brains out; G-d d--n me, if I don't. (2:235)

And so on for a full page. What fascinates is what is not being said, and how
Johnson's represents what is not being said. Fly's discourse, if one can call it
that, is like a pie to the face of polite speakers of English, or more specifically,
socially sanctioned language. The author of *Plain Reasons for the Growth of
Sodomy* does not have to describe the sodomitical act because his readers will
understand what he implies. Defoe can call "bawdy" language "Sodomy of
the Tongue," and his readers will understand the metaphor. At the very
least, it is morally wrong, ill mannered, and self-consciously transgressive in
middle-class society. Anyone can fill in the gaps in the representation of Fly's
words, and if not, even the most naive reader knows *why* the gaps are there.
This depiction of pirate verbal abuse is a word game that compels the reader
to see into the pirate's mind, or at least the mind as Johnson represents it.
Fly's censored profanity is so distinctive because it parallels the language that
we know. We can all fill in the blanks; however, the way Johnson represents
Fly is both alien *and* familiar. The speech's deviation lies in the ways readers
must *imagine* profanity as "Sodomy of the Tongue."

The exuberant use of profanity contrasts pirates with sailors in eighteenth-
century literary representations. However, language at sea contrasts pirates
and sailors with landlubbers who speak "normal" English because seamen
use specialized sea terminology. The seamen's dialect is further complicated
by the makeup of the sailors on board a pirate ship: men from all over
Europe who speak an alphabet-soup patois (Redicker, 150, 162–69, 278). If
English, Dutch, Portuguese, Arabic, French, Spanish, and other languages
are combined into a singular tongue, a sailor cannot understand it unless he
has been initiated into its mysteries.[27] Indeed, Edward Ward in *The London-
Spy* has a lot of fun representing the sailor's speech. Ward overhears sailors
talking in a tavern, and uses that opportunity to lampoon the sailors and
make their language almost unintelligible:

> They swear and so forth and talk a funny way "The Devil D—n the Ratlings
> of these Wooden Shrouds, for I have broke my Shings against 'em; I had
> rather run up to the Cross Trees of the Main topmast in a Storm, than six
> Rounds of these confounded Land Ladders, after the Drinking a Kan of Phlip
> or a Bowl of Punch."[28]

Sailors speak a strange language—almost English but not familiar. What *are*
Cross Trees or Land Ladders, anyhow? The pirate's "Sodomy of the
Tongue" shows that pirates deviate even from the ordinary seaman's lan-

guage. The way Fly's dialogue gets recorded works to horrify everyone and point up the transgressive "nature" of an already fallen language. Ordinary seamen may swear as much as pirates, but their oaths do not get written down. Johnson reproduces Captain Fly's oaths precisely to emphasize their transgressive nature. Captain Fly revels in the profanity, in the "sodomy" of his tongue in ways impossible for individuals tied down by conventions of decorum.

A century later, an edition of the *General History* dated 1825 represents Captain Fly's speech in the third person: "Upon Mr. Atkinson's desiring to have his liberty with the others, Capt. Fly refused it with the most horrid oaths and imprecations."[29] A century has "tamed" Captain Fly considerably. A reader must now base an understanding of the "horrid oaths" not on dialogue by Johnson (a vernacular that creates a kind of piratical "character" "horrid" in its baseness), but on the mythological construction of the piratical subject. Fly's character is a construct and is refracted by representations of all the pirates. Johnson used his explicit representation of Fly's profanity as one of the building blocks for the foundation of pirate mythos.

The reader of 1825 knew what the "horrid oaths and imprecations" signified. In other words, the Fly of Johnson is portrayed as transgressive to readers in the 1720s in ways that the Fly of the 1825 edition does not have to be. By an edition of 1860, Fly has been excised from the volume.[30] Moral behavior, the internalization of cultural standards, is so embedded, as Foucault would argue, that for the reader explicit language transgression by a pirate like Fly no longer needs to be forthrightly represented. Fly's transgressive language is part of the cultural knowledge of the piratical subject.

There is more to pirate deviance than language difference. Despite their utterly masculine embodiment, Johnson's pirates at times embrace an effeminate outward deportment and dress at odds with their reputations. For example, in the chapter "Of Captain Martel" Johnson represents pirate cross-dressers who self-consciously parody the beau. In one sense, of course, the pirates are lampooning class differences. In the early eighteenth century, however, the sodomite began to be depicted as effeminate and feminized, as historians like Trumbach and Greenberg have shown us. A "correspondent" to the *General History*, who was captured by the pirate Martel, writes,

> Notwithstanding the melancholy Situation I was in, I could not refrain laughing when I saw the [pirates] who went on board the *Greyhound*, return to their own Ship; for they had, in rummaging my Cabbin, met with a Leather Powder Bag and Puff, with which they had powder'd themselves from Head to Foot, walk'd the Decks with their Hats under the Arms, minced their

Oaths, and affected all the Airs of a Beau, with an Aukwardness would have forced a Smile from a Cynick. (2:334)[31]

The complications in this passage are fascinating. To use the critic Lennard Davis's terminology, Johnson is "framing" it through the correspondence of a sea captain. This captain relates the story of pirates who use his powder in order to make fun of a "Beau." We easily picture the pirates as great hairy masculine men, particularly since we have read about their violent and profane ways and seen engravings in books. These powdered pirates parody the effeminacy of a certain kind of masculinity, represented by the beau and, implicitly, by the effeminate sodomite — that "Man of Clouts."

During the Restoration effeminacy as portrayed by the fop figure did not necessarily constitute sexual identity. By the 1720s, however, the beau and the effeminate sodomite were embodied in ways that were much more intertwined. One need only to read the short novel *Love Letters between a Certain Late Nobleman and the Famous Mr. Wilson* (1723) to see how this change occurred.[32] Wilson — a young beau-about-town — cross-dresses in order to sexually excite the "Late Nobleman." What follows in the short novel is a passionate physical affair between two men.

Johnson's pirates find the powder in the first place in the cabin of the man who is amused by their burlesque: a sea captain. Presumably, this sea captain powders himself as well. Who is being feminized here? The pirates, already implicitly homoeroticized even though they are masculine in their deportment? The captain — the pirate's masculine nemesis — whose powder is used and is certainly not representing himself as effeminate? Society, which makes the powdered "beau" a paragon of fashion but likewise feminizes the sodomite? The pirates' parody becomes very ambiguous for readers, who must envision what they know of the pirate and balance that with what they see in "everyday" life.

The objects of the parody are not only the pirates who "mince their oaths" — as much as the correspondent would like to think — but also the correspondent himself, whose powder creates these dandified pirates. On the other hand, homoerotic noise suggests that the pirates are being parodied as well, despite their genuinely masculine image. The "noise" insinuates that a mincing pirate is not too far out of the realm of possibility, that something about the pirate makes his parodic effeminacy disturbing, if effeminacy marks homoerotic identity as well as the class difference represented by the beau.

The parodic behavior of the pirates in the Martel chapter is further complicated by the reader's awareness of pirate dress. The pirate's costume, like the sailor's, is distinctive. Put together from the clothes of dead or captured sailors, booty, and what they can scrounge up, their clothing was patched and falling apart. After months of staying unwashed, the pirate wore whatever he could or whatever the captain could find. For example, Woodes Rogers, in his *Voyage*, tells the readers how his crew was dressed: "We had six Taylors at work for several weeks to make them Clothing, and pretty well supply'd their Wants by the spare Blankets and red Clothes belonging to the Owners; and what every Officer could spare, was alter'd for the Mens Use" (107). However, some pirates were known for their sartorial flair. Indeed, at times Johnson emphasizes their singular appearance as part of their transgressive characterization. For example, "Calico Jack" Rackham—remembered because he captained the ship on which the "female pirates" Mary Read and Anne Bonney served—got his nickname because of his outrageous dress.[33]

Captain Roberts, about whom Johnson writes in the most detail, is a snappy dresser, even for a dandified pirate:

> Roberts himself made a gallant Figure, at the Time of the Engagement, being dressed in a rich crimson Damask Wastcoat, and Breeches, a red Feather in his Hat, and a Gold Chain Ten Times round his Neck, a Sword in his Hand, and two pair of Pistols hanging at the End of a Silk Sling, which was slung over his Shoulders (according to the Fashion of the Pyrates). (1:213)

Even during battle, Captain Roberts dresses in a glamorously dazzling way at odds with the aggressively masculine embodiment maintained by the pirates themselves—Blackbeard comes to mind as the most obvious example—and their chroniclers. However, Roberts's foppish dress and its effect on his behavior are mitigated because he "is said to have given his Orders with Boldness, and Fire" (Johnson, 1:213). Roberts refuses to allow the refined impression he makes on an audience—or his enemies—to influence the way he *acts* as a pirate: "with Boldness, and Fire."

Roberts may wear gold chains and fling silk slings over his shoulder "according to the Fashion of the Pyrates," but he is a pirate, first and foremost, who like Captain Fly can swear oaths, and, like Blackbeard, fight to the death. Roberts revels in the explicit dichotomy between his behavior and his distinctive costume. Roberts can shout to his crew, "We would set Fire to the Powder with a pistol, and go all merrily to Hell together" (Johnson, 1:179), but he wears clothing parenthetically dismissed by Johnson as "fashion." "Fashion" was a word loaded with contemptible, unmanly connotations in the early eighteenth century. But fashion shared by the pirates suggests that their world was in fact a society, with its own standards of fashion.

In the preface to the second edition Johnson writes, "I presume we need make no Apology for giving the Name of a History to the following sheets, though they contain nothing but the Actions of a Parcel of Robbers" (1:A4r-v, 2d ed.). This "Parcel of Robbers" may prey on innocent sailors and merchants of the sea and are indeed criminals. However, they are also portrayed by Johnson as antiheroes who buck tradition and live by their own rules. These rules challenge conventional depictions of masculinity and masculine desire.

6

A Brave, a Just, an Innocent, and a Noble Cause

[I]f there is one common Enemy, we have the less need to have an
Enemy in our Bowels.
—Daniel Defoe, *The Shortest-Way with the Dissenters*

Every Herb, every Shrub and Tree, and even our own Bodies, teach us
this Lesson, that nothing is durable or can be counted upon. Time
passes away insensibly, one Sun follows another, and brings its
Changes with it.   —Charles Johnson, *General History*

Captain Roberts's biography is by far the longest in the *General
History*.[1] Johnson says that this is because Roberts "ravaged the Seas longer
than the rest, and of Consequence there must be a greater Scene of Business
in his Life" (1:A4r). Captain Roberts is intended to represent all the pirates:
"we found the Circumstances in *Roberts's* Life, and other Pyrates, either as
to pyratical Articles, or any Thing else, to be the same, we thought it best to
give them but once, and chose *Roberts's* Life for that Purpose, he having
made more Noise in the World, than some others" (1:A4r). The "noise"
that Roberts makes is no "noisier" than that of other pirates. Undeniably
certain pirates from the first volume will be better remembered because of
their individual exploits: Avery, Blackbeard, and Bonnet are the most obvious examples. In Roberts, however, Johnson finds the pirate whom he can
most usefully represent as both criminal and hero. This dichotomy most
obviously is exemplified by *The King of Pirates*, an "autobiography"; by
Captain Singleton, explicitly a novel; and by the fictional chapter "Of Captain Misson" in volume 2 of the *General History*. With Captain Roberts,
Johnson is able to build a "history" that pulls together such facts as trial
records, a list of articles, and names of men condemned, as well as an

accretion of detail and a number of anecdotes, all of which work to create a "real" history of a pirate. Using Roberts as his defining pirate, Johnson can analyze many of the transgressive qualities of the pirate and demonstrate *how* the pirate comes to transgress in conflicting heroic and criminal ways.

As a way of trying to stereotype the pirates, however, this approach backfires. Johnson positions Roberts near the end of the first volume, so that Roberts is preceded by many other pirates, each of whom exhibits a distinct individuality or personality. Further, in volume 2 Johnson emphasizes the peculiarities of many different pirates, beginning with the memorable Captain Misson. The history of one pirate cannot contain all the variations of character displayed in pirate history. And variations of individuality undermine Johnson's attempts to "tame" pirate representations through Roberts's history.

For example, the "democratic values" of the pirate, well known before Johnson's and Defoe's books, are foregrounded throughout the *General History.*[2] When pirates "went on the account" they usually wrote up articles that detailed the distribution of the booty as well as prescribed their behavior on board the pirate ship. The articles are "one of the most egalitarian plans for the disposition of resources to be found anywhere in the early eighteenth century" (Rediker, 264). Further, "The pay system represented a radical departure from practices in the merchant service, Royal Navy, or privateering. It leveled an elaborate hierarchy of pay ranks and decisively reduced the disparity between the top and bottom of the scale" (Rediker, 264). Besides percentage scales that regulated the distribution of booty based on a pirate's position on board ship, the articles might include prohibitions against deserting, fighting, stealing, and "meddling" with women. The articles even included a kind of insurance that detailed specific reparations for loss of limbs or eyes. "The articles also regulated discipline aboard ship, though 'discipline' is probably a misnomer for a system of rules that left large ranges of behavior uncontrolled" (Rediker, 265).

The distinction between rules and "uncontrolled behavior" interests me. "Behavior" is defined by the system that the pirates are rebelling against. Roberts's articles serve as signs for Johnson's commentary on the political, and thus cultural, dangers of piracy. But the articles complicate the way Johnson represents Captain Misson and other "radical" pirates. The pirates' articles demonstrate the extent to which the pirate milieu opposed the political structures of conventional society and the economic structures of mercantile seafaring.

According to Johnson, Captain Roberts and his crew "formed a Set of

Articles, to be sign'd and sworn to, for the better Conservation of their Society, and doing Justice to one another. . . . How indeed *Roberts* could think that an Oath would be obligatory, where Defiance had been given to the Laws of God and Man, I can't tell" (1:169). Johnson explicitly represents Roberts and his men as being a "society," but they are outside "the Laws of God and Man." At the same time—even though the men have a society— he is unable to comprehend why they would have articles in the first place since they are so deplorably criminal. Johnson assumes here that any "oath" replicates conventional society's values. The pirates, however, have created their own society—as Johnson has demonstrated throughout the *General History*. Their oath, then, is given within the terms of camaraderie in their own transgressive world.

Sodomites had a secret society as well, as numerous pamphlets make clear.[3] Molly clubs were gathering places for sodomites in early-eighteenth-century London. But these clubs represent a secret society within the conventional structures of English society. Johnson himself sets up the pirates as creating a "society," with a moral system in "defiance" of the world. The pirates, who "defy" the "Laws of God and Man," are, as we have seen, the masculine alternative to the hero, opposed to the legitimate sea merchant and the hierarchical economic system that he represents. The difficulty for Johnson lies in representing the pirates as *hostis humani generis* and at the same time avoiding the contradiction that they morally and economically support one another at sea.

After listing Roberts's articles—a model, we are told, for other pirates' regulations—Johnson comments on each one. For example, article 5 declares that the pirates must make every effort "*To keep their Piece, Pistols, and Cutlass clean, and fit for Service*" (1:170). The article itself is straightforward: make sure your gun is ready to fire. Johnson adds embellishments that serve to confirm the reader's impression of the pirate:

> in this they were extravagantly nice, endeavouring to outdoe one another, in the Beauty and Richness of their Arms, giving sometimes at an Auction (at the Mast,) 30 or 40 £ a Pair, for Pistols. These were slung in Time of Service, with different coloured Ribbands, over their Shoulders, in a Way peculiar to these Fellows, in which they took great Delight. (1:170–71)

These embellishments to the forthright article emphasize both the pirate's extravagance and his "peculiarities," his love for costume and display. The depiction of Captain Roberts in his finery demonstrates a necessity for Johnson to mark all the pirates as "other," both in the earlier descriptions of the costumes of Roberts and his brethren, and in this description of the need to keep their weapons "fit for service." In addition, "30 or 40 £ a Pair, for Pistols" was an enormous sum in 1724. That the pirates are willing to "auction" their guns for that much money suggests either the kind of property that may be important to them (their guns, here) or their cavalier disregard for money at all (there's always more where that came from when the whole world is your enemy).

However, at the same time they may not be quite as "other" as he maintains, given his construction of their world. Precisely because the pirates have a society defined by the articles, their separate world may be a little too close for comfort. The articles show that these criminals have their own cultural and legal system. Johnson must elaborate on the articles to demonstrate that the pirates still differ from members of English society. That he reproduces the articles in the first place implies a way to complicate the reader's understanding of the pirate: Is he hero or villain? Is he civilized or bestial?

Johnson is very careful in this respect. He reemphasizes the implied perversion of the piratical articles:

> These, we are assured, were some of *Roberts*'s articles, but as they had taken Care to throw over-board the Original they had sign'd and sworn to, there is a great deal of Room to suspect, the remainder contained something too horrid to be disclosed to any, except such as were willing to be Sharers in the Iniquity of them. (1:172)

This is a tantalizing passage. Not only does Johnson rely on hearsay and innuendo, but he also manages to hint at dark—or perhaps even sexual—misbehavior. It is hard to tell what he is getting at, what is "too horrid to be disclosed." But the "noise" of pirate transgression interrupts his commentary and makes the reader ask exactly what "Iniquities" the pirates may be "Sharers in." Is Johnson "suspecting" some misdeed other than the usual pirate misbehavior, that is, plundering, looting, and pillaging? If so, what horrible secrets lie behind the missing articles? Norman O. Brown argues that "the mythical archetypes of the race . . . say things which it is still not possible to say in any other way" (219). The literal demonization of these "mythical archetypes" suggests several alternatives for a depiction of hyper-masculine identity that is inclusive of homoerotic desire.

Given the coded ways deviant sexuality was talked about in early-eighteenth-century England, it is not going too far out on a limb to suggest that the "dark secrets" can signify sexual transgression.[4] For example, in *The*

Conspirators, "Britannicus" compares the authors of the South Sea Bubble to Roman degenerates like Catiline, who "married several times, but chiefly, as People suspected, for the Convenience of strengthening himself by *Alliances* with *Great Men*, rather than out of any Affection for the *Ladies*." Britannicus takes the innuendo a bit further than is usual:

> For if we may believe some Authors, he had a most *unnatural* Tast [*sic*] in his *Gallantries*: And in those Hours when he gave a Loose to Love, the Women were wholly excluded from his Embraces. . . . There are some Vices, which give too gross Ideas, to be repeated by the Names that are afix'd to them.[5]

Catiline indulges in vices that are "too gross" to name. Britannicus uses Catiline and ancient Rome to comment on a dreadful economic situation caused by implicitly deviant sexual desire. Roberts and his men—who live in a transgressive world—likewise wreak havoc on the economic status quo. It is not a misinterpretation, I would argue, to suggest that homoerotic desire is implicit in Johnson's commentary on the pirates' articles.

Indeed, the physical expression of deviant sexuality is not entirely prohibited by the articles, as Johnson implies in article 6:

> *No Boy or Woman to be allowed amongst them. If any Man were found seducing any of the latter Sex, and carried her to Sea, disguised, he was to suffer Death;* so that when any fell into their Hands . . . they put a Centinel over her to prevent ill Consequences from so dangerous an Instrument . . . ; but then here lies the Roguery; they contend who shall be Centinel, which happens generally to one of the greatest Bullies, who, to secure the Lady's Virtue, will let none lye with her but himself. (1:171)

Although boys and women are not "allowed amongst them" because of their "disruptive influence," there are neither implicit nor explicit prohibitions against sodomy.[6] Either the idea of sodomy is so beyond the pale that Johnson cannot articulate why boys should not be "amongst them," or it never occurs to him that boys can *be* a sexually disruptive influence. We know from naval records that cabin boys could be as young as twelve or thirteen. They could easily become pirates if the situation warranted (and this is exactly what happened to the very young Singleton in Defoe's novel). Additionally, there are no bans against "meddling" with boys: only women are specified as sexually threatening. Whether or not sodomy occurred is, as I have argued, beside the point. What *is* to the point is the dead silence in the space between gendered relations in the "real" world and those in the world of the pirates. The pirates' well-known physicality, exemplified by their violence, costume, and profanity, complicates homosocial and hetero-sexual depictions of their identity that ignore pirate sexuality.

I have described the articles at length because their importance to pirate culture allows us to see that their dissemination, in fact, portrays a "world" of the pirates, a world with its own laws and proscribed behavior. Those laws are mutable, however, and change from pirate gang to pirate gang. Although the articles specifically prohibit women from being brought on board a pirate ship, two of the most famous pirates from the "golden age" were women disguised as men: Mary Read and Anne Bonny.

According to a recent historian of piracy, "Whether Anne and Mary were in fact the passionate but faithful mates of two of their fellow pirates or whether they were whores is beside the point. No one disputes the facts of their dramatic careers which equalled those of the most dashing pirates."[7] It is *exactly* the point that Read and Bonny were sometimes "passionate but faithful mates" and other times "whores." This dichotomy is precisely how Johnson and later writers characterize Read and Bonny, with novelistic detail. But here the author sweeps aside the fictive qualities of Johnson's biography to privilege Read and Bonny's "dramatic careers which equalled those of the most dashing pirates." The trial record deals with the facts of the crime rather than the perhaps more interesting personal details of the "female" pirates, the place where Johnson focuses his attention.[8] Read and Bonny would never be remembered if, first, they weren't women, and second, their stories didn't emphasize the "whore"/ "faithful mate" dichotomy.

Even though the meager "facts" of these female pirates do not stand up to this dichotomous scrutiny, Read and Bonny are still represented as either whores or faithful mates. Any "facts" about their lives and "dramatic careers" are based on Johnson's representation in the *General History*. In "The Life of Mary Read" Johnson writes, "some may be tempted to think the whole Story no better than a Novel or Romance; but since it is supported by many thousand Witnesses . . . the Truth of it, can be no more contested, than that there were such Men in the world, as *Roberts* and *Black-beard*, who were Pyrates" (1:117). Read and Bonny's backgrounds before they turn pirate sound like the stuff of romance novels, a fact most historians pick up. But most historians do not question these fictive details.[9] Why are their back-grounds described in greater detail than those of any other pirate in Johnson's book? First, Johnson suggests that despite the fact that these pirates are women, it is no odder that there are female pirates than "such Men" as the most famous pirates, Roberts and Blackbeard. Representations of Read and

Bonny's explicit sexuality, oppositionally gendered in a predominantly homosocial world, alleviate the anxiety caused by the libertine homoerotic implications of the all-male pirate world. Second, these representations of the female pirates, in turn, subvert conventional gender norms for the reader because Anne Bonny and Mary Read are pirates in the first place. And pirates are, with the exception of Read and Bonny, masculine men who bond with other men. Finally, Johnson bases his history on "thousands" of witnesses.

As in Defoe's fiction (think of the prefaces to *Robinson Crusoe* or *Roxana*), Johnson asserts testimony based on his own authority as the writer in order to establish the "truth" of his story. Otherwise, the history of Read and Bonny could be taken for a "romance" or "novel." Just think of all the tales of buried treasure in the following centuries. Or in the most sensational pirate act, where is the "evidence" that Captain Avery kidnapped and married the Great Mogul's granddaughter? Unlike the stories of Read and Bonny, the outrageous stories of the male pirates do not need such verification. In other words, pirates live in such a *male* culture, with *male* bonding and pseudolibertine excess as the defining features of their culture, that the very oddness of the trangsressive female pirate demands that the "truth" be told, that it be "verified" by witnesses, particularly in a book explicitly titled a "history."[10]

Johnson and the popular and academic writers who follow tell the same story: both of the female pirates were raised as boys, for convoluted reasons that involve adultery, illegitimate birth, and poverty (1:119, 130). In a time of changing gender roles and definitions of identity, the implications of their upbringing raise many questions. In fact, Mary Read "becomes" a man through her own skill at replicating masculine roles. Read's cross-dressing skill—at least in Johnson's highly anecdotal narrative—demonstrates the transparency of an essential sexual "nature."

Before she went to sea Read joined the army, where "she behaved herself with a great deal of Bravery, yet she could not get a Commission, they being generally bought and sold" (Johnson, 1:119). Read was never discovered and so she was never kicked out of the army. It seems odd, then, that it is not her *gender* but her class that disables her career. In fact—discounting her gender—Read's case is similar to that of many soldiers and sailors in eighteenth-century England who could not afford to buy their commissions.

Read shares her tent with another soldier. After a long infatuation for both of them, which is of course confusing to the man she loves since he thinks she is a he, Read "found a Way of letting him discover her Sex, without appearing that it was done with Design" (1:120). Johnson leaves the details of her lover's discovery unclear. Later writers, however, play with variations on Read seducing the man by letting her tunic open up to her lover's delight and surprise. But Johnson tells us that when the soldier "thought of nothing but gratifying his Passions with very little Ceremony . . . [Read] prov'd very reserved and Modest . . . so far from thinking of making her his Mistress, he now courted her for a Wife" (1:120). As a soldier—a member of conventional society—Read is portrayed less as an amazonian warrior than as a faithful mate: an object of sexual desire.

Read's modesty, then, is a part of her female "character." It is significant, I think, that at this point she is not "at war against all mankind" but in the service of her country: "The Story of two Troopers marrying each other, made a great Noise, so that several Officers were drawn by Curiosity to assist at the Ceremony, and they agreed among themselves, that every one of them should make a small Present to the Bride, towards House-keeping, in consideration of her having been their fellow Soldier" (1:120). In the topsy-turvy world of Mary Read, she is given a wedding present *not* because she is a woman marrying a soldier, but because she is herself a fellow soldier. Johnson writes that two *soldiers* marry, not, I emphasize, that everyone recognizes that a soldier marries a woman whom he and everyone else thought was a male soldier. This may be a small distinction, but gender games are rampant in this chapter. Nothing is as it seems to be.

Soon Read becomes a widow. She goes to sea and joins Captain Rackham's pirate ship. Usual prohibitions against women on board pirate ships are ignored, since Read is still cross dressing. Guess who else is on the ship?

> [Read's] Sex was not so much as suspected by any Person on board till, *Ann Bonny* . . . took a particular Liking to her; in short, *Ann Bonny* took her for a handsome young Fellow, and for some Reasons best known to herself, first discovered her Sex to *Mary Read*; *Mary Read* knowing what she would be at, and being very sensible of her own Incapacity that Way, was forced to come to a right Understanding with her, and so to the great Disappointment of *Ann Bonny*, she let her know she was a Woman also. (1:122)

Mary Read is dressed like a man, and she becomes a pirate and the lover of that dandy "Calico Jack" Rackham himself. Read is depicted as both a "faithful mate" and a "warrior woman." However, she just happens to come across *another* female pirate. These ships were small; sometimes hundreds of pirates were packed in them. Yet nobody on board knows that these two men are in fact women. At the same time, Bonny "took a particular liking" to Read, but was unable to follow through on her desires because Read was not inclined with lesbian tendencies. What are the gender and sexual issues at play here? Johnson goes to a lot of trouble to "prove" that Bonny and Read are women—through their coincidental meeting, their love affairs with fellow pirates, their pregnancies—once they actually turn pirate. The "facts" are lost to history by the romantic mythologizing that preserves the hetero-centric status quo.

Less important to later writers (and this *has* been "lost" in pirate histories) is the idea that despite the almost universal injunctions against women on board pirate ships, these women serve alongside the homosocialized pirates. Johnson writes that both of them are "of a fierce and couragious Temper" (1:132). So on the one hand, the female pirates are admired for their bravery—just as Blackbeard is depicted as a "couragious Brute." On the other hand, the historians are titillated by two women surrounded by hundreds of men who can't figure out that Read and Bonny are women, unless the love affairs are a "secret."

Next comes a very interesting point in Read's biography in which gender does *not* play such an explicit part: "A young Man," Johnson writes, "ask'd [Read] what Pleasure she could have in being concerned in such Enterprizes, where her Life was continually in Danger, by Fire or Sword; and not only so, but she must be sure of dying an ignominious Death, if she should be taken alive" (1:125). Read replies,

> She thought it no great Hardship, for, were it not for that, every cowardly fellow would turn Pyrate, and so infest the Seas, that Men of Courage must starve:—That if it was put to the Choice of the Pyrates, they would not have the Punishment less than Death, the Fear of which, kept some dastardly Rogues honest; that many of those who are now cheating the Widows and Orphans, and oppressing their poor Neighbours, who have no Money to obtain Justice, would then rob at Sea, and the Ocean would be crowded with Rogues, like the Land, and no Merchant would venture out; so that the Trade, in a little Time, would not be worth following. (1:125)

Who is speaking here? A female pirate? A male pirate? Just a pirate? Why, in all of the *General History*, is Mary Read given the most articulate voice to justify piracy? As I have argued, the ways that early-eighteenth-century writers represented piracy are very complex: a dialectic of admiration and disgust for their transgressive homosocial world and economic criminality. What is interesting to me is that the women *have* to be women in order for sexuality to be disclosed on board a pirate ship. Yet the gender of Mary Read seems to matter a great deal in order for piracy to be defended so explicitly in the *General History.*

It is in fact necessary for a "female pyrate" to ventriloquize a justification for the pirate trade. On the one hand Read is a passionate fighter, a pirate *par excellence.* On the other hand she is a "faithful mate"—both faithful to her captain and faithful to her lover. But she is a woman—and her gender allows her to defend the indefensible without causing unease for the reader. But it is all still complicated by the dichotomy of sexualized object and amazonian warrior.

The terms of the "reality" of the female pirates are based on the usual "truths" that Johnson works with in telling the history of a pirate. He swears that the tale of Mary Read and Anne Bonny "is supported by many thousand Witnesses, I mean the people of *Jamaica*" (1:117). At the same time, he says that although this wild story may *sound* like a "romance," it is not. Any beliefs in the story of the female pirates, then, have to be based on the same assumptions about "history" that one makes about the authenticity of any of Johnson's pirate stories, or *any* eighteenth-century fiction and histories based on the narrator's protestations of "truth." The only real evidence is the author's word.

Mary Read and Anne Bonny: passionate whores, faithful mates, women warriors, cross dressers. The "female pirates" are in fact so overdetermined as "feminine" at the same time that they are singled out for their "masculinity"—their ferocity with a sword, their incredible bravery, and Read's articulate defense of piracy—that their gender questions the meaning of their inclusion in the *General History.* The point, finally, is that the anxiety created by an absent heterocentric foundation in stories of the pirate world requires gendered tranquilizing, and the female pirates are the sedatives. Sedatives, that is, until we see how complex their representation is: "whores" or "passionate mates," "feminine" yet embodying very "masculine" characteristics.

"Of Captain Misson" is the most familiar of the chapters in the *General History.* Misson and his crew are a different sort of pirate gang than that to which readers of the *General History* have become accustomed. Much like Captain Singleton and his companion, Quaker William, they kill only out of necessity. Misson and his men do not fly "old roger" or the "black flag," usually a skull and crossbones on a black background. Instead they fly a white flag, the customary banner of peace. Misson's mentor, Caraccioli, says to the crew, "As we then do not proceed upon the same Ground with Pyrates, who are Men of dissolute Lives and no Principles, let us scorn to take their colours: Ours is a brave, a just, an innocent, and a noble Cause; the Cause of Liberty. I therefore advice a white Ensign, with Liberty painted in the Flag" (Johnson, 2:16). As important as the flag's color—an ironic reversal of pirate self-identification—is the fact that "Liberty" is painted on it. These men "at war against Europe" assert that they do not consider themselves pirates. Yet, like their "dissolute" opposites, they also set up a world defiantly outside European culture. They proclaim the "Cause of Liberty," in this case liberty for criminals. The piratical subject's position as both criminal and alternative to the masculine hero becomes complicated by Johnson's distinction between "good" pirates and "bad" pirates. Johnson's literary representation of the "radical" pirate and the reality of the legally defined pirate become deeply intertwined by volume 2 of the *General History*. Like Defoe's fictive protagonists Robinson Crusoe, Moll Flanders, Colonel Jack, and Captain Singleton, Misson desires a "home"—a place for himself— that resists conventional ideologies. For Misson, the desire is explicitly class-based. Unlike Singleton, Misson has a history: he is from French nobility, but unfortunately is a second son. Like Singleton and Crusoe, Misson is of a "roving temper" (Johnson, 2:2). Unlike them, Misson is supported by his father, who buys him a berth on a ship. As he sails around Europe, Misson becomes intrigued by Catholicism and visits Rome, where he meets his mentor, a deist and dissenting priest named Caraccioli. They join arms and eventually turn pirate. Caraccioli argues that the pirate life is good for Misson because

> [Misson] might with the Ship he had under Foot, and the brave Fellows under Command, bid Defiance to the Power of *Europe*, enjoy every Thing he wish'd, reign Sovereign of the Southern Seas, and lawfully make War on all the World, since it wou'd deprive him of that Liberty to which he had a Right by the Laws of Nature. (2:12–13)

Whether Misson is the second son of a nobleman or an ordinary sailor, Caraccioli asserts *any* man's right of "liberty" because it is "natural."

Even though Captain Misson's account is like a conventional novel— with a beginning, a middle, and an end—his story is just one of a larger narrative. New pirate histories follow "Of Captain Misson," so that even though Misson's story is over, others that precede and follow it complement his narrative. One critic has characterized "Of Captain Misson" as "a sketch of political theories rather than a study of human beings."[11] This analysis is correct as far as it goes, but "Of Captain Misson" is about only one pirate, surrounded by the stories of many other pirates.

To grant literary worth to one chapter outside the context of the others results in a reductive understanding of the *General History* and its significance for pirate history as well as the development of the novel. In the preface to the first volume of the *General History*, Johnson writes that "had [the pirates] all united, and settled in some of those Islands, they might by this Time, have been honoured with the Name of a Commonwealth, and no Power in those Parts of the World could have been able to dispute with them" (1:vi, 2d ed.). Misson and his crew may be "good" pirates, but their colony has to be placed in the context of the society as it is characterized for all the other pirates, what Johnson calls "a Refuge of Thieves and Outlaws" (1:vi).

Captain Avery, for example, sets up a Madagascar colony in direct contrast to Misson's own democratic utopia in Madagascar. Avery's only desire is to raid ships and make himself rich. Despite his memorable piratical acts such as plundering the ship of the Great Mogul, Avery steals not only from ships that stray in his wake, but also from his fellow pirates. Johnson writes that Avery and his crew headed to Madagascar, "intending to make that Place their Magazine . . . but *Avery* put an end to this Project, and made it altogether unnecessary" (1:31). He runs away with the treasure that he and his men have accumulated. Thus Avery is not only *hostis humani generis*, but *hostis pirati generis* as well. He is a thief who steals from his own comrades. How does a legal definition of piracy work in a world that defines itself outside any of the laws that pertain to all "mankind"? The literary representation of the piratical subject—fictional or "real"—upsets definitions that totally criminalize the pirate.

Misson never existed. Without crediting Johnson, Gosse writes that "This unique pirate came of an ancient French family of Provence" (*Pirates' Who's Who*, 210). He might as easily have written that this "unique pirate" came of a great literary imagination, whether or not Johnson was Defoe. While details about any specific pirate's life may be questioned, the inclusion of Misson in Gosse's book determines his actual existence.

Gosse, like so many other pirate historians, takes the *General History* at face value. As I have said, whether or not a pirate actually existed is beside the point. "Of Captain Misson" is significant because in it Johnson explicitly heroicizes the "enemies against all mankind." Consequently, he both creates the myth of the "democratic" pirate and contradicts all the other stories of the pirates' depravity he has written thus far.

"Of Captain Misson" is in the exact center of the two volumes of the *General History*.[12] The location of Captain Misson's "history" confounds readerly reactions to the stories of the other pirates that bookend this chapter. Its placement as the first chapter in volume 2 also foregrounds what some critics believe to be Defoe's representation of an ideal government. For example, neither Hill nor Novak takes Misson's story at face value.[13] However, Hill writes, "I think we may conclude that [Defoe] was reproducing the substance of what he had been told [by pirates]. Some pirates must have seen themselves as egalitarian avengers. How are we to explain the radical element in these pirate yarns or fantasies?" (165). Hill argues that Defoe's narrative of a utopian pirate society may help us "to understand how those on the margins of society adapted themselves to a world which seemed increasingly hostile" (180). Even the most revisionist pirate historians overdetermine the place of the "real" radical pirates in revisionist English history.[14] The most radical of the pirates whom Johnson represents are, after all, creations of his imagination. However, Hill and Rediker make important points that try to recontextualize the pirates outside the mythological framework of literary representation. Their analyses undoubtedly help us to understand both the undervalued relevance of the pirate to eighteenth-century culture and the reasons pirates might explicitly choose their way of life "at war against all mankind."

More important than an example of the hard-to-prove political extremism of the pirates, I believe, is the way that "Of Captain Misson" works as realistic fiction, and thus proves its utility for Hill's argument by demonstrating how fiction and reality reflect one another. Even the way Misson's story is broken up and resumed with the chapter on the real-life Captain Tew—fiction within the reality of "fact"—parallels the structure of Defoe's more familiar novels, particularly *Captain Singleton*. A good portion of *Captain Singleton* combines the adventures of Singleton and Avery. In *Captain Singleton*, Defoe uses a fictional form to tell a coherent narrative about the ideological awakening of a pirate. This, too, shares similarities with Defoe's other fiction.

For example, in *Robinson Crusoe* Defoe creates the "Island of Despair," which becomes a capitalist—but ultimately unworkable—utopia. Similarly, Johnson imagines a kind of democratic utopia with Misson's colony on Madagascar. Defoe's representation of Crusoe's island is read as a serious meditation on economic philosophy, whereas "Of Captain Misson" has been neglected in critical discourse. This neglect of "Of Captain Misson" is because Misson's story is perceived as fact, and has been ignored by most literary historians. Crusoe's story, in contrast, is determinedly fiction, despite claims of "truth" in the preface.

In both cases, the island settlement breaks down. In "Of Captain Misson," Misson is killed and the story ends, the dream destroyed along with its leader. In *Robinson Crusoe*, Crusoe leaves his island in the care of others, and, we discover in the *Farther Adventures*, conflicts between the English and the Spanish as well as attacks by "savages" contribute to its downfall. However, unlike Misson, Crusoe continues his adventures; his story does not end with the demise of his colony, because he sails away from it for particular reasons. Crusoe's need to fulfill his goals for economic aggrandizement is determined by his unsure sense of identity; his interests go in other directions.

Novak is one of the very few critics who read "Of Captain Misson" as an example of Defoe's economic philosophy (or, for that matter, consider the chapter at all as a significant piece of literature). Consequently, he is more interested in the chapter as a work of utopian fiction than as a history of one of many notable pirates. He writes that "Defoe was more interested in dramatizing proletarian utopian ideals than in developing the inner workings of Misson's mind. The novelette is unified by its epic theme, not by its study of character or its episodic plot" (iii). The problem with Novak's characterization of this work is that he disregards the rest of the *General History* and presumes that Defoe is the author. Notions of "inner workings of Misson's mind" presuppose that "Of Captain Misson" ought to be treated either as a "realistic" novel that privileges the inner life of its hero or as an articulation of Defoe's utopian beliefs, what Novak terms "epic themes." In fact, Johnson is working toward more complex goals than this either/or distinction; "Of Captain Misson" complicates the lives of all the pirates in the *General History*.

In other words, their homosocial world has been an uneasy union of the demonic and the heroic, and the economically transgressive and the culturally transgressive throughout. The subjectivity—or "inner workings"—of the pirate, however unstable, has already been established through the characterizations of all the other maritime criminals about whom Johnson has written, as well as all the literary artifacts and newspapers. Johnson confuses the character of the pirate further by turning Misson into a paragon of egalitarian virtue *despite* his identity as a pirate. Johnson demonstrates the instability of identity in the conventional world through his depiction of the pirate.

I suggest that a "good" pirate subverts the conception that all pirates were "bad": "Desperadoes, who were the Terror of the trading Part of the World" (Johnson, 1:17). Standards of "badness" are already complex because Johnson represents some pirates, such as Blackbeard, as "heroic" despite their "badness." We empathize with both the "good" and the "bad" pirates. Misson and the other pirates become the means to interrogate and question the "reality" of normative subjectivity, represented by Defoe's more accessible and obviously fictional—but no less transgressive—characters such as Crusoe and Singleton.

Captain Misson enables Johnson to talk about an egalitarian government. "Realism" in "Of Captain Misson" is centered on the economic system of these pirates, not their domestic relations with one another. Sexuality itself is not implied because Johnson is setting up Misson's government in direct opposition to the *form* of English power and control. Unlike the other pirates in the *General History*, slippery rovers who sail the seven seas, Misson and Caraccioli band together to create a government in absolute resistance to the English system. The "bad" pirates about whom we have read in the first volume were irresistibly "noisy." Despite the focus on a political critique in "Of Captain Misson"—and the focus on "Of Captain Misson" by critics such as Novak—the alternative masculinity of these other pirates impresses readers. These readerly responses threaten the egalitarian critique represented by Misson's colony. The transgressive camaraderie of these other pirates suggests that normative sexuality is complicit with the "Oppression, Poverty, and all the Miseries of Life" (2:15) that caused Misson and his crew to turn pirate in the first place.

"Of Captain Misson" is a striking contrast to Defoe's *Robinson Crusoe*. Like Crusoe's island, which Crusoe has "peopled" with English pirates, Catholic Spaniards, and "savage" men and women, Misson's democracy contains women—albeit "savage" women—and is composed of different races and nationalities. But Misson is not their "governor," the title Crusoe takes to rule his island. Instead, all the pirates in Misson's crew meet; Caraccioli "spoke to the Necessity of lodging a supream Power in the hands of one. . . . That such a Power however should not be for Life, nor hereditary, but determinate at the end of three Years, when a new Choice be made by the State, or the Old confirm'd for three Years longer" (2:100). The "supream Power" is called "Lord Conservator." He stands in direct contrast to the monarchs of Europe because he is chosen by the people, who are the state. Like England, which has a parliament, Libertalia has a senate, but that senate is made up of all the men in the country: it is an all-male commonwealth, what Johnson calls "a Democratical Form, where the People were themselves the Makers and Judges of their own Laws, the most agreeable" (2:100). Libertalia is the logical extension of a pirate world that might be termed a "society against the state."

Novak points out that Libertalia is "Defoe's best expression of political and social ideals which he admired but considered unworkable" (iii). These ideals are "unworkable" because Misson and his men set up egalitarian legal structures. Besides, the government *does* work, at least for a time. The possibility of their replication within conventional structures simply is not a part of the early-eighteenth-century political economy. This utopian community takes the pirate myth as far as it can go, given the transgressive "nature" of pirate communities and the articles that govern the pirates' behavior. Misson, in a speech to his brother pirates, says, "[we] were no Pyrates, but Men who were resolved to assert that Liberty which God and Nature gave [us] and own no Subjection to any, farther than was for the common Good of all" (2:14). Although Misson denies that he and his men are pirates, they still *act* like pirates because they prey on other ships and live outside the boundaries of European laws. On one level the difference between Misson and other pirates lies in Misson's articulate espousal of "democratical" virtues, which Johnson sets up in opposition to English and French government.

Novak suggests that "Although Defoe apparently thought that democracy was the ideal form of government, he may have regarded it as impractical." In one sense, Novak is wrong. The colony is not "destroyed through its very basic belief in human equality," as Novak argues. While Libertalia has its own internal tensions, it is actually destroyed by an attack by natives from the interior of Madagascar. Pirates are so unstable in their representation, exemplified by the whole *General History*, that prospects for the success of Libertalia seem remote to begin with. The "good" pirates—represented by Misson and his brethren—are in opposition to the "bad" ones, such as Blackbeard, Avery, and Low, pirates who are determined by their violence and their criminality, rather than by the "ideals" of a government.

If "Of Captain Misson" were only a means for Johnson—or Defoe for that matter—to articulate his vision of an "ideal" government, I would not attach importance to its place in the *General History*. However, the chapter complicates the representations of already unstable depictions of heroic and criminal pirates. It demonstrates that pirates can imagine an "ideal" egalitarian government. Even more significant, the "liberty" that Misson espouses goes much further than "egalitarian" values.

The "liberty" that Misson envisions suggests all kinds of freedom. Notions of "liberty" become wrapped up with sexual and economic standards regulated by English hegemony. Johnson's depiction of "liberty" shows how close the piratical subject's transgressive identity—identity embodied by such individuals as Blackbeard, England, and Roberts—and Johnson's representation of that identity are to the heroic character exhibited by Misson. Even though Libertalia could not survive, the other pirates about whom we have read continued to roam the seven seas. For Johnson and the readers, egalitarianism is part of the pirates' threat as well as their allure.

7

Solemn Imprecations and Curses
Captain Singleton's Search for Identity

The ordinary story of the pirate, or the wicked man in general, no matter how successful he may have been in his criminal career, nearly always ends disastorously, and in that way points a moral which doubtless has a good effect on a large class of people, who would be very glad to do wrong, provided that no harm was likely to come to them in consequence.
        —Frank R. Stockton, *Buccaneers and Pirates of Our Coasts*

Captain Singleton and, to a lesser extent, *The King of Pirates* represent the most compelling union of implicit homoeroticism and sanctioned economic transgression in Defoe's canon. In these two works, the piratical subject is embodied by both the "real" Captain Avery (who, with Captain Kidd and Blackbeard, was the most notorious of late-seventeenth-century and early-eighteenth-century pirates) and Defoe's fictional Captain Singleton. Defoe's use of the trope of the pirate challenges critical histories that reduce the "novel" to middle-class experiences of "self" and economics.[1] *Captain Singleton* is not supplemental to Defoe's "major" accomplishments, as critics tend to argue, nor is it haphazardly plotted or constructed.[2]

I have proposed that homoerotic desire is implicit in early-eighteenth-century representations of the piratical subject, particularly in the *General History*. The "noise" of homoeroticism can be located in *Captain Singleton* as well, not only through the instability of the piratical subject's opposition to both the feminized, effeminate sodomite and the masculine hero but also through the anxiety that this sexualized "nature" generates for twentieth-century critics. I intend to analyze homoeroticism rather than ignore it in *Captain Singleton* and then to imagine the homoerotic subject in the context of all the attributes that construct "subjectivity." The attributes—such as class, gender, religion, politics, and sexuality—all contribute to the complexity of the masculine individual. A recognition of homoeroticism as an alternative—and positive—means of identifying masculine individuality provides an alternative way to reread this lesser known work. Further, a homoerotic analysis suggests ways to recover and put into perspective other narrative forms with which Defoe experimented.

In 1720, the year after the great success of *Robinson Crusoe*, Defoe published *Captain Singleton*, his most famous novel with a pirate setting.[3] This novel is not structured like *Crusoe*; rather, it is broken into two seemingly disparate halves. When read through a homoerotic analysis, the two parts form a whole and the randomness helps explain a transgressive protagonist who shares similarities with the sodomitical subject. To investigate the sodomite—and by extension, the pirate—"will never deliver [him] per se; but only . . . relational structures precariously available to prevailing discourses."[4] These "relational structures" show how *Captain Singleton* is a template for an alternative model of fiction. This alternative model, further, acknowledges the power of heterocentric definitions within the genre of the novel.

Of all Defoe's novels currently in print, *Captain Singleton* remains one of the least known today, and the least understood.[5] The title page shows, however, Defoe's fictional manipulation of some of the iconic cultural metaphors in early-eighteenth-century England. These metaphors, significant in the years Defoe wrote his great fiction, must be placed in historical context if we are to grasp the implications of *Captain Singleton* for the history of the novel. The title page reads:

> Containing an Account of his being set on Shore in the Island of *Madagascar*, his Settlement there, with a Description of the Place and Inhabitants: Of his Passage from thence, in a Paraguay, to the main Land of *Africa*, with an Account of the Customs and Manners of the People: His great Deliverances from the barbarous Natives and Wild Beasts: Of his meeting with an *Englishman*, a Citizen of *London*, among the *Indians*, the great Riches he acquired, and his Voyage Home to *England*: As also Captain *Singleton's* Return to Sea, with an Account of his many Adventures and Pyracies with the famous Captain *Avery* and others.

Like *Captain Singleton*, *Robinson Crusoe*—Defoe's most popular novel—uses "piracy" as a selling point to potential readers. In *Captain Singleton*, however, piracy is the guiding trope and is foregrounded to a far greater extent than in *Crusoe*. The title page focuses attention on the first half of the novel, in which Singleton crosses the mysterious "dark" continent. His adventures as a pirate, however, are suggested with much less detail. It is enough for readers to see that this book is an "account" about "Madagascar" and a "pirate." The brutal, exotic preconceptions—as we have seen, so dominant in early-eighteenth-century popular culture—will allow the readers to fill in the details.

The tensions between the apparently realistic account of exploration and the legendary status of the pirate, if interrogated, reveal that *Captain Singleton* is an important novel in the development of both modern and eighteenth-century notions of subjectivity. *Captain Singleton* seems an unstable text to twentieth-century readers because traditional criticism reads backwards to try and define an essential subject as the *raison d'être* of acceptable "realistic" fiction. The novelty of its title character—a pirate hero—coupled with the exotic settings leads to critical dismissal of the novel's importance and intent. For example, some critics believe that in his novels Defoe was working toward what have become critically validated notions of psychological realism. Other critics argue that Defoe used fiction to address his concerns about the English economy.[6] If he is successful, as in *Robinson Crusoe*, Defoe is able to negotiate the complex relations between the rise of capitalism and the rise of the domestic psychological subject.[7] *Captain Singleton* "fails" as a novel because of its fragmented nature and Defoe's difficulty in portraying the emergence of subjectivity at a moment of early-modern history. Although arguably we can see a progressive middle-class hero in *Robinson Crusoe*, Singleton poses obstacles because his psychological makeup is not "real" in the modern sense. And he is a pirate: his behavior is not acceptable within the confines of early-eighteenth-century notions of heterocentric identity.[8]

Singleton's milieu is not only a fictional world in which the absence of women questions paradigms implicit in any discipline's version of "history." As we have seen, early-eighteenth-century representations of traditionally gendered desire are alien to the maritime world of the pirate as well. These tensions form the narrative's framework, a structure read differently by eighteenth-century readers than by twentieth-century critics. The disjointed elements that form the narrative framework of the novel make sense if we recognize that Singleton's outlaw behavior as a pirate parallels his subjective desires as a transgressive erotic subject: to become rich on the one hand, and to find "home" or a place in society on the other. *Captain Singleton* presents a different kind of psychological realism that challenges the validity of normative sexuality.

In this chapter I shall analyze the second half of *Captain Singleton*, generally overlooked in the criticism of the book. After I examine Singleton's early career as a pirate, I shall pay careful attention to the relationship that builds between the title character and his companion, Quaker William. The novel's first half has received most of the critical attention in recent years because it can be seen as a precursor to such novels as *Heart of Darkness* and other colonial and postcolonial works.[9] This section of the novel is indeed important, and I shall briefly discuss it. However, we need to consider *Captain Singleton* as a cohesive whole. By focusing on the second half of the novel, we can see how these two parts fit together. We shall see that Singleton's journey across Africa, his return to England as a rich man, and finally his decision to go on the account all point toward the hero's search for an identity. This search questions the terms of masculine sexual desire both in England and in the transgressive homosocial world of piracy.

Shortly after the novel opens, young Singleton and a group of sailors are marooned on Madagascar after they attempt a mutiny. They escape to the east coast of Africa, and Singleton relates an account of his journey across the vast, uncharted continent by boat and on foot. Nothing in the men's journey suggests transgressive economic or cultural desire. Their wealth establishes the terms for their nontransgressive camaraderie; their goal is to reach civilization, to return to the conventional world. They are rewarded for their perseverance by the accumulation of gold and ivory, which they literally stumble over as they make their way west through jungles and across deserts. "I thought I had enough already," the fabulously rich Singleton says just before he returns to England, "and all the Thoughts I had about disposing of it, if I came to *Europe*, was only how to spend it as fast as I could, buy me some Clothes, and go to Sea to be a Drudge for more" (132). For Singleton, wealth means nothing because he has nothing on which he desires to spend it.

This point is driven home by Singleton's experiences when he returns to England midway through the novel. His return marks a change in the narrative. A fantastic travelogue that catalogs the wonders of Africa becomes the story of Singleton's adventures as a pirate. However, he does not go on the account until he loses his fortune. "Thus ended my first Harvest of *Wild Oats*," he says of his African adventure, "the rest were not sowed to so much Advantage" (137). Singleton is embarrassed by the way he frittered away his fortune in England: "the rest Merits to be conceal'd with Blushes, for it was spent in all Kinds of Folly and Wickedness" (137–38).

Singleton's return to England and disenchantment with what he finds there signal a shift toward a desire for the transgressive camaraderie he will find once he turns pirate. Were Singleton's experiences in England—"conceal'd with Blushes"—homoerotic or "heterosexual"? Defoe does not let us know. However, the sexual connotations implicit in the loss of his fortune—his "oats" that "were not sowed to so much Advantage"—are provocative because he stays silent and does not tell the reader what his "Folly and Wickedness" are. More significant, however, Singleton literally misses his chance to buy into English society through marriage and property. As Moll Flanders and Colonel Jack both recognize, someone without property—and Singleton has said he does not even desire property—is always an outsider, as are pirates such as Avery and Misson.[10] His trek across Africa proves to Singleton that he is a successful if reluctant leader. He is dubbed "Captain Bob" by his companions (35), and he and his men profit enormously from their journey. Prudent investments such as buying property or marrying well ought to be just as profitable when he returns "home" to England. But these desires for a normal life leave Singleton cold. He does not "fit in" with the "ill company" he finds in his birthplace. He is an outsider; former "friends" are now spoilers who take advantage of his wealth and his naïveté. They let him know that he has "nothing to expect of them farther than I might command it by the force of my money" (138). Singleton loses his vast fortune and decides "that it was Time to think of farther Adventures" (138). His undetermined identity precludes allegiance with or affection for his homeland. He resolves to return to sea—wide open and not restrained by land-based conventions—to live in the only place he can possibly call home. With his resolution we come to the second half of the novel, in which Singleton wholeheartedly embraces the pirate way.

Singleton discovers that the pirate's transgressive world provides fulfillment and pleasure that the easy accumulation of wealth in Africa—riches without work—never did. John J. Richetti points out that Singleton's two-year stay in England leads him into his pirate adventures, and "is manifestly a continuation of that aversion to restrictive identity and that drive towards the possession of a dynamic process."[11] Richetti's observation is valid as far as it goes, but he does not fully appreciate the motivation that drives Singleton away from a "restrictive identity." After he loses his money, Singleton discovers that he has no place in England. He reveals what the trek across Africa and his earlier behavior only suggested: "I that was, as I have hinted before, an original Thief, and a Pyrate even by Inclination before, was now in my Element, and never undertook any Thing in my Life with more particular satisfaction" (140).

As a pirate, Singleton must work hard for his profit; he finds a camaraderie among these self-made outcasts that he felt neither crossing Africa nor among the "ill company" of his homeland. Singleton's "Inclination" toward piracy suggests that he will find a bonding with the "brethren of the sea" that he has not found elsewhere. If profit has no meaning for Singleton, then he has an "Inclination" toward piracy for other, perhaps unaccountable reasons. Singleton's rejection of a "restrictive identity" leads inevitably, I think, to transgressive desires not predicated on birth, marriage, and property and the social identity they promise. Singleton suspects that he can find some satisfaction among these men who bond both economically and culturally in an outlaw world unrestricted by the economic and cultural conventions of English society.

The pirate exploits take over as the narrative drive of the novel once Singleton decides to follow his "Inclination." He signs himself on a ship bound east and, he says, "I fell into Company with some Masters of Mischief" (138). One of these "Masters," Harris, becomes his mentor. Harris reveals his plans to mutiny and asks Singleton to go along with him on the account: "He then asked me if I would swear to be secret, and that if I did not agree to what he proposed, I would nevertheless never betray him; I readily bound myself to that, on the most solemn Imprecations and Curses that the Devil and both of us could invent" (138). Singleton sees in Harris a kindred spirit, someone else born to be an outsider and a pirate by "Inclination." Is Singleton attracted to the "secrecy" of the mutiny, the chance to "bind" himself to a band of outlaws? Or does he look forward to a chance for very public—if transgressive—deportment, to show the world that he is his own man? The transgressive culture of piracy is more alluring than any wealth he might accumulate, as his earlier adventures in Africa suggest. I would argue that Singleton jumps at the chance for camaraderie. By swearing "Imprecations and Curses," he can become a member of a group that recognizes a "kindred spirit" and accepts him as he is.

Harris introduces him to the gang's leader, a Captain Wilmot, who welcomes Singleton "with a great deal of Joy" and becomes a key player in Singleton's pirate adventures. Singleton tells us that he was "well prepared for all manner of Roguery" and thus further emphasizes his sense of "home" that the pirate world should offer him (139). It is, perhaps, no coincidence that Singleton's new friend and leader shares the name of the most infamous libertine of the seventeenth century, John Wilmot, earl of Rochester. Since the actuality of pirate life is left vague in Singleton's narrative, a recognition of Wilmot's link to Rochester allows the reader to imagine the pirate world as a place of libertine excess. Further, Defoe relies on the reader's knowledge of pirate life to fill in the blanks. Eighteenth-century readers had easy access to pirate stories found in newspaper accounts, trial records, and other ephemeral literature. As we have seen, these readers knew that pirates were *hostis humani generis*. And of course, we know that pirates declared *themselves* "at war against all mankind."

Defoe suggests the affinities that the pirate shares with the libertine through his representation of the pirate's disruption of both trade and culture. Singleton follows his "true Inclination" "to consort with the most famous Pyrates of the Age" (139) in a pseudolibertine world not constrained by "Conscience" or the values imposed on it by the domestication of erotic or economic desires. Moreover, Captain Wilmot's "joyous" welcome is effectively suggestive for the reader not only because of Defoe's allusion to Rochester, but also because of Rochester's notorious bisexuality. The warm welcome by the great libertine's namesake—coupled with the notoriety of "the most famous Pyrates" such as Avery, Blackbeard, or Kidd that any reader could envision—only strengthens Defoe's suggestive linking of the libertine and the pirate. These men are outsiders, a "gang . . . prepared for all manner of roguery." Singleton enthusiastically enters into a life of secrecy and dissolution.

At this stage of Singleton's career—narrated in hindsight by an older, retired Singleton—the pirates lead lives that echo the accounts of debauchery by Restoration libertines such as Rochester. The difference between these pirates and the libertines, of course, lies in how the pirates reveal their "roguery." For the libertine, "roguery" was sexual conquest, be it sodomitical or "heterosexual." This sexual conquest was a display of power by men who delighted in all kinds of excess. Further, the libertine showed his power through an anarchic refusal to bow to any conventions—sexual or cultural. The libertine represented by Rochester and others, however, came from the aristocracy and could afford to assert his power through excess.

The pirate Wilmot's gang comes from a different class altogether. As we have seen, the pirate's sexual behavior was left out of eighteenth-century pirate accounts. These highly transgressive cultural aspects of their all-male society complicate the homosocial constructs of pirate camaraderie that ignore sexuality. The pirate—Defoe and other writers suggest—is a kind of libertine of the seven seas who thumbs his nose at convention. Indeed, the gang belongs to no class at all, for they "declare war against all mankind." Since they have turned their backs on normative society, they are defined as pirates—and *only* pirates—and thus defined by their transgressive cultural *and* economic defiance. Any debauchery takes place at sea away from societal restraints. Their threat to society is criminal because they wreak havoc on maritime trade, yet they are represented in print by their "otherness," their violence, cruelty, and over-the-top performance when they wreak that havoc. Furthermore, the pirates' well-known delight in the physical is explicitly overdetermined by Johnson, Defoe, and other early-eighteenth-century writers. Their behavior is characterized by violence, costume, and profanity, as well as a propensity to drink, play, and make merry, all to outlandish excess. Defoe thus links the economic menace of the pirates to the libertine excesses of the aristocracy, through the pirates' disruption of the economic and cultural status quo—and implicitly the sexual status quo as well.

For example, the gang's first act is "making an Agreement, that whatever was taken by either of our Ships, should be shared among the Ship's Company of both" (141). These financial arrangements, shared by most early-eighteenth-century pirates, have fascinated both eighteenth-century and modern chroniclers of piracy. As Marcus Rediker has demonstrated, the articles suggest a "democratic" society of murdering marauders. They establish how the criminalized pirates' financial agreements differ from other maritime payment systems. The pirates—unlike ordinary seamen—are freed from economic dependency on employers from their home countries. This economic freedom, then, allows the pirates freedom from all kinds of restraints. They are thus able to declare themselves "at war against all mankind" not only economically but culturally as well.[12]

Singleton could just tell us about his cruel piratical acts—how he "murthered the People in cold Blood, tying them Back to Back, and throwing them into the Sea" (144). But then the book would be nothing more than a criminal tract, what one critic would call a "frivolous" crime novel because it has no "moral" underpinning.[13] Singleton's stories of barbaric cruelty disappear, however, when his mentor, Harris, dies and Quaker William is introduced into the story. From this point onward *Captain Singleton* differs significantly from other Defoe novels because its hero becomes involved in a stable emotional and economic relationship with another man that lasts the rest of the book.

As a result of his relationship with William, Singleton's way of defining himself undergoes a transformation. Singleton evolves from a libertine pirate who "murthered the People in cold Blood" to a man who defines himself in an affectionate relationship with a Quaker pirate. Their relationship will become an alternative to the transgressive bonding of the pirate world or to an identity based on property and marriage. Before William becomes the center of his world, Singleton's pirate acts depend on the physical power he and his gang wield over any ships that stray into their path. Like any pirate worthy of the name, Singleton loots, pillages, plunders, and murders. With the introduction of William, the focus of Singleton's desires shifts. His desire for economic aggrandizement coupled with violence shifts to personal affection and pacifism centered around another person. An emotional attachment develops between two men whose business just happens to be piracy.

One of Defoe's most fascinating characters, William is a religious dissenter who refuses to shed blood, but is happy to join Singleton's gang and share in the booty. Defoe turns tradition topsy-turvy and redefines the criminalized pirate through his characterization of William, a Quaker pirate. William, despite his professed Christianity and pacifism, has no compunction about "turning" pirate. He manages to have it both ways. Indeed, William's sensible, businesslike mind—as well as his enthusiastic though passive assistance—enables the gang to become richer and richer. He becomes Singleton's inseparable companion, and is culpable in the pirates' crimes. Yet he is always represented as an "advisor." He never participates in the bloodshed but always helps Singleton and his men to profit from their crimes. William offers counsel on the least dangerous ways to plunder unlucky vessels that cross the pirates' path.

William is, too, the ultimate "outsider" on board the pirate ship. As a dissenter, he is outside mainstream English political and religious culture; but he also remains aloof from pirate culture because he refuses to take up the sword even as he dives wholeheartedly into their "trade." He is thus implicated in all the criminal acts without participating in the actual violence. The figure of William suggests that the pirate, if stripped of his libertine aspects, differs little from other traders: he is constructed by a desire for profit. Through William's participation—and the ways Defoe represents his "character"—we see the correlation between the more usual libertine pirate's immoral criminality and the uncertain morality of what William calls "money without fighting" (154), that is, legitimate trade.

After Quaker William joins the gang, the pirates rove the Indian Ocean, taking ships and amassing enormous treasure. He offers crafty suggestions on financial opportunities that for the pirates would have overlooked in order to get at the loot in conventionally violent ways. He and Singleton have an exchange about the desires of the pirate shortly after they meet:

> Why, says *William* gravely, I only ask what is thy Business, and the Business of all the people thou has with thee? Is it not to get money? Yes, *William*, it

is so, in our honest Way: And wouldst thou, says he, rather have Money without Fighting, or Fighting without Money? I mean, which wouldst thou have by Choice, suppose it to be left to thee? O *William, says I,* the first of the two to be sure. (153–54)

Defoe complicates the usual literary representation of the violent, blood-thirsty pirate in the characters of William and Singleton. These two men are not brutal murderers whose desire for ill-gotten gain is associated with their uncontrolled behavior. They are, however, criminals who cause economic havoc. Paradoxically, their crimes go unpunished even as they increase their wealth. But in the context of British culture and society, they are still *hostis humani generis,* and they still live in a transgressive world from which women are excluded. Singleton has already insisted that he has an "Inclination" for the pirate way and has no desire to turn his life around. What does it mean to be "inclined" if pirates are both economic criminals and outrageous antiheroes? The only way Singleton knows to make a profit is to plunder the "enemy," legitimate traders. At the same time, he feels comfortable only with the camaraderie of men in a world of libertine outlawry. His desires, then, seem to be satisfied by his pirate way of life. Further, piracy is a "business" to Singleton, and an "honest" one at that, with, he suggests, different standards for honesty.

Defoe is exposing the English government's hypocrisy and ambivalence toward renegades like Singleton. As we saw in chapter 2, piracy was, of course, legally sanctioned during times of war with the issuance of letters of marque for privateers such as William Dampier and Woodes Rogers. However, during peacetime, privateers and navy men were left without employment, so they often went on the account. During piracy's "golden age" the British government issued proclamation after proclamation giving clemency to pirates who turned themselves in to the authorities.[14] This strategy would work for a time, but the pirates simply took the pardons they were offered and went back to their old "trade," forcing the government to deal with the havoc in the Caribbean or the Indian Ocean all over again. Whatever schemes the British government used to stamp out piracy, nothing seemed to work, and in fact pirates set up semipermanent colonies in the Caribbean and on Madagascar. Singleton himself settles briefly in Madagascar, legendary seat of pirate "government." Given the demonized and complex status of the pirate within maritime law, how can we make sense of Defoe's heroicization of Singleton's criminality?

In an extraordinary pamphlet attributed to Defoe, the anonymous author argues that trade with the Madagascar pirates might prove profitable for Britain. "In the last Place," the author reasons,

> though it was not thought consistent with the Honour of the Nation to grant the pirates of *Madagascar* a Pardon, yet since they have establish'd and form'd themselves into a kind of regular government, it would not be more dishonourable for the *South-Sea* Company to trade with them, than it was for the People of Italy to hold a Commerce and friendly Correspondence with the First Founders of old *Rome*, who were but a Company of Publick Robbers.[15]

The author uses a sort of "if you can't beat 'em, join 'em" argument, coupled with the potent but peculiar comparison of the pirates to Romans. Romans, of course, were usually characterized as embodying features of British strength. Here, Romans are "a Company of Publick Robbers," and Rome is linked to the completely illegitimate "government" of Madagascar. Thus the author of the pamphlet acknowledges the power that the pirates have asserted for themselves in the Indian Ocean. Moreover, the tract demonstrates—at least in part—the ambivalence that some English felt toward the pirates of the Indian Ocean. The author suggests that although the pirates have not exactly reformed, they have created a home for themselves with a "kind of regular Government" that ought to be recognized as such. The end result of explicitly criminal acts potentially offers credible profit for the British economy. By using these comparisons, the author is on the verge of depicting trade as a kind of state-sanctioned piracy.

Whether or not the author of this pamphlet is Defoe, Defoe himself made a similar point a decade earlier in his *Review of the State of the British Nation*:

> for if it be lawful to admit them to Pardon, and if it be lawful to take what they have by Force, it must be lawful to take it as a Condition of admitting them to come in—And all this, supposing they cannot easily or without Hazard or Blood, be otherwise reduc'd—Let them offer their illgotten Money, then I am clear, it will be well gotten money to us.[16]

From Defoe's argument here we can see the similarities to the author's argument in *A True Account . . . of the South-Sea Trade*.

Defoe is making a similar point in *Captain Singleton*. Flying in the face of pirate legend and mythology, William and Singleton show piracy's similarities to "legitimate" business. Singleton has told William that he would just as soon be a nonviolent pirate, if he could get rich that way. Pirate histories—including the *General History*—contradict Defoe's depiction of Singleton and his gang as budding pacifists, as we all know from our cultural knowledge of bloodthirsty freebooters. Even Captain Misson establishes a colony on Madagascar with the intent of continuing his piracies. In *Captain Singleton*, Defoe hints at the pirates' affinity with legal trade, and further, the pirates themselves have a code of honor—their articles—where profit is concerned. What kinds of pirates are these, who do not revel in calling for quarter, who free their victims instead of throwing them overboard, or try to avoid slitting their quarries' throats?

Defoe raises uncomfortable questions for those who condemn piracy outright. Perhaps the line between legal and illegal trade is a little too fine, as is suggested in the anonymous pamphlet, Defoe's argument in his *Review*, *Captain Singleton*, and the legalized piracy by such privateers as Dampier, Funnel, Rogers, and Cooke. With William's help, Singleton manages to accumulate enough illegal riches to think about giving up piracy and settling down permanently. Defoe has suggested that at least in part Singleton's lack of an identity is based on his lack of property; as we have seen, Singleton remained an outsider even after he had collected enough capital to buy property in England. The ending of the novel undermines the apparent return to the status quo, a final recovery of lost normative subjectivity. Singleton's uncertain desires become focused on his relationship with William. Their affection for each other offers an alternative to a normative identity based on "heterosexual" psychological desire. The relationship between the two men suggests that homoerotic affection—at least for Singleton—can displace normative desires for property and by extension middle-class stability.

All the disparate parts of *Captain Singleton* that construct the title character's search for an identity—the African journey, the outrageous pirate adventures, the enormous profit—come together when William and Singleton agree to turn their backs on the pirate life but still remain outside conventional society. In a fascinating dialogue, indirect in its meaning, the two men talk about Singleton's desires. The dialogue is reminiscent of the initial meeting between Harris and Singleton. "If thou dost not like what I am going to propose to thee," William tells Singleton, "thou shalt promise me not to make it publick among the Men" (255). Singleton's response reminds the reader of the "solemn Imprecations and Curses" he shared with Harris: "I will not, *William, says I,* upon my Word, and swore to him very heartily" (255). Further, Singleton is willing to agree to any of William's terms, with a notable exception: "In any Thing, *says I, William,* but leaving me, I will; but I cannot part with you upon any Terms whatever" (255). The affectionate language here is extraordinary when compared with Singleton's earlier incarnations in Africa, his discussions with Harris and Wilmot, or, in a broader sense, the language used by other Defoe characters such as Captain Avery in *The King of Pirates*, Moll Flanders, or Robinson Crusoe. Unlike these other Defoe characters, William and Singleton share a language not dependent on economic diction for its effect. Furthermore, the "terms" that Singleton agrees to are contingent on the two men staying together.

William wants Singleton to give up "trading," "for no body trades for the sake of Trading, much less do any Men rob for the sake of thieving" (256). William's arguments have no precedents in other Defoe novels. Crusoe's whole self, for example, is based on his desire to profit and trade, as critics have shown.[17] At the end of *Colonel Jack* (1722) the title character, by this time a powerful and rich trader, is a prisoner in the Spanish colonies because he could not resist the opportunity for illicit trade. In a reversal of *Crusoe*'s end, when Crusoe promises "farther adventures," or the ambivalent ending of *Colonel Jack*, William suggests that the pair run away together and return "home" to England: "Why truly, *says William* . . . it is natural for most Men that are abroad to desire to come Home again, especially when they are grown rich, and when they are (as thou ownest they [sic] self to be) rich enough, and so rich, as they know not what to do with more if they had it" (256). "Why, Man, I am at home," Singleton replies, "here is my Habitation, I never had any other in my Life time" (256). He has no notion of "home" other than his life at sea as a pirate, as he told the reader when he first went on the account. His pirate "Inclination" is far more "natural" than anything he can expect to find in England. William is confused by Singleton's response and pushes him to explain. Madagascar, Singleton replies, has felt more like home and "has been a fortunate Island to me more than once, as thou knowest, *William*" (257). "*William* was quite stunn'd at my Discourse," says Singleton, "and held his Peace" (257). William is "stunn'd" not only because Singleton feels more at home at sea living among the pirates but also because his "Projects are come to nothing, and gone" (257). Singleton is curious about William's "Projects" and pushes him further. He tells William, "I do not say I like this roving cruising Life, so well as never to give it over; Let me hear if thou canst propose any thing beyond it" (257).

Because Singleton shows some interest, William gets to the point. With tears in his eyes, he tells Singleton, "*That there was something to be thought of beyond this way of Living*" (258):

> Why, *William, says I,* what was that?
>
> It was *Repentance, says he.*
>
> Why, *says I,* did you ever know a Pirate repent?
>
> At this he started a little and return'd, at the Gallows, I have one before, and I hope thou wilt be the second.
>
> He spoke this very affectionately, and with an Appearance of Concern for me. (258)

The gist of their conversation suggests that William would like them to return "home" to England and become members of conventional Christian society. Moreover, Singleton himself recognizes the affection William shows and is moved by William's tears, even if Singleton does not see the point of repentance. Singleton has no notion of Christianity or religion of any kind. Further, he tells William that it is pointless even to think about repentance until they quit the pirate life. Once they do, he tells William, "I'll begin there with you with all my Heart" (259). William is touched by Singleton's response, "and if he had Tears in his Eyes before, he had more now, but it was from a quite differing Passion, for he was so swallow'd up with Joy, he could not speak" (259).

Singleton is moved by William's reaction as well; indeed, their roles are reversed. "As I have commanded you all along, from the Time I first took you on board," he tells William, "so you shall command me from this Hour; and everything you direct me, I'll do" (259). William has gone from sorrow that Singleton does not understand his request to "Joy" that Singleton has agreed to do what he asks "with all my Heart." What seems a simple Christian repentance, however, is complicated by Singleton's ignorance of both religion and "home." Singleton repents because he has allowed William to become the center of his life. He can put all his trust in William because he has depended on William for profitable advice. More significant, with William's guidance he has given up the outrageous libertine aspects of piracy while remaining a criminal, and is considering giving up the pirate way altogether to live with William.

I quote at length from this section of the novel because it is of great importance for an understanding of how *Captain Singleton* works as a coherent text. Singleton has been, as he cries in his sleep, "*a Thief, a Pirate, a Murtherer, and ought to be hanged*" (269). He has profited enormously from his pirate adventures, and he has had no sense of "home" other than the libertine, transgressively homosocial world of his fellow freebooters. In his discussion about repentance, Singleton makes a connection with William. Even if Singleton knows nothing of "repentance," he is still moved by

William's talk and the affection William shows for him. Further, the affectionate language between the two men, despite—or perhaps because of—its diction of religious conversion, gives Singleton an attachment, a way "home" even, that he has not felt elsewhere in the novel.

The ambivalence in Singleton's talk with William recalls his entry into piracy. It is as if William shares affinities with Singleton's dead mentor, Harris. Like William, Harris asks Singleton to go to a private place. Like William, Harris asks Singleton if he had "a Mind for an Adventure that might make amends for all past Misfortunes" (138). Singleton's response to Harris is much like his answer to William: "yes, with all my Heart, for I did not care where I went, having nothing to lose, and no Body to leave behind me" (138). The difference is, of course, that Singleton does not bind himself to William by "solemn Imprecations and Curses." Instead Singleton is bound by William's affection and desire to "save" him. Although Singleton has no understanding of repentance or reformation, he does understand that he can leave behind the pirate way and find a "home" with William. That leave-taking, I would argue, establishes a kind of male bonding different from the anarchy of consistently unstable pirate desire. But it is not coded sexually in any way that early-eighteenth-century popular culture would have understood sodomy. Sodomitical behavior was seen as a criminal act that disrupted the societal status quo, not a way to define oneself as a desiring subject. Their relationship is closer to Foucault's definition of identity that links sexuality with desire between two subjects. William and Singleton have established a bond based on their desires for one another, an affectionate—but not necessarily nonsexual—union of two selves.

Current historians of sexuality are of course unable to pinpoint the exact moment when sodomy became a crime that merged the act with the actor. An analysis of *Captain Singleton* demonstrates how complex an interlocution of sexuality in the late seventeenth and early eighteenth centuries can be. I am not arguing, I want to emphasize, that pirates were all sodomites. As I have said, there is no evidence that they were and the notion is, in fact, beside the point here. I am arguing that Singleton and William's relationship moves beyond a self-conscious disruption of power—which pirates have always been known for—to a paradigm that brings these two men together because of their mutual desires. This paradigm is still, of course, a disruption of power and the status quo, but that disruption is secondary to their own desires.

The two men retire from piracy and turn their booty into diamonds. Singleton thinks about William's suggestion as they roam across the Middle

East toward Europe. "The Nature of Repentance," Singleton tells William, "includes Reformation, and we can never reform; how then can we repent?" (266). In this case "reform" takes on multiple meanings. On the one hand, "reform" means to pay back the booty they have taken from so many ships. On the other hand, in the Christian terms of repentance, "reform" suggests a rejection of the pirate way of life to which Singleton has an "Inclination," a life that he is unable to separate from his own internalized sense of self. William replies with a reasonable suggestion that takes into account the practicality of reformation. It would be impossible to return the booty to the original owners. He suggests that they should keep the fortune "with a Resolution to do what Right with it we are able" (267). Singleton then repents, but he repents to the *legalized* definition of piracy, the crimes that they have committed. He does not repent the lives they have led as demonized pirates whose identities are linked with the transgressive world in which they live.

The transgressive camaraderie of the pirate world—and William and Singleton's relationship in particular—is not a part of that repentance because they are still together and still embody the cultural desires of the pirates: to be apart from men and women in the normative society of England. Further, their feelings for one another are cemented by their affectionate speech. William, Singleton says, "was my Guide, my Pilot, my Governor, my every thing, and took care of me, and all we had" (271). In this speech Singleton combines religious diction with maritime diction. It is with William that Singleton decides to spend the rest of his life. Defoe has spent the entire novel setting up Singleton as the hero, and Singleton has spent the entire novel as a man with unfulfilled desires. Repentance is his only choice when the one connection he makes is with another man who demands that he "repent." It seems to me that it is inevitable that he turn to William—the dissenting figure in the novel—and that he become "every thing" to Singleton. William is the one person who has shown affection and concern for Singleton that go beyond economic aggrandizement. As a dissenter, William is—like Singleton—an outsider. He is, therefore, the one person with whom Singleton desires to spend the rest of his life.

Homoeroticism, then, because it is linked in the sense of "affection" to the desire between two men, becomes implicated in repentance in ways that the libertine sexuality of the pirates in the book does not, and in ways that normative society cannot offer them. Repentance—for Singleton and William—becomes the foundation for their affectionate relationship in both the present and the hereafter. For Singleton, that repentance becomes the foundation for, I would argue, implicit homoerotic desire for William. Any traditional ideas of the pirate as a libertine outlaw collapse by this point in the novel. William and Singleton are inseparable, both literally and symbolically; these two "reformed" pirates change the terms for male-male bonding to something quite different from either economic transgression or notions that link sodomy with power as enacted by the libertine. Singleton is at last realizing that he need not wander the world any farther because he found what he desired all along: stability and security with Quaker William. He is finally discovering that his own identity begins and ends with Quaker William: "I am loath to part with you so long as to go to the Bottom of the *Persian* Gulph," Singleton tells William as William leaves to do some trading. William is gone much longer than he said he would be; Singleton is distraught because for the first time he sees a future for himself: "I began to be very uneasy about *William*, sometimes thinking he had abandoned me" (260). By the end of the novel, Singleton cannot imagine a life without Quaker William.

That Singleton repents, reforms, and tries to restore all he has taken does not mean that he and William will live as "normal" people. On the contrary, they begin entry into society first by dressing as Persians who, like the historical pirates, speak a private language "as was sufficient to make us able to talk to one another so as not to be understood by any Body, though sometimes hardly by our selves" (272). It seems as if even though Singleton may have trouble at times understanding what William says to him, he does on a deeper level understand the real affection the two men share. Their return to Europe is marked by their continued outsider status and the remarkable symbiosis they share. They never see themselves as part of society, but only as living within that society.

Defoe has created a situation in which Singleton longs for a "home" but at the same time is neither a pirate nor an Englishman. He neither owns property nor rebels against ownership as a definition of identity. Singleton's only connection with others is a desire to spend the rest of his life with his friend William. Given the clear echoes of the Book of Ruth in their conversation, it is curious that no one has pointed out the vividly loving language that Defoe employs when William speaks to Singleton: "William look'd very affectionately on me; nay, *says he*, we have embarked together so long, and come together so far, I am resolved I'll never part with thee as long as I live, go where thou wilt, or stay where thou wilt" (274). The emotional desire implicit in the affectionate words that William and Singleton speak to each other here and elsewhere in the novel contrasts with the language of economic and erotic desire spoken by the usual Defoean characters, like Moll Flanders, who routinely conflates sex and money, or Captain Avery when he comes upon the Great Mogul's granddaughter.

In a way, William's and Singleton's words echo the language of Moll and Avery or even the language of Singleton himself when he stumbles across gold in Africa. The difference from these other outlaws or Singleton's earlier incarnation in Africa is that Singleton and William verbalize their affection. These men do not desire objects: money, jewelry, or women's bodies. Rather, their desire is a reciprocal yearning for each other: William cares for Singleton's soul and Singleton desires to be led by William. There is, however, a complication to this religious foundation. Unlike Crusoe, Singleton never has the kind of epiphany that demonstrates true faith. Instead, as the novel ends, Singleton finds what he has been looking for all along through the "terms" he agrees to: he repents in order to live out his life in domestic solitude with Quaker William.

Singleton still retains some control over his return to England and still reflects some of the ways piracy has influenced his sense of self. He tells William he will return to England on four conditions. First, they will disclose themselves only to William's sister. Second, they will wear beards "after the *Grecian* Manner . . . that we may pass for *Grecians* and Foreigners." Third, they will speak English only in private. And finally, "That we will always live together and pass for brothers" (277). Singleton's conditions embody some of the characteristics of the transgressive pirate. Like the fanciful, colorful dress and alien language of the pirates, their clothing and their speech will distinguish them from their neighbors. Like the pirates who call themselves the "brethren of the sea," Singleton and William live together as "Greeks," and rich Greeks at that.

In the novel's penultimate paragraph, Singleton lists all the wealth that the two men have accumulated, "with all of which I arrived safely, and some time after married my faithful Protectress, *William's* Sister" (277). The marriage, I would argue, becomes nothing more than a fig leaf—like their costume and language. Indeed, the way that Singleton characterizes his marriage is strikingly similar to Crusoe's famous dismissal of his own marriage and his wife's death in one sentence.[18] Singleton's marriage, like Crusoe's, symbolizes his intent to remain in England. However, the marriage is subordinated to the wealth Singleton accumulated with William and their disguise as "Greeks" with all the connotations that implies. The effect is to reemphasize the deep affection that has developed between the two men throughout the latter half of the novel and the desire Singleton shows for William.

They will not spend their lives together *as* brothers, in a kind of benign homosocial camaraderie; instead they will "*pass* for brothers," a significant distinction. They will define themselves to others in a relationship that others can understand, and in turn live as *they* desire. Underneath the costume, language, and presumed camaraderie of these ex-pirates lies something else, the implications of homoerotic desire exemplified by their Greek disguise and by their affectionate relationship that goes far beyond camaraderie. The choices that Singleton makes are tied up with shifting definitions of self and the difficulties inherent in defining identity as a function of sexuality— whether deviant or not. Singleton has given up being a pirate for being a Christian, but he is still an outsider. He can never "fit in," but all the same he has found a "home" and has learned what to do with his "property." All this stability is contingent on his own desire for William and William's reciprocal affection.

Richetti writes that at the end of the novel Singleton "is his own man, something else behind the disguise, as he was really something else behind his various other roles." However, what Richetti goes on to describe as a "myth of a residual person behind the visible social personality" is, more accurately, the establishment of a nontraditional identity.[19] Singleton has found a home, but it is a secret transgressive world within the boundaries of heterocentric English society. Defoe's construction of the desiring subject finally sets *Captain Singleton* apart from *Robinson Crusoe*, *Roxana*, and *Moll Flanders*. Unlike these other, more familiar novels, *Captain Singleton* ends with a sense of closure. This closure is discomforting for critics of Defoe and the novel. The subversive happily-ever-after ending questions the normative terms that critics use to construct the antecedents for the origins of the novel. Further, Defoe's ending challenges the standards by which individuality must be integrated with and defined by social norms.

8

Robinson Crusoe and "True Christian" Identity

To me the Impiety of this Part of the Book, in making the Truths of the Bible of a Piece with the fictitious Story of *Robinson Crusoe*, is so horribly shocking that I dare not dwell upon it; but most say, that they make me think that this book ought to be printed with *Vaninus*, and *Freethinker*, and some other Atheistical Tracts, which are condemn'd and held in Abhorrence by all good Christians.
　　　　　—Charles Gildon, *The Life and Surprizing Adventure of Mr. D----- De F--*

No political arithmetic can make a calculation of the number of true Christians while they live blended with the false ones, since it is not only hard, but impossible, to know them one from another in this world.　　—Daniel Defoe, *The Serious Reflections of Robinson Crusoe*

　　　　The success of *Robinson Crusoe* as an early masterpiece of the modern novel has relied on criticism that takes into account only the events that lead up to and include Crusoe's stay on the island. The incidents that occur after his rescue and in *Robinson Crusoe*'s two sequels are dismissed as tangential to Defoe's first and greatest attempt at fiction.[1] In *The Reluctant Pilgrim*, for example, Hunter writes that the *Farther Adventures* and the *Serious Reflections* "seem . . . to have been separately conceived" (ix-x). *Robinson Crusoe*, on the other hand, has a definite form that contributes to the book's continued power:

> *Robinson Crusoe* is constructed on the basis of a familiar Christian pattern of disobedience-punishment-repentance-deliverance, a pattern set up in the first few pages of the book. . . . Crusoe's continual appraisal of his situation keeps

the conflict at the forefront of the action throughout, for his appraisal is not the superficial, unrelated commentary some critics have described, but rather an integral part of the thematic pattern set up by Crusoe's rebellion and the prophecy of his father that Crusoe "will be the miserablest Wretch that was ever born." (Hunter, 19–20)

Hunter is correct, as far as he goes, but he sells Defoe—and Crusoe—short by limiting his discussion to *Robinson Crusoe.*

Like other critics, Hunter argues that Crusoe's "deliverance" ends with his rescue; the last section of the book does not count or is reduced to an epilogue. The emphasis on volume one while dismissing the two sequels can explain Crusoe's behavior, and allows Hunter and other critics to find the "thematic pattern" in the novel. In the last lines of *Robinson Crusoe,* Crusoe writes that he has more to tell of his life after his rescue. "All these things," he says, "with some very surprizing incidents in some new adventures of my own, for ten years more, I may perhaps give a farther account of hereafter" (299).

The implications of Crusoe's "farther account" are important for a new reading of *Robinson Crusoe* that can embrace all of Defoe's fiction without excluding his less familiar novels. Crusoe's offering of a "farther account" suggests that the sequels challenge and extend Defoe's "thematic patterns." The *Farther Adventures* and the *Serious Reflections* are not the "failures" they have been called.[2] If we look at all three novels and consider that Crusoe's stay on the island is one adventure out of many, then Crusoe's characterization, apparently a transparent merging of a belief in providence and middle-class economic values in the first novel, becomes increasingly indefinite in the *Farther Adventures.* If his "serious reflections" are read along with *Robinson Crusoe* and the *Farther Adventures,* what seems to be a random series of events can be seen to anticipate and parallel the structure of *Captain Singleton.* Crusoe is on a quest to determine his identity, a tension between homo eroticus and homo economicus that finally—implicitly in the *Farther Adventures* and explicitly in the *Serious Reflections*—becomes displaced by a narrative that emphasizes violent and radical religious faith.

Of course, it can and has been argued that the narrative voice of the *Serious Reflections* represents a persona for Defoe. We cannot read the *Serious Reflections* as a continuation of the kind of story that Defoe has been writing in the first two Crusoe books. However, let us accept that Defoe was not working toward an "invention" of the novel (Ian Watt's assumption in *The*

Rise of the Novel). Instead Defoe wrote the book as a continuation of the kind of moral instruction that he asserts is the purpose of the first two books. The *Serious Reflections* does not contain the "entertaining" episodes found in the first two novels that might divert the reader from the book's overtly didactic purpose. However, one can also argue that the "persona" *is* Crusoe's voice, since over the course of two novels we have seen the development of a mutable character: Robinson Crusoe himself. If read as a second sequel, the *Serious Reflections* is the culmination of all the stories and "incidents" that Defoe relates in the first two Crusoe novels: an answer to Gildon's critique quoted in the epigraph at the start of this chapter.

Crusoe's religious beliefs in *Robinson Crusoe* are transformed into religious zeal in the *Farther Adventures* and the *Serious Reflections*. The "zeal"—particularly in the *Serious Reflections*—is a violent exaggeration of the faith that Crusoe professes on the island. Hunter's "reluctant pilgrim"—a man who converts out of necessity—is transformed into a crusader who wants to exterminate any people who are not Christians or who refuse to convert to Christianity. This extremism—a religious desire made explicit by violence—displaces the inferred sexual and economic desires that define the modern individual. And the modern individual is, of course, the character of Crusoe, a character archetypical in Western literature who exemplifies Defoe's genius as a novelist.

Throughout the first two novels, Crusoe's "wandering inclination" takes him from one adventure to another. Defoe had to write the *Serious Reflections* in order to conclude Crusoe's story definitively, to bring an end to his unrelenting rambling. Crusoe says, "I have frequently mentioned the unconquerable impressions which dwelt upon my mind and filled up all my desires, immovably pressing me to a wandering, travelling life, and which pushed me continually on from one adventure to another, as you have heard" (*Serious Reflections,* 110). Unlike Captain Singleton, who found a home and an identity in a relationship with Quaker William, Crusoe, in hindsight, wants to resolve or understand his "inclination" to travel, to find some meaning that "pressed" him to wander. His "desires" are similar to Singleton's roving inclinations. Crusoe, in the first two novels, travels the world in order to discover who he is, to find some way to negotiate the conflicting demands of society that equates identity with the desire for property and marriage, or domestic stability. If Defoe had not written the *Serious Reflections*, it would be easy to imagine Crusoe wandering the globe in the *Farther Adventures* volumes 3, 4, 5, *ad infinitum*, until he dies in some foreign land. The third volume, however, brings together all the disparate elements of property, trade, and middle-class domesticity—represented by the colonization of his island, his profit from trade, and his barely mentioned marriage—implicit in the first two novels. The representation of religion both at the end of the *Farther Adventures* and in the *Serious Reflections* becomes the means to understand his inability to settle down.

Based on his experience as a traveler and his observations of different religions, Crusoe determines that the English "are the most religious nation in the world" (*Serious Reflections,* 159). However, he makes a distinction between Christian practitioners of what he calls "negative religion" and "true religion": "The negative Christian I speak of is so full of himself, so persuaded that he is good enough, and religious enough already, that he has no thought of anything unless it be to pull off his hat to God Almighty now and then, and thank Him that he has no need of Him" (167). Negative Christians go through the motions of religious piety; they profess but do not practice true Christian principles. In this passage, Crusoe could be alluding to his own experience, his own several crises of faith, when he was marooned on the island in the first of the Crusoe novels. Necessity and fear drove him toward repentance and providence when he was alone and his life was threatened by disaster. All the signs of providence that moved Crusoe toward repentance on the island meant nothing after his rescue in the first two novels. The chaotic ending of *Robinson Crusoe* becomes clearer if we take Crusoe's "reflections" as seriously as Defoe intends.

In the most significant passage in the *Serious Reflections,* Defoe makes clear the motivations behind Crusoe's conversions and "wandering inclination." Crusoe writes that for the hypocritical Christian, negative religion "is the opiate that doses his soul, even to the last gasp; and it is ten thousand to one but the lethargic dream shoots him through the gulf at once, and he never opens his eyes till he arrives in that light where all things are naked and open" (167). As an old man, Crusoe anticipates Marx by more than a hundred years.[3] Further, he seems to anticipate Norman O. Brown's argument that religion and dreams—both significant aspects of the Crusoe novels—"are expressions, distorted by repression, of the immortal desires of the human heart" (Brown, 13). The "opiate" is both the material success he had on the island and the "profitable and diverting" incidents that occur one after another in the *Farther Adventures* (vii). Crusoe is able to make sense of his "diversions" because through his experience and age he "arrives in that light where all things are naked and open" and becomes a "true Christian." Defoe, unlike Marx, makes a distinction between "negative" and "true" religion; that distinction, in turn, enables Crusoe to make some sense out of his "wandering years" and give meaning to his past. By professing "true Christianity" as an old man, Crusoe shows how he was deluded by his easy "profit." Further, his "wandering inclination" was symptomatic of his lack of faith. But both negative and true religion are symptomatic of the repression of his desires. Religion for Crusoe becomes the means to make sense of an identity that has eluded him for seventy years.

"True Christianity" is not, to Crusoe, a benign or dissenting version of the Puritanism that he professed when he was marooned on the island. In the *Serious Reflections*, Crusoe suggests a "subscription" to raise an army and destroy the infidels. "Ten millions should be asked," he says, "to be subscribed for sending a strong fleet and army to conquer heathenism and idolatry" (237). This attitude contrasts sharply with his reaction to the cannibals in *Robinson Crusoe*. He is fearful and bewildered when he first discovers the footprint and then sees the cannibal feasts, but he finally asks himself "what authority or call I had, to pretend to be judge and executioner upon these men as criminals. . . . How do I know what God Himself judges in these particular cases?" (177). The difference, then, between his belief on the island and his belief at the end of his life is a zeal that, while not unusual in early-eighteenth-century England, is astounding in its violence in the context of Crusoe's own life. In both *Robinson Crusoe* and the *Farther Adventures*, religion plays a significant role in Crusoe's adventures, but there is always the sense that Crusoe's conversions are temporary. Toward the end of the *Farther Adventures*, however, his religious beliefs become stronger. His final "conversion" in the *Serious Refections* comes out of the beliefs he professed in the *Farther Adventures*.

In the author's preface to the *Farther Adventures* Defoe writes,

> The second part, if the Editor's opinion may pass, is (contrary to the usage of second parts) every way as entertaining as the first, contains as strange and surprising incidents, and as great a variety of them; nor is the application less serious and suitable, and doubtless will, to the sober as well as ingenious reader, be every way as profitable and diverting. (vii)

Defoe was a notorious pen-for-hire; but he insists that his sequel is not written to cash in on the success of the first Crusoe novel. The critical determinism that *assumes* that the *Farther Adventures* is aesthetically less successful or a hastily written sequel ignores the importance of the sequel to an understanding of *Robinson Crusoe* itself.[4] The tendency to downplay the importance of the *Farther Adventures* is based on the inclination to dismiss *any* sequel as less perfect than the original, a point Defoe himself suggests in his preface.

But the *Farther Adventures* was enormously popular in eighteenth-century England and went through seven editions by 1747, only two fewer than *Robinson Crusoe.* It was published initially in August 1719, just four months after the first edition—and enormous success—of *Robinson Crusoe.*[5] Defoe's situation is exacerbated because of his own reputation as a hack and his chameleon-like ability to assume authorial expertise no matter what the political circumstances. His prefaces, then, tend to be read with a jaundiced eye and can lead critics like Watt to conflate Defoe the author with Crusoe the narrator. However, the very instability of authorial intent in the preface allows a complicated reading across the novels themselves, since the reader cannot know exactly *how* to take the author's meaning.[6]

Crusoe and Singleton—the piratical subject *par excellence*—share an "inclination" to see the world. That "inclination" leads Crusoe to leave England and join the homosocial camaraderie of the sailor's world. Like Singleton, he has a desire to make his travels profitable; unlike Singleton, he never desires to use that profit to make a home in England. He is, in fact, discontented by the "middle life" his father desired for him when he returns at the end of *Robinson Crusoe.* With Singleton and Quaker William's "Greek" relationship, Defoe provides a perverse sense of closure to *Captain Singleton. Robinson Crusoe,* on the other hand, ends with the promise of more to come, presuming that the popularity of the novel warrants a sequel.

Near the end of the *Farther Adventures* Crusoe says "with some truth, that if trade was not my element, rambling was; and no proposal for seeing any part of the world which I never had seen before, could possibly come amiss to me" (214). When Crusoe—who has accumulated great wealth through his efforts—says, "trade was not my element," the reader might be forgiven for taking this with several grains of salt. However, Crusoe is telling *a* truth. To focus only on his mercantile endeavors ignores the reasons that "rambling" was his "element." Trade indeed provides the narrative drive for this book, in much the same way that Crusoe's taming of his island provides the motivation for *Robinson Crusoe* and piracy drives the second half of *Captain Singleton.* He *is* a success in "trade," but trade by itself is less significant to Crusoe than his "rambling"—his ambivalence about returning home—in the *Farther Adventures.* Critics locate the heart of *Robinson Crusoe,* indeed its "thematic meaning," in the "inner life" of his character. Unlike Singleton, whom we have examined, or Moll Flanders, Roxana, or Colonel

Jack, Crusoe's constant self-awareness—in *Robinson Crusoe* at least—stands as a paradigm for like novels written over the past 250 years.[7] It is no less interesting, however, to suppose that Defoe's idea of "character" is unstable precisely because that character does not fit into normative, middle-class paradigms of identity. In other words, notions of religion and dissent implicit in much of Defoe's other work make Crusoe's character less stable than critics suppose, if the *Farther Adventures* and the *Serious Reflections* are not ignored.

Once Crusoe is rescued, he makes sure his "tyrannical" government—as he describes it in the *Farther Adventures* (304)—can succeed without him when he returns to England. Crusoe says that by his constant reflections about God and the meaning of his exile on the island, "I gained a different knowledge from what I had before" (*Robinson Crusoe*, 140). The island teaches him to rely on his belief in God. "In a word," Crusoe says, "the nature and experience of things dictated to me, upon just reflection, that all the good things of this world are no farther good to us than they are for our use" (140). But after his rescue, Crusoe's self-reflection and desire to learn about his inner life, so much a part of the heritage of the novelistic tradition, disappear until the overtly didactic but strangely fascinating *Serious Reflections*, published the next year in 1720.

In the *Farther Adventures* Defoe offers all the entertainment and "strange and surprising incidents" that he gave in the first novel. He also insists on the moral importance of both works for "the sober as well as the ingenious reader." Defoe is objecting to critics like Charles Gildon, who wrote in 1719 after the publication of *Robinson Crusoe*, "I hope, Dear D—, that you have taken more care of Probability and Religion than you have in this; tho' I am afraid you are too harden'd a Sinner in these Particulars."[8] The constant movement and travel in the *Farther Adventures*—with little time for the kind of reflection admired by readers of *Robinson Crusoe*—tend to overshadow exactly what the "surprising incidents" might represent for the "sober" but "ingenious reader" of the novel.

This disjunction between inner reflection by the reader—at least in the second half of the *Farther Adventures*—and outward plot movement is made more apparent by the focus on Crusoe's "inner life" in the first novel. Crusoe himself realizes in hindsight the direction his inclination to ramble is taking him:

> But I was gone a wild-goose chase indeed, and they that will have any more of me must be content to follow me through a new variety of follies, hardships,

and wild adventures; wherein the justice of Providence may be duly observed, and we may see how easily Heaven can gorge us with our own desires, make the strongest of our wishes be our afflictions, and punish us most severely with those very things which we think it would be our utmost happiness to be allowed in. (*Farther Adventures,* 187)

If Crusoe, like Singleton, is unable to stay at home but must travel the world, the "lessons" that he and the reader learn must end with the first novel, because in the sequel Crusoe once again interacts with the world as if he never learned the lessons on the island. While Gildon notices this tension, later critics simply ignore the plot shift by ignoring the *Farther Adventures* or declaring it aesthetically inferior.

As the lack of scholarship on the *Farther Adventures* demonstrates, the "ingenuity" of the reader that Defoe presumes has been ignored by traditional criticism. To reject the second Crusoe novel as inferior is to miss the ironic point: Crusoe—perhaps more of an "everyman" than didacticists or moralists would like to think—did not learn anything from his stay on the island.[9] He admits as much in the first paragraph of the *Farther Adventures*:

Any one would think that, after thirty-five years' affliction, and a variety of unhappy circumstances, which few men, if any, ever went through before, and after near seven years of peace and enjoyment in the fulness of all things, grown old, and when, if ever, it might be allowed me to have had experience of every state of middle life, and to know which was most adapted to make a man completely happy; I say, after all this, any one would have thought that the native propensity to rambling, which I gave an account of in my first setting out in the world to have been so predominant in my thoughts, should be worn out, the volatile part be fully evacuated, or at least condensed, and I might, at sixty-one years of age, have been a little inclined to stay at home, and have done venturing life and fortune any more. (1)

In this long, digressive justification for his desire to "ramble," Crusoe's reasoning hinges on his "experience of every state of middle life." Just as he wanders the globe to try and find "meaning" for his existence, his pen wanders the page to justify his "inclination." He tries to understand why a life of plenty and comfort results in an edgy desire to "venture life and fortune" on the uncertainty of travel. Middle-class life—even with the material comfort he lacked on the island—leaves him unhappy or dissatisfied. Like Captain Singleton and Roxana, he is unsure of his "place" in the world despite his fame, family, and wealth.

The *Farther Adventures* can be read as a fictionalized version of the travel books so popular in the early eighteenth century. For instance, when Crusoe talks about the people, sights, and society of China (250, 268, 270) or his trip through the steppes of Russia and the Mongolian desert (281), the reader is reminded of such privateer/authors as Woodes Rogers, Edward Cooke, and William Dampier.[10] But from the beginning, the *Farther Adventures*, like *Captain Singleton*, is more than an imitation of a travelogue by a privateer. The narrative is instead the logical development of a character who finds that nothing or nobody—except Friday—is important in the "real" world. Crusoe showed this tendency in the first novel, although then it was based on his relationship with God. Indeed, Crusoe often writes that he purposefully does not intend to give detailed descriptions of coast lines and the flora and fauna of the places he visits as the travelogue writer does. Instead, Crusoe undertakes or describes a different kind of travel, a search for self-knowledge that the reader discovers along with him in *Robinson Crusoe*. The reader and Crusoe find out in the *Farther Adventures* that "self-knowledge," that is, belief in providence and satisfaction derived from material success, were attainable only when Crusoe was alone on the island. Crusoe may be *born* into the middle state, but his "happiness" hinges on travel, a restlessness in stark contrast to the middle state his father desired for him.

What happens if the terms of validation for *Robinson Crusoe* are reversed, if we suppose that the *Farther Adventures* is the more important volume? Crusoe's "rambling"—read in the context of his time on the island—becomes neither a quixotic gambol halfway around the world, nor a picaresque novel, nor an imitation privateer journal. Instead, the overarching goal—more important than the individual incidents—is to return to his island, and then, after he is marooned in Bengal, to get back to England. The travels in the *Farther Adventures* become a reversal of the static, inward search for self-knowledge in *Robinson Crusoe*. In this first novel, Crusoe *makes* a home on his island and recreates a sense of material and domestic comfort, since money is worthless on the island. When his Edenic, self-contained world is threatened by cannibals, then overrun by Spaniards and pirates, he retreats to the fears that haunted him before he read the signs of providence.

As he watches the pirates' cruelties near the end of the first volume, Crusoe says, "This put me in mind of the first time when I came on shore, and began to look about me; how I gave my self over for lost; how wildly I looked around me; what dreadful apprehensions I had; and how I lodged in the tree all night for fear of being devoured by wild beasts" (250). If Crusoe's paradise can be invaded by outsiders—whom he compares to "wild beasts"—what will happen to him when he returns to the outside world itself, to "civilization"? Like Gulliver, who reacts with undisguised disgust toward his countrymen on his return to England after his stay with the Houyhnhnms, Crusoe will discover that all the fears represented by the cannibals he had avoided for his last ten years on the island can come true, at the same time that his desires cannot be satisfied. But once he returns to England, after his narrow escape from wolves in the Pyrenees, Crusoe says, "I was inured to a wandring life . . . I could not resist the strong inclination I had to see my island" (*Robinson Crusoe*, 297). Even though Crusoe spent all those years alone on a deserted island for the most part happily, he also discovers that civilization can be as dangerous as the unknown. The lust for travel is too strong to ignore, however; he has not learned the lessons of his twenty-seven-year displacement from society, despite the safety provided by his material and domestic success in London.

After his return, the only thing that keeps Crusoe in England is his wife. She dies, as the reader learns in the famous paragraph at the end of the first Crusoe novel. At the beginning of the *Farther Adventures,* Crusoe says, "When she was gone, the world looked awkwardly around me. I was as much a stranger in it, in my thoughts, as I was in the Brazils when I went first on shore there; and as much alone, except as to the assistance of servants, as I was in my island" (7). Always feeling like an outsider at home—both before he left at eighteen and after he returns at the age of fifty-five—he had at least a semblance of "home" when he lived in England, married, with young children. The death of his wife leaves him isolated in ways that make him see the tedium of everyday life for an Englishman with an inclination to travel. His "inclination," however, runs deeper than a desire to see the world. Bored in England, frustrated by the "middle state," Crusoe looks back with nostalgia at the way life was for him when he survived alone and, as critics like to emphasize, the ways he looked inward to find justifications for his solitude by signs of providence.

The apparently simple goal of Crusoe's story in the *Farther Adventures*—to return to his island—becomes complicated by his assertion that "there was something which certainly was the reason and end of life, superior to all these [material] things, which was either to be possessed, or at least hoped for, on this side of the grave" (8). Defoe's plotting of the novel gives further complication to Crusoe's initial design. Although Crusoe aims to find out what had happened to his "subjects" in his absence, that impulse to return to his "kingdom" results in a trip from England to South America to Asia and finally back to England through Russia and Europe. As the reader discovers, Crusoe is a man torn by both his inability to settle down and his inability to view the world as an impartial traveler. This understanding of his reasons to ramble might relieve him of the scrapes in which he finds himself. He is a quintessential provincial Englishman in his responses to the sites he visits, but also a man metaphorically without a country. Crusoe looks for something that he desires—he is not sure what—but that mysterious something eludes him, until he looks back on his life in the *Serious Reflections*.

Toward the end of the *Farther Adventures* Crusoe is forced to spend the winter in Siberia with an exiled Russian prince. The prince, he decides, is a "truly great man." He is content in his banishment because, Crusoe says, the prince "showed that his mind was so inspired with a superior knowledge of things, so supported by religion as well as by a vast share of wisdom, that his contempt of the world was really as much as he had expressed" (307). After so many years alone on an island, Crusoe has had the chance to get to know his own "mind." He explicitly professed "contempt of the world" when he was marooned. The prince's story, then, is both emblematic of Crusoe's time alone and, for the reader, suggestive of the unhappiness that causes Crusoe's wandering inclination in the second novel. His wife is dead, Friday is dead, and he has been left behind by his own sailors. He is an old man who must, in fact, find his way home, in his case a "home" that we know has left him unsettled and unhappy. Crusoe cannot express his own "contempt of the world" except through analogous stories such as the tale of the exiled prince. And Crusoe believes that this prince has learned to control his desires through "a superior knowledge of things."

Both Crusoe and Captain Singleton return to an England of strangers. As the first half of Singleton's story comes to an end, he says, "I had neither Friend, Relation, nor Acquaintance in *England*, tho' it was my Native Country" (137). Singleton is "betrayed" by friends and loses all the money that he accrued in his trek across Africa. Crusoe, on the other hand, returns to his "Native Country," keeps his money, marries, and has a family. Singleton says that the first half of his life "may be said to have begun in Theft, and ended in Luxury; a sad Setting out, and a worse Coming home" (138). Crusoe's trials began when he left home. His isolation on the island began "in Theft" because he went against his instincts and became involved in slavery. Like Singleton, Crusoe has new trials when he tries to settle down at the end of *Robinson Crusoe*. His return "ended in Luxury," and enables him to buy a ship or "property"—only to begin his wandering and his afflictions all over again. The parallels between Crusoe and the piratical subject Captain Singleton are striking. Both men are unable to settle down, to find a "home" in England. Both men are searching for a sense of identity that does not have to be defined by ownership of property or domestic stability.

Given the opportunity to travel again, Crusoe jumps at his nephew's offer to go to sea with him, and asks, "What devil . . . sent you of this unlucky errand?" (*Farther Adventures,* 10). His deliverance from tedium—the middle state that he vowed to resign himself to after his rescue from the island—he attributes to "the existence of an invisible world" and "the occurrence of second causes with the ideas of things which we form in our minds, perfectly [p]reserved, and communicated to any in the world" (9). The providence that earlier enabled him to keep faith on the island has been transformed into those "thoughts" that tell him to go on board a ship again, exactly what, as he says, "compleated my ruin" in the first place (*Robinson Crusoe,* 40). His unsettled "nature" requires his claim that "it would be a kind of resisting Providence if I should attempt to stay home" (*Farther Adventures,* 11). Providence for Crusoe in the first two novels is the sign that gives him the justification to do what he intended to do anyway.

When Crusoe returns to his island he learns of the trials that his settlers went through. The pirates who settle with the Spaniards are distinctly different from the heroic piratical subjects of the *General History* and *Captain Singleton*. The pirates in the Crusoe novels are *hostis humani generis,* criminals with no redeeming qualities, "rogues," "villains," and "brutes" (*Farther Adventures,* 45, 46). They exhibit none of the mythic qualities we have seen in other eighteenth-century depictions. Homoerotic desire is absent from the representations of these pirates, and absent from representations of the Spaniards who settle Crusoe's island. The Spaniards were usually represented as "bad" in eighteenth-century texts, not only because they were Catholic but also because of their massacres of Native Americans in Mexico and Peru.[11] In the *Farther Adventures,* by contrast, Crusoe's Spaniards are morally superior to anyone, including any British citizens:

> And here I must, in justice to these Spaniards, observe, that let the accounts of Spanish cruelty in Mexico and Peru be what they will, I never met with seventeen men, of any nation whatsoever, in any foreign country, who were so universally modest, temperate, virtuous, so very good-humoured, and so courteous as these Spaniards; and as to cruelty, they had nothing of it in their very nature; no inhumanity, no barbarity, no outrageous passions, and yet all of them men of great courage and spirit. (83)

The Spaniards—England's enemies—have the qualities embodied by people in the "middle state" described by Crusoe's father: "temperance, moderation, quietness, health, society, all agreeable diversions, and all desirable pleasures" (*Robinson Crusoe*, 28). These are not the usual Spaniards at all. However, Defoe has to set these men up heroically in contrast to the criminalized pirates. Through Defoe's representation of the Spaniards, Crusoe can reassert his authority over his subjects and his island. The Spaniards are no more "legitimate" as settlers than the pirates or even Crusoe himself. They all arrive uninvited to the island. However, the Spaniards show their willingness to carry out Crusoe's wishes. Therefore he can leave them in control of the island that he "tamed" in the first place.

Compare these heroically embodied Spaniards (saints, if Crusoe's world would allow such "idols") with the pirates, who destroyed the "plantations" of some of Crusoe's settlers:

> When the three [pirates] came back, like furious creatures, flushed with the rage which the work they had been about had put them into, they came up to the Spaniards, and told them what they had done, by way of scoff and bravado; and one of them stepping up to one of the Spaniards, as if they had been a couple of boys at play, takes hold of his hat, as it was upon his head, and giving it a twirl about, sneering in his face, says he to him, "And you Seignior Jack Spaniard, shall have the same sauce if you do not mend your manners." (49)

The pirates in the *Farther Adventures* are the antithesis of the Catholic Spaniards. They are without redeeming qualities, unlike the title characters of *The King of Pirates* or *Captain Singleton*, both of which were written within a year of the *Farther Adventures*. Crusoe's pirates—unwilling to take care of themselves in any way—exhibit none of the dichotomous pirate traits that fascinated early-eighteenth-century readers. Defoe even compares them to children—"boys at play"—to emphasize their distance from the usual pirates, who were serious in their enmity to the world. A representation of the more complex piratical subject—the antihero who is both valorized and vilified in early-eighteenth-century England—would make it difficult for Defoe to show these pirates' redemption.

Crusoe allows "liberty of Conscience" on his island (*Robinson Crusoe*, 248). These are strong words with explicit political connotations for Defoe's English readers. This liberty anticipates Captain Misson's democratic utopia. Further, Defoe, the author of *The Shortest-Way with the Dissenters* twenty years before and other works that justify "liberty of Conscience" in the face of great resistance, shows how such a society can live in peace.[12] The Spaniards and the pirates, from different countries and with different religions, live together in the same community.[13] This "liberty of Conscience" is problematized, however, because the island almost falls apart. The pirates, unlike the Spaniards, refuse to help make the island habitable. It takes the arrival of Crusoe and the establishment of a unique kind of Christianity, tolerated by *all* the islanders, to control the pirates and establish a new order on the island.

Atkins, the worst of the pirates, never ceases to pester and harass the Spaniards until he and his crew are brought together with the Spaniards by a common fear of "cannibals." When Crusoe returns, Atkins has settled down and is in fact living with a native woman, though without the benefit of marriage. When Crusoe gives the Spaniards and the pirates the opportunity to marry, the Spaniards refuse because "some . . . had wives in Spain, and the others did not like women that were not Christians, and all together declared that they would not touch one of them; which was an instance of such virtue as I have not met with in all my travels" (77). Defoe the ironist plays with the expectations of the readers. Spaniards, England's most notorious enemies (but *not* the enemies of "all mankind") are the most virtuous men in either volume. Not only do they refuse to marry non-Christians, they refuse to have sex with them. Even though Crusoe himself is unable to settle down, Defoe is making an important moral and political point about the significance of marriage and stability, but at the same time complicates his construction of the island. The reader is left to wonder how long the island can remain habitable if it is "peopled" by nonpropagating settlers, or, as in the case of Misson's Libertalia, how long the island can remain "European" if Europeans are propagating with natives. Defoe's imagination is a little extreme in this depiction of a group of men who have been marooned for many years, particularly given the context of the maritime world and the sexual proclivities of the sailor.

This contrasts sharply with depictions of pirates in Defoe's other works. In *Captain Singleton* and *The King of Pirates*, the single status of the pirates is foregrounded. And in the *General History,* a work probably not by Defoe but surely influenced by him, pirates are always either unmarried or ambiguously attached, with the notable exceptions of Blackbeard and his fourteen wives, Rackham and his cross-dressing female lover, and Misson and his Libertalia. These exceptions—all overdetermined or parodic instances of heterosexual behavior—contrast with the transgressively homosocial world of the other pirates in the *General History*. If the pirates are to be brought into Crusoe's society, they must marry, even if their marriages are to native women. However, these pirates deviate from English norms in another way because they are married in a Catholic ceremony. The detail with which Defoe narrates the marriage of Will Atkins to his wife suggests that dissent from the Church of England is the norm on Crusoe's island. The "liberty of Conscience" Crusoe allows makes him resort to deceit so that a French priest—whom he had earlier rescued and brought with him to the island—performs the ceremony for the reformed pirates.

In order to convince the pirates of the necessity of a "legal" marriage, Crusoe says to Atkins that he has "no doubt but they were married in the sight of God, and were bound in conscience to keep them as their wives; but that the laws of men being otherwise, they might pretend they were not married, and so desert the poor women and children hereafter" (136–37). To Crusoe, the importance of the ceremony lies in the legal ramifications of marriage for the wives and children. Crusoe's concern is ironic since "desert the poor . . . children hereafter" is exactly what he did when he abandoned his young children after his wife's death. He tells the pirates that a marriage "was not only to prevent any scandal, but also to oblige them that they should not forsake [their wives], whatever might happen" (*Farther Adventures,* 138). Crusoe is "despot" of his island and is ultimately responsible for his subjects' behavior. The wedding, therefore, is not only to "protect" the wife and children, but also to cover up any possible scandalous behavior and to screen Crusoe's island from potential sexual and economic repercussions these transgressive relationships between pirate and heathen might reveal. Perhaps more important, the marriages serve to civilize the island and its inhabitants. By forcing the pirates to marry, Crusoe is building a society that replicates England and goes against usual depictions of the pirate world. Crusoe's society provides stability for the island based on the relations between different kinds of property: land, wives, and the harvest that each produces—and typical pirates have neither land nor wives.

The marriage—and its ties to property—and the avoidance of scandal are very similar to the relationship between Quaker William and Captain Singleton. In order to prevent "scandal," William and Singleton live as "Greeks"; further, they promise never to "forsake" one another, and live together on their own bit of property in England. A subversive tension permeates the ending of *Captain Singleton,* as we have seen. Likewise, the tension between English moral conventions and the world of Robinson Crusoe and his island is very strong in the *Farther Adventures.* The tension lies not only in the marriage of the reformed pirates to native women but in

Crusoe's encouragement of liberty of conscience on his island. He wants the pirates to marry, but allows a French priest to handle the ceremony. This is in itself a striking representation of religious tolerance. Of course, one could argue that Crusoe has no choice, because the Frenchman is the only clergyman around. However, Crusoe rationalizes the moral virtues of the Catholic priest:

> It is true this man was a Roman, and perhaps it may give offence to some hereafter if I leave anything extraordinary upon record of a man whom, before I begin, I must, to set him out in just colours, represent in terms very much to his disadvantage in the account of Protestants; as, first, that he was a Papist; secondly, a Popish priest; and thirdly, a French Popish priest. (121)

The "French Popish priest" has three strikes against him, yet Crusoe insists that he perform the marriages. A more threatening religious man to early-eighteenth-century English readers—other than a satanist in league with the devil, or an idol worshiper—Defoe could not have come up with. However, this priest is a paragon of Christian virtue, a "true Christian," not drugged by the opiate of "negative religion." In fact, Crusoe says to the priest after they talk about Christianity, "How far . . . have I been from understanding the most essential part of a Christian, viz., to love the interest of the Christian Church, and the good of other men's souls!" (131). In *Robinson Crusoe,* Crusoe spent years alone because he had no "interest of the Christian Church" and never thought of the "good" of others. His experience on the island told him that toil, thrift, and belief in providence would affect his spiritual and thus material well-being. Now he sees that not only his own soul, but the souls of others must be "saved" if the "interest" or stability of his island is to be maintained.

The priest's embodiment as a "true Christian" is undercut, however. For the reader there is a tension between the specificity of Christian religious belief and the "scandal" that Crusoe fears might blacken his island's reputation. Furthermore the financial connotations of "interest" indicate how economic and religious social convention both play a large part in Crusoe's thinking, despite his continual subversion of convention through his rambling and his inability to settle down. After he has once again put his stamp of authority on the island, Crusoe leaves his "subjects" to fend for themselves. He has reasserted his power over them, turned pirates into "true Christians," and left his island in the capable hands of the Spaniards, who will presumably continue to "profit" from their hard work and religious convictions. The marriages of the pirates demonstrate the compelling desire

Crusoe has to reaffirm convention at the same time he is unable to conform to convention himself.

As we have seen, Crusoe never thinks about marriage and "settling down" before he is rescued in the first volume. When Crusoe's wife dies at the end of *Robinson Crusoe*, he dismisses not only her death, but the marriage as well in one sentence (248). Crusoe's relationship with Friday is delineated much more clearly and at much greater length than his union with his wife. This connection is fascinating to read in the context of both Crusoe's marriage and the marriages of the pirates to their native wives. In part because I see the homoerotic connotations in Crusoe and Friday's relationship—and similar relationships in the *General History* and *Captain Singleton*—I see the desire exhibited by Crusoe toward Friday as distinct from the usually uncomplicated master/slave dichotomy that critics tend to observe.[14] After Crusoe rescues Friday from cannibals and teaches him English and about Christianity, the two men return to England together. There is no question that Friday is an essential part of Crusoe's life. In fact, his unusual status as "companion" and "servant"—never "slave"—is taken for granted in the *Farther Adventures* until he is killed off midway through the novel.

Friday's death scene begins as an amusing episode after the excessive moralizing that accompanies the marriage of Will Atkins and his native wife. Crusoe and his ship are sailing down the eastern coast of South America and are set upon by "a hundred and six and twenty" canoes filled with furious natives (178). Neither side can communicate with the other, until Crusoe sends Friday to "go out upon the deck and call out aloud to them in his language, to know what they meant" (179). Friday attempts to talk to the natives. They pay no attention to Friday's efforts; instead, "six of them, who were in the foremost or nighest boat to us, turned their canoes from us, and stooping down, showed us their naked backsides; just as if, in England, saving your presence, they had bid us kiss—" (179). Unfortunately, Friday is killed in the ensuing fusillade: "Friday cried out they were going to shoot; and unhappily for him, poor fellow, they let fly about three hundred of their arrows, and to my inexpressible grief killed poor Friday" (179). The humor of the situation works in two ways. Not only does it undercut the significance of Friday's death because mooning natives are a striking image. Defoe's use of the humor also unmasks the depth of Crusoe's response to his loss because the attack comes as such a surprise to the reader.

Crusoe, so nonchalant when his wife dies, becomes "so enraged with the loss of my old servant, the companion of all my sorrows and solitudes, that

I immediately ordered five guns to be loaded with small shot, and four with great, and gave them such a broadside as they had never heard in their lives before, to be sure" (179). Friday's death has an indelible effect on Crusoe, an effect that permeates the entire second half of the novel, just as his father's presence is never completely out of Crusoe's—or the reader's—consciousness in *Robinson Crusoe*. The repressed violence that Crusoe had shown toward the cannibals in *Robinson Crusoe* in the years before he rescued Friday is unleashed by Friday's death. Religion, which had been the means to create a working society and economic stability on his island both when he was alone and when he returns, manifests itself as a violent hatred of "heathens" and "pagans." Friday, not always visible in the *Farther Adventures* before his death, is the catalyst for Crusoe's reactions toward non-Christians in the remainder of the novel and toward "negative Christians" in the *Serious Reflections*.

Crusoe makes a point of saying that it is not "the ill manners of turning up their bare backsides to us" that aggrieved him. Instead, the natives "killed my poor Friday, whom I so entirely loved and valued, and who, indeed, so well deserved it, I not only had been justified before God and man, but would have been very glad, if I could, to have overset every canoe there, and drowned every one of them" (180). Crusoe's response to the natives' actions contrasts with his reaction to the massacre of an entire town by his sailors, a few pages later in the novel. In that instance, Crusoe is horrified by his men's actions, and for weeks berates them because they horribly overreacted to the killing of one of their own by a group of Madagascar natives. When Friday is killed, Crusoe's response is as violent as that of his men will be, although he manages in part to repress that violence. The affection Crusoe shows toward Friday is quite different from the affection he professes when he introduces the slave boy Xury in *Robinson Crusoe*.

As a young man, years before he is initially shipwrecked on his island, Crusoe is captured by a Sallee pirate. He makes his escape with Xury, for whom Crusoe shows some fondness. After they make their escape and are sailing along the coast of Africa, Xury offers to go on shore, to risk certain death from "savages" or "lyons and tygers" (*Robinson Crusoe*, 47). "I asked him why he would go; why I should not go and he stay in the boat; and the boy answered with so much affection that made me love him ever after" (47). The "affection" that Xury shows and the "love" that Crusoe asserts contrast sharply with Crusoe's reaction to Friday's death. After Crusoe and Xury are rescued by the Portuguese captain, Crusoe ends up selling Xury.

Even though he protests that he is "loath to sell the poor boy's liberty," he does, for sixty pieces of eight (54). And that is the last the reader hears of Xury.

In contrast, memories of Friday keep intruding into Crusoe's thoughts. When he speaks of Friday, Crusoe can barely repress the bubbling emotions that come through the prose. He describes the way the "natives . . . always add two *e's* at the end of the words where we make one . . . nay, I could hardly make Friday leave it off, though at last he did" (*Farther Adventures,* 182). This memory sets Crusoe off once again in a digression about his late friend:

> And now I name the poor fellow once more, I must take my last leave of him, poor honest Friday! We buried him with all the decency and solemnity possible, by putting him into a coffin, and throwing him into sea; and I caused them to fire eleven guns for him; and so ended the life of the most grateful, faithful, honest, and most affectionate servant that ever man had. (182)

There is no indication that sexual relations took place between Friday and Crusoe. Rather, it is more significant that Crusoe lives in a homosocial world in which affection for Friday causes him to be devastated at Friday's death, indeed, devastated in ways that elude him when his wife dies. In Crusoe's world, conventions of religion and master/slave relationships mask and discipline the love and affection that are explicit and the eroticism that is implicit in their relationship.

The implicit sexuality in Crusoe's world can be seen in the retelling of the Crusoe story in an amusing little pornographic novel from the 1960s entitled *The Secret Life of Robinson Crusoe.* "Humphrey Richardson" (surely a pseudonym) writes in the introduction,

> And the tale that follows is nothing more or less than an attempt to visualize and to recapture the secret side, the neglected aspect of Robinson Crusoe's life, a life led in a world perhaps less devoid of at least the thought of women (in the practical absense of their carnal presence) than an XVIIIth Century journalist's version of the story has led us to suppose.[15]

What follows is an at times hilarious retelling of the Crusoe story. Toward the end of the short novel, after Crusoe has tired of fantasies and onanism, he sets his eyes on Friday and "he would possess the unhappy lad. Possess him furiously."

Each night, Friday lies awake and waits for a drunken Crusoe to come into his bed:

Robinson staggers over to the bed. He reaches down, grabs the undershorts, pulls. His fumbling hands find their way to the fly. . . . Finally pulls the garment off. Friday hides his timid nudity. "Hey, by God! Turn over, d'ye hear!" Robinson bellows.

Shocking scenes like that.[16]

I quote at length from this "complete and unexpurgated" book because Crusoe and Friday act out what is implicit in the Crusoe character: sexual desire made manifest by its very silence in Defoe's novels. Other, more serious books, such as J. M. Coetzee's *Foe* and Maurice Tournier's *Friday*, suggest hidden sexual desire as well. In *Friday*, for instance, the island literally becomes Crusoe's lover: "Then, with strength renewed . . . he would turn to press his loins to the huge, warm female body, to furrow it with a plow of flesh."[17] Part of the fascination with the Crusoe story, I would argue, is this "secret" side of Crusoe's life. We hear about his relationship to God, we read in great detail his taming of the island. But if we are reading about a fully "psychological" human being in Defoe's depiction of Crusoe, much is also left out. Bataille is absolutely correct when he argues that "eroticism is that within man . . . which calls his being into question." Bataille asserts that religion and eroticism are but two sides of private experience: one sacred and one profane. "Private experience" (and what else do we get in *Robinson Crusoe* but the title character's own account of his private experience?) and religion and eroticism are dialectical and inextricably linked.[18]

Of course, when Crusoe and Friday live together in England, the terms of their relationship change because a "civilized" man and a "savage" would be watched by all of Crusoe's acquaintances in London. However, the island is a world where different rules apply, and Crusoe attributes his friendship with Friday to providence (206). The transgressive nature of their relationship—not entirely subordinated by notions of servitude and slavery— is in fact sanctioned by the signs of providence. Crusoe and Friday rescue honorable Spaniards, and Crusoe is able to create his own little "kingdom," a homosocial world in which gendered difference is entirely absent from representations of human relationships.

If Friday's death scene were the only example of the "affection" between Crusoe and his servant, then this would be an effort to make a mountain out of a very small molehill. Friday's affection for Crusoe, however, is equally strong, and not simply because Crusoe saved Friday from being the main course at a cannibal feast. In *Robinson Crusoe*, Crusoe offers to let Friday return to his own people. Unhappy with Crusoe's proposal, Friday says, "What you send Friday away for? take, kill Friday, no send Friday away?"

(227). Surprised by Friday's response, Crusoe says, "In a word, I so plainly discovered the utmost affection in him to me, and a firm resolution in him, that I told him then, and often after, that I would never send him away from me, if he was willing to stay with me" (227). The relationship between Friday and Crusoe must then be read in the context of both *Robinson Crusoe* and the *Farther Adventures*. Their conversation, reminiscent of the affectionate vows between Quaker William and Captain Singleton, is a transgressive speech, a window into the affectionate, possibly homoerotic world implicit in both *Robinson Crusoe* and the *Farther Adventures*. Crusoe extends his promise to "never send him away" *only if* Friday chooses to stay with Crusoe. By looking at the *Farther Adventures* in addition to *Robinson Crusoe*, we can see the ways Crusoe's relationship with Friday extends through both volumes, and see that his stay on the island is not entirely detached from the later events in both novels.

After Friday's death, Crusoe's journey loses the purpose that it had as means to an end: to return to England. For the remainder of the *Farther Adventures*, Crusoe becomes embroiled in one violent incident after another. Many of these events metaphorically resemble his encounters with wolves at the end of *Robinson Crusoe*. Indeed, Defoe uses the image of the wolf more than once implicitly and explicitly as an effective analogy to Crusoe's response to the world. The episode with the wolves toward the end of the novel is one of the most puzzling and seemingly arbitrary sequences in *Robinson Crusoe*. Modern critics are unable to make sense of this scene. What does it have to do with anything else in the novel? Is it nothing more than sensationalism tacked on for readerly excitement? The wolves attack Crusoe, Friday, and their party as they travel through the mountains between Spain and France in "the severest winter all over Europe that had been known in the memory of man" (285). A less literal representation of this lupine image is repeated twice more in the *Farther Adventures*. If both parts are read together, the deceptively capricious inclusion of the wolves in the first novel begins to take on meaning that does not have to be explained away as aberrant in an otherwise coherent masterpiece.

In the long chase sequence at the end of *Robinson Crusoe*, the wolves present horrifying and violent images of "devils," gruesome death, and senseless appetite that parallel and make real Crusoe's fears of cannibals on the island. However, Defoe's description of the wolves' attack and Crusoe's self-defense reads like a war between two well-organized armies. In the wilds of the mountain passes, Crusoe and his party are assaulted by "troops of wolves" (293):

We were not gone half over the plain, but we began to hear the wolves howl in the wood on our left, in a frightful manner, and presently after we saw about a hundred coming on directly toward us, all in a body, and most of them in a line, as regularly as an army drawn up by experienced officers. (292)

Like these wolves, both the cannibals whom Crusoe and Friday attacked to save the Spaniards and the heathens whom Crusoe will attack in the *Farther Adventures* "howl" and make similar frightful noises. The wolves, however, are overcome, and retreat before Crusoe and his companions can inflict further damage. They have more "sense," it seems, than the "heathen" cannibals and Chinese and "Tartar" pagans. Even though they show some sense, the wolves are horrifying to Crusoe. It is inexplicable to Crusoe that he meets such "hellish creatures" (293) when he is so near civilization and "home." He says, "I think I would much rather go a thousand leagues by sea, though I were sure to meet with a storm once a week" than cross those mountains again (296).

When the wolves reappear in the *Farther Adventures* they recall both the wolves Crusoe met in the mountains and his fear of the cannibals. In the *Farther Adventures* Crusoe says that his colony "had, as I may say, a hundred wolves upon the island, which would devour everything they could come at, yet could very hardly be come at themselves" (102). Near the end of the novel Crusoe has allowed religion, even fanaticism (since other Christians try to dissuade him from his actions) to take over his identity. He again uses a lupine image, this time to describe the Chinese "heathens." Defoe's use of the wolves works to unveil the purpose behind Crusoe's unrest: he is disinclined to marry again and settle down. Instead, he is "inclined" to travel. And he wants to get away from an England he does not really know, nor wants to know.

The trope of piracy appears more frequently than the wolves in the Crusoe novels. The fear of pirates and piracy is never far below the surface of the *Farther Adventures*. After Friday's death, the ship sails halfway around the world to Madagascar. While they are at the island made famous by pirates such as Avery and Kidd, one of the most vivid episodes in the book occurs. Interacting and trading with the natives of Madagascar, Crusoe and his men believe they are on friendly terms with them. Unfortunately, one of the sailors rapes a native woman during the night, and then disappears. The sailors—without Crusoe—go in search of their comrade, believing he is held hostage in the natives' "city." Defoe writes, "and so it was indeed, for there they found the poor fellow, hanged up naked by one arm, and his throat cut" (198). Enraged by their comrade's murder, the men go on a horrible rampage. "They swore to one another they would be revenged," writes Defoe, "and that not an Indian who came into their hands should have quarter; and to work they went immediately, and yet not so madly as by the rage and fury they were in might be expected" (198–99). Here the sailors act with the ferocity of the pirates when they raid a ship. The ferocity is also reminiscent of the wolves' insatiable appetites and military precision when they meet Crusoe and his party in the mountains.

As Crusoe notices, at first the sailors are able to control their passions. In a sort of inverted way, they are reasonable in their methodical reprisal. Instead of ransacking, looting, and murdering the "Indians," they set about burning the houses of the sleeping natives. As more and more of the natives wake up and come out of their houses to see what is the matter, the sailors give in to their passions and massacre all of them. What begins as a systematic retribution for the murder of their friend becomes a holocaust of a whole village. All this time, Crusoe is on board his ship with his nephew. They see the flames coming from the shore and decide to try to put a stop to the massacre. Crusoe says, "I must confess I never was at the sacking a city, or at the taking a town by storm . . . I never had any idea of the thing itself before, nor is it possible to describe it, or the horror which was upon our minds at hearing it" (201). The sailors act like the wolves in *Robinson Crusoe*, stripped of all restraint, and indeed show the brutish nature of the pirates. The sailors' uncontrolled passions are unmasked. Their unmasking demonstrates the horrible "nature" of mankind to Crusoe.

In *Robinson Crusoe*, Crusoe describes the sight when they come upon the wolves' carnage in the mountains: "But here we had a most horrible sight; for riding up to the entrance where the horse came out, we found the carcass of another horse, and of two men, devoured by the ravenous creatures . . . as to the man, his head and the upper part of his body was eaten up" (293). Crusoe describes in detail his entry into the Madagascar village:

> plain now to be seen by the light of the fire, lay four men and three women killed; and, as we thought one or two more lay in the heap among the fire. In short there were such instances of rage altogether barbarous, and of a fury beyond what was human, we thought it was impossible our men could be guilty of it. (202)

Defoe depicts the scenes of horror here in the same kind of detail he uses to describe the minutiae of Crusoe's life on the island in the first novel. The numbers of natives, how the wolves' victims and the sailors' victims die, and the detail of the barbarity and carnage are a vivid reminder of just how lively a writer Defoe can be. Defoe ties together the "natural" violence of the wolves and the overwrought violence of the sailors. Further, the two scenes anticipate Crusoe's violence toward the Asian "heathens" near the end of the *Farther Adventures*. Defoe—probably inadvertently—shows that there is a fine line that separates Christian violence and anti-Christian, uncivilized violence. All these examples serve to question and complicate the meaning of Crusoe's plans for a religious "war" at the end of the *Serious Reflections*.

At this point Crusoe does not know why the sailors have turned so brutal, although he can understand the "madness" of the wolves, because they are starving to death. He says of the scene on Madagascar, "I was so terrified in my thoughts at this outrageous attempt, that I could not stay there, but went back to my own men, and resolved to go into the middle of the town through the fire . . . and put an end to it" (203). He berates the men for their barbarity, and they in turn show him the body of their murdered comrade. Crusoe admits that

> I was urged then myself, and at another time would have been forward enough; but I thought they had carried their rage too far, and I thought of Jacob's words to his sons Simeon and Levi, "Cursed be their anger, for it was fierce; and their wrath for it was cruel." . . . nay, my nephew himself fell in with them, and told me in their hearing that he was only concerned for fear of the men being overpowered; for as to the people, he thought not one of them ought to live . . . and I, seeing it quite out of my power to restrain them, came away pensive and sad, for I could not bear the sight, much less the horrible noise and cries of the poor wretches that fell into their hands. (204–5)

Crusoe uses similar diction when he describes coming upon the cannibals for the first time in *Robinson Crusoe* (172). The ways he attributes "inhuman" character to the sailors and his nephew through his description of the "poor wretches," and his sadness at their inhumanity demonstrate a concern for the natives that Crusoe has hitherto not shown. He implies that what upsets him is the sailors' inability to restrain their passions. What is masked, I think, is Crusoe's desire, this displacement of unknown, unfulfilled wandering into violence. The conflation of the wolves, the "cannibal" anxiety, and the sight of his own people acting like savages suggests that Crusoe is lost in the world, neither "despot" nor "subject." These men, who act like pirates although they are not, threaten Crusoe's sense of identity predicated on authority and control.

After Crusoe witnesses the massacre by the sailors, he complains loudly and at length about the violence and moral blindness of their actions. The sailors become so tired of his constant lecturing and moralizing that they tell Crusoe "they will have nothing to do with me any more, neither on board or on shore; and if I came on board, they would all go on shore" (211). Crusoe is left behind in Bengal:

> Here I had the particular pleasure, speaking by contraries, to see the ship sail without me; a treatment, I think, a man in my circumstances scarce ever met with, except from pirates running away with a ship, and setting those that would not agree with their villainy on shore; indeed this was next door to it both ways. (212–13)

Although Crusoe does not call the mutineers "pirates," he sees their action as piratical. Ironically, even his nephew, the captain of the ship, goes with his men. Crusoe is left behind, once again a stranger—without family—in a strange land.

Now that the ship has sailed away, Crusoe is at a loss: "I had a kind of impatience upon me to be nearer home, and yet the most unsettled resolution imaginable which way to go" (217). Just getting home is not enough for Crusoe; this indecision reflects the ambiguity of his desires. He and his partner buy a ship together and decide to trade throughout Asia. The two men agree that not only will they return to Europe, but they will make some profit as well. He says to his partner, "I shall pursue it so eagerly, I shall never let you lie still" (218). Once again, Crusoe acts before he thinks. His desire for money gets him into trouble, just as it did when he dealt in slaves in *Robinson Crusoe*.

Crusoe's latest troubles begin when he is mistaken for a pirate because, unfortunately, the ship that they buy belongs to someone else. He does not know he owns a stolen ship, but his desire to make money—or perhaps the perfidy of the pirates—gives him away to the authorities as the possible pirate. The difference between his "ill-fate" in the *Farther Adventures* and the troubles he encounters in *Robinson Crusoe* is that providence itself never enters into Crusoe's thoughts in the former. Religion is not yet the driving force that will take over the end of the novel and give him the reason to go home.

If Crusoe can be mistaken for a pirate, anyone can be. In this case, it is Crusoe's word against his accusers'. Crusoe is so upset by the accusation that he never stops to consider that his circumstances preclude his guilt. The "real" pirates who originally stole the ship do not resemble Crusoe and his crew in the least (246). But his imagined guilt is, I believe, a recognition of his vulnerability. The sense of insecurity that enables him to imagine he is a pirate ties into his reactions to cannibals and the massacre of the Madagascar "Indians" by his own sailors. Indeed, his guilt at being a pirate invades his dreams:

> I . . . scarce slept a night without dreaming of halters and yardarms, that is to say, gibbets; of fighting and being taken; of killing and being killed; and one night I was in such a fury in my dreams, fancying the Dutchmen had boarded us, and I was knocking one of their seamen down, that I struck my double fist against the side of the cabin . . . so that it not only waked me out of my sleep, but I was once afraid I should have lost two of my fingers. (245–46)

Even though he and his crew are not pirates, they are forced to act like pirates, to internalize their own presumed guilt. Not only is Crusoe accused of piracy, he chooses to run away as if he were guilty rather than risk the presumption of innocence. The lines between legitimate trade and piracy are blurred when Crusoe is mistaken for a pirate. When Singleton cries out, "*I am a Thief, a Pirate, a Murtherer, and ought to be hanged*," he is reliving his life of crime through his dreams. Crusoe is only *accused* of piracy, yet in his dreams he imagines himself a pirate. The legal representation of the pirate—embodied by the criminals on Crusoe's island—and the piratical subject—a literary representation—suggest that Crusoe's "guilt" is not based on anything criminal he might have done. Instead, his "guilt" is based on a recognition that his sense of self is ambiguous and transgressive, a fact that he can admit only in the repressed form of dreams. In order to assuage that guilt, then, Crusoe allows newfound religious belief—even fanatic belief compared to his "conversions" in *Robinson Crusoe*—to take over as the driving force behind his actions.

Crusoe never establishes his innocence, although he and his partner manage to get rid of their ship without being caught. "For my part," Crusoe says, "I had a weight taken off from my heart that I was not any longer to bear; and . . . we resolved to go no more to sea in that ship" (248). In fact, Crusoe never returns to sea in the *Farther Adventures*. The sea has always been a representation of Crusoe's—and Singleton's—wandering without particular aim; now, however the journey "home" across China and Russia takes over the novel, as it did for Captain Singleton when he and William head back to England over land. Crusoe's trek, then, provides the narrative impetus that will close the book.

Unlike Singleton, however, Crusoe has no companion or partner with whom to share his life. Coupling provides closures for certain other Defoe novels: think of *Captain Singleton* or *Moll Flanders*. Like the open-ended novels *Roxana* and *Colonel Jack,* the *Farther Adventures* ends ambiguously. Religion—what Crusoe calls "true Christianity" in the *Serious Reflections*—accompanies all his actions throughout the remainder of the *Farther Adventures.* This religion becomes increasingly zealous, culminating in the destruction of the Asian idol in the *Farther Adventures* and his call for a holy war at the end of the *Serious Reflections.*

Crusoe breaks with his partner and becomes a traveler, paradoxically with no particular interest in the sights he sees. Crusoe is one of the most annoying tourists who ever traveled around the world, unimpressed by anything that does not replicate or try to imitate English and European custom.[19] He is particularly distraught by the paganism he discovers and the European admiration of the "heathen's" civilization:

> It is very observable that we wonder at the grandeur, the riches, the pomp, the ceremonies, the government, the manufactures, the commerce, and the conduct of [the Chinese]; not that it is to be wondered at, or indeed, in the least to be regarded; but because, having first a true notion of the barbarity of these countries, the rudeness and the ignorance that prevails there, we do not expect to find any such things so far off. (*Farther Adventures,* 256)

In other words, it is a wonder that these wretched heathens have gone as far as they have, given their non-Christian ways. In fact, the Chinese world cannot be compared to the European world. "Where are their cities to ours," Crusoe asks, "for wealth, strength, gaiety of apparel, rich furniture, and an infinite variety?" (256–57). As he joins a caravan and goes deeper into Asia, west toward Russia and home, he becomes more and more appalled by what he sees. The "heathens" begin to look as they act: dirty, ill-clothed, belligerent—and Crusoe believes—ignorant and "stupid" (285). The more heathenish these people are to Crusoe, the more angry he becomes. His religious belief causes him to become more intolerant. Finally, giving in to the kind of outrage shown by the sailors who wipe out the Madagascar village, Crusoe decides that something must be done to teach these "worst and most ignorant pagans" a lesson (282). We see Crusoe's beliefs evolve from a providential reliance on the wisdom of God's ways—"How do I know what God himself judges in this particular case?" (*Robinson Crusoe* 177)—to a conviction at the end of the second novel that Crusoe himself is entitled to play God by asserting his faith and resorting to violence.

Soon after Crusoe and his caravan cross into "the Muscovite dominions," they stop for the night in a village (*Farther Adventures,* 283). There Crusoe comes upon "an idol made of wood, frightful as the devil, at least as anything we can think of to represent the devil can be made" (284). For the first time since he left his island many years before, Crusoe has a profound and immediate conversion; he decides he must do something about these heathens and their "devil worship." His behavior seems extreme because at the same time that he spouts "Christianity" the reader sees Crusoe behaving exactly the way his men in Madagascar did. This Crusoe is not the man of the previous novel, who decides to spare the cannibals. Nor is he the Crusoe who is able to repress his most violent tendencies when even Friday is killed. Instead, this man is a religious fanatic who "resolves" that a violent course of action is necessary.

Crusoe sees no irony in his determination to destroy the heathens' idol. "So I related the story of our men at Madagascar" to a Scotsman, Crusoe says, "and how they burnt and sacked the village there, and killed man, woman, and child for their murdering of one of our men, just as it is related before; and when I had done, I added that I thought we ought to do so to this village" (286). When Crusoe is confronted by heathenism, violence is a logical action. Completely forgotten is Crusoe's "pensive and sad" reaction to his sailors' horrific massacre of the Madagascar village. Crusoe and the Scotsman creep into the village at night, pull some of the "pagans" out of their huts, tie them up, and burn down the idol. "We supposed," Crusoe says, that they "had been about some of their diabolic sacrifices" (292). Crusoe and his companions force the "heathens" to watch their "monstrous idol" blow up, and satisfied with a job well done, return to their encampment. In a shift of belief confusing to the reader, Crusoe decides that he can be judge and executioner against "heathens" who are ignorant of Christianity. He has no island, no family, no friends; instead, newfound religious belief, what he calls "true Christianity" in the *Serious Reflections*, gives him a sense of identity.

The destruction of the "idol" is the last major adventure in the novel. He writes at the end of the *Farther Adventures*, "I am preparing for a longer journey than all these, having lived seventy-two years a life of infinite variety, and learnt sufficiently to know the value of retirement, and the blessing of ending our days in peace" (323). As Crusoe got farther away from "civilization," the world became more and more dangerous, the people more heathenish, and his own "true Christianity" more important as the foundation for his identity. Now that he is finally headed home, he no longer desires profit or cares to wander, because he believes he has found what he has been looking for since he first left home as a young man. The reader discovers that "true Christianity" displaces all Crusoe's unfulfilled economic and sexual desires. Crusoe's sense of identity—based on "true Christianity"—enables him to return home with a newfound purpose.

In the *Serious Reflections* Defoe finally demonstrates the alarming repercussions of that purpose. Most of this little-read book is filled with chapters such as "Of Solitude" or "Of Honesty in Promises."[20] Defoe writes in the preface, "here is the just and only good end of all parable or allegoric history brought to pass, viz., for moral and religious improvement" (xii). All Crusoe's anecdotes about spiritual improvement are conventional, until, as we have seen, his chapter "Of Religion." The distinctions he makes between "negative religion" and "true Christianity" highlight Crusoe's change from wanderer and self-serving profiteer to religious crusader. His religious identity at the end of both the *Serious Reflections* and the *Farther Adventures* overwhelms any of the "moderate" temperament he so admires in the Russian exile, that "true Christian" whom he met on his final journey "home" to England.

Religion has been a part of *Robinson Crusoe* and the *Farther Adventures* all along. As Defoe says in the preface to the *Farther Adventures*, "The just application of every incidence, the religious and useful inferences drawn from every part, are so many testimonies to the good design of making it public, and must legitimate all the part that may be called invention or parable in the story" (vii). Whether or not one reads Defoe's protestations as a cynical attempt to justify the adventures in the novels, as Gildon did, a pious reader will still look for "the religious and useful inferences" in both *Robinson Crusoe* and its sequel. Crusoe brought Christianity to Friday and his father, the pirates and their wives, and he found it himself during his years alone on the island. But what began as an intellectual and spiritual battle for "souls" in *Robinson Crusoe* and the *Farther Adventures* turns into a plan for an out-and-out war "against the kingdom of the devil" (*Serious Reflections,* 239). In the midst of the common pieties Crusoe repeats in the *Serious Reflections* comes a violent, narrowly defined Christianity that advocates killing and war "in behalf of the Christian worship" (239). Crusoe asserts that if "talk" and persuasion do not work, then force must be used. He advocates burning temples and pagodas—which he has already done—and "destroying" "priests and dedicated persons of every kind" (239). In an understatement, Crusoe says, "This is all the coercion I propose . . . yet I insist that we may by force . . . suppress paganism, and the worship of God's enemy the Devil" (239). By destroying idols, places of worship, and the pagan spiritual leaders, firm Christian leadership will carry the day against the "infidels." Christianity will be spread over the world, and Crusoe himself—who never felt at home in England—will finally feel at home in the world because all the world will be reconstructed in the terms of his own religious beliefs, just as his time alone reconstructed the island into his own "kingdom."

In the *Serious Reflections,* Defoe suggests that religion displaces all the masked emotions and desires that are implicit in Crusoe's character. "Profit" and property as they define personal psychological stability—in the terms that make Crusoe happy on the island—are an ideal that eludes him when he returns to England at the end of the first novel. When he is traveling the globe, both trying to get home and avoiding it, he is still searching for something. Religion displaces his own desires, whatever they may be. The displacement becomes clear in the final lines of the *Serious Reflection:*

> All I can add is, I doubt no such zeal for the Christian religion will be found in our days, or perhaps in any age of the world, till Heaven beats the drums itself, and the glorious legions from above come down on purpose to propagate the work, and to reduce the whole world to the obedience of King Jesus— a time which some tell us is not far off, but of which I heard nothing in all my travels and illuminations, no, not one word. (243)

This is an extraordinary passage. Crusoe is skeptical that "man" can do much good prior to the millennium, but he finds what amounts to an apocalyptic identity. Even though he doubts that anyone else will share his religious zeal, he still offers suggestions for converting the whole world to his Christian belief. In fact, Crusoe tries to "play God" by waging war on the heathens; he has become what Gildon—one of Defoe's harshest contemporary critics—accused Defoe of doing in *Robinson Crusoe.*[21]

Crusoe's quest for identity is resolved, finally, by his newfound zeal at the end of the *Farther Adventures.* The *Serious Reflections* is the logical conclusion for a trilogy that tries to stabilize a sense of self based on desire. Crusoe found peace of sorts on the island, but that was an ideal. The island enabled him to construct a homosocial world in which profit and property were static. As homo economicus he could not go anywhere because profit itself depends on the exchange of capital. He found some stability in his relationship with Friday—a perhaps transgressive homoerotic relationship—but that stability ended when Friday was killed. Further efforts at profit were undercut by his misidentification as a pirate. The movement toward religious faith in both *Robinson Crusoe* and the *Farther Adventures* is a logical progression because assertions of faith, of giving oneself over to God's purposes rather than one's own questioning or quest, becomes a narrative, as well as a means of ensuring closure for that narrative. Religion for Crusoe is, as Brown writes in arguing for "a way out of history," a way for him "to enter that state of Being which was the goal of his Becoming": to find an identity for himself in a world from which he is always alienated.[22]

All three Crusoe novels suggest that the only way to transcend sexual and economic desire—to break away from *any* transgressive position that questions normative heterocentric identity—is through an unshaking belief in God and "true Christianity." Crusoe—after all his wandering—finds a kind of peace in his old age when he believes that the millennium approaches. Writing his *Reflections*—and granting that his persona is a character—gives him the discursive means to assert an identity not dependent on profit or middle-class domesticity. Profit—the accumulation of property—as a means to justify Christian belief is transformed into a belief in the apocalypse. Ironically, Gildon was right to be "horribly shocked" by *Robinson Crusoe* (Gildon, 25). Crusoe found "happiness" on the island: profit and domesticity, resulted from "conquering" and transforming the island into an ideal state. Unfortunately, Crusoe is unable to "conquer" the world. In the *Serious Reflections*, his belief transfers his resistant passion for travel and dissatisfaction with middle-class domesticity into a system that allows Crusoe to "play God" and impose his "true Christianity" on the rest of the world. Sexuality and economy drop out of Crusoe's life, but religious passion—an obsession with Christianizing the world—replaces those needs.

Notes

NOTES TO THE INTRODUCTION

1. Captain Charles Johnson [Daniel Defoe?], *A General History of the Robberies and Murders of the Most Notorious Pyrates* (London, 1724, 1728), 1:99–100. Cited parenthetically in the text by volume; the second edition (also 1724) of volume 1 is noted where it is used.

2. B. R. Burg looks at pirate sexuality in *Sodomy and the Pirate Tradition* (New York: New York University Press, 1982); Marcus Redicker and Robert C. Ritchie look at the economic and political effects of early-eighteenth-century piracy in, respectively, *Between the Devil and the Deep Blue Sea* (Cambridge: Cambridge University Press, 1987) and *Captain Kidd and the War against the Pirates* (Cambridge: Harvard University Press, 1987). All cited parenthetically in the text.

3. Indeed, this paucity of evidence undermines Burg's popular but historically flawed *Sodomy and the Pirate Tradition*.

4. John J. Richetti, *Defoe's Narratives* (Oxford: Clarendon, 1975), 65; Joel H. Baer, " 'The Complicated Plot of Piracy': Aspects of English Criminal Law and the Image of the Pirate in Defoe," *Eighteenth Century Culture* 14 (Madison: University of Wisconsin Press, 1985), 3–16. First published in *Eighteenth Century Life*, 23, no.1 (winter 1982): 17.

5. Jonathan Goldberg, *Sodometries: Renaissance Texts, Modern Sensibilities* (Stanford: Stanford University Press, 1992). Cited parenthetically in the text.

6. Robert E. Lee, *Blackbeard the Pirate: A Reappraisal of His Life and Times* (Winston-Salem, NC: John F. Blair, 1974), 24.

7. Robert C. Ritchie, "Samuel Burgess, Pirate," in *New Approaches to the History of Colonial and Revolutionary New York,* ed. Conrad Wright and William Pencok (Charlottesville: University of Virginia Press, 1988), 115.

8. This introduction is the logical place to bring up the question of authorship and Defoe. Since John Robert Moore published *Defoe in the Pillory* in 1939, *A General History of the . . . Pyrates* has been attributed to Defoe, usually without any questions. Indeed, when Manuel Schonhorn published his edition of the *General History* in 1972, Defoe was given credit for the book on the title page. And so it stood until 1988, when P. N. Furbank and W. R. Owens published *The Canonisation of Daniel Defoe* and devoted a chapter to the question of whether Defoe wrote the

General History. While they do not completely demolish Moore's attribution of the *General History* to Defoe, they have very serious doubts that Defoe in fact wrote the book. Indeed, Marcus Rediker, among the foremost maritime historians, doubts very much that Defoe wrote the *General History.* All this doubt and conjecture presupposes a kind of authorship that twentieth-century critics grant writers. As Paula Backscheider points out, Defoe had a very different idea of the author's role. In *Daniel Defoe: His Life* (Baltimore: Johns Hopkins University Press, 1989), Backscheider writes that Defoe devised a "method of publication . . . during the time of his greatest productivity in the reign of Anne. He had divided the work and begun to use both of his sons" (371). Despite the division of labor devised by Defoe, he still had control of his product. Moreover, the idea of the author was, as Backscheider implies, different in the early eighteenth century. As Furbank and Owens demonstrate, since few of Defoe's writing came out under his own name, many attributions made to Defoe rest on shaky evidence or shoddy scholarship. See Furbank and Owen, *The Canonisation of Daniel Defoe;* and idem, *Defoe De-Attributions* (London: Hambledon Press, 1994). We do not know who Johnson was, nor do we know anything about the circumstances of the writing of the *General History.*

9. Robert Louis Stevenson, *Treasure Island* (London: Cassell and Company, 1883).

NOTES TO CHAPTER I

1. *Unparallel'd Cruelty; or The Tryal of Capt. Jeane of Bristol* (London, 1726), 24. Cited parenthetically in the text.

2. Indeed, Captain Jeane had "punish'd several with a more than ordinary Severity; and particularly, that he once cut a Piece of Flesh out of the Inside of a Boy's Thumb, making an Orifice as low as the Bone, and two Inches round, which he fill'd up with Salt, to torture him for some very small Offence he was chargeable with."

3. Pierre Clastres, *Society against the State*, trans. Robert Hurley in collaboration with Abe Stein (Oxford: Basil Blackwell, 1977), 159.

4. William Funnel, *A Voyage round the World Containing an Account of Captain Dampier's Expedition into the South-Seas in the Ship St George, in the Years 1703 and 1704* (London, 1707).

5. *Weekly-Journal,* 9 July 1720.

6. Woodes Rogers, *A Cruising Voyage round the World* (London, 1712). Cited parenthetically in the text.

7. See Pat Rogers, *Defoe: The Critical Heritage* (London: Routledge, 1972); Manuel Schonhorn, *Defoe's Politics: Parliament, Power, Kingship, and* Robinson Crusoe (Cambridge: Cambridge University Press, 1991); J. Paul Hunter, *The Reluctant Pilgrim: Defoe's Emblematic Method and Quest for Form in* Robinson Crusoe (Baltimore: Johns Hopkins University Press, 1966), among others.

8. George Shelvocke, *A Voyage round the World by the Way of the Great South Sea. . . . By. Capt. George Shelvocke, Commander of the Speedwell, Recovery, &c. in this Expedition* (London, 1726). Cited parenthetically in the text.

9. John Dean, *A True and Genuine Narrative of the Whole Affair Relating to the Ship Sussex, as Sent to the Directors of the Honourable East India Company* (London, 1740), 12. Also see *An Authentick Relation of the Many Hardships and Sufferings of a Dutch Sailor, Who Was Put on Shore on the Uninhabited Isle of Ascension, by Order of the Commadore of a Squadron of Dutch Ships* (London, 1728). In this pamphlet, the narrator is forced by circumstance, as he says, "to make water in my scoop and drink it, thinking it was better than Salt Water" (24). Cited parenthetically in the text.

10. Edward Barlow, *Barlow's Journal of His Life at Sea in King's Ships, East and West Indiamen and Other Merchantmen from 1659 to 1703*, transcribed by Basil Lubbock (London: Hurst and Blackett, 1934). Cited parenthetically in the text.

11. N. A. M. Rodger, *The Wooden World* (London: Fontana Press, 1986), 126–27.

12. Page 134 of Kidd's trial transcript.

13. See Rogers, *A Cruising Voyage round the World*, esp. 121–31; and Edward Cooke, *A Voyage to the South Sea, and round the World* (London, 1712), 36–37. Several books and articles were written about Selkirk, including Isaac James, *Providence Displayed: or, The Remarkable Adventures of Alexander Selkirk, of Largo, in Scotland* (Bristol: 1800); and the anonymous *Crusoniana; or Truth versus Fiction, Elucidated in a History of the Islands of Juan Fernandez* (Manchester, 1843); *The Gentlemen's Magazine*, March 1788, 206–8.

14. See, for example, Rogers, *A Cruising Voyage round the World*, 14, 34, 39, 234–36.

15. William Betagh, *A Voyage round the World. Being an Account of a Remarkable Enterprize, Begun in the Year 1719, Chiefly to Cruise on the Spaniards in the Great South Ocean* (London, 1728), 2. Cited parenthetically in the text.

16. R. W., *The Sailors Advocate* (London, 1728), 4.

17. *Plunder and Bribery Further Discover'd, in a Memorial Humbly Offer'd to the British Parliament* (London, 1712), 44.

18. Rodger, *The Wooden World*, 164.

19. *The Sailors Advocate*, 34–35.

20. *The Sailor's Advocate II* (London, 1728), 22, 23.

21. *Observator* 3, no. 5 (3 February 1705).

22. Barlow also has things to say about the press later in his career. *Barlow's Journal*, 405–6.

23. *Weekly-Journal*, 16 February 1717, 57.

24. *Barbarian Cruelty; or, An Accurate and Impartial Narrative of the Unparallel'd Sufferings and Almost Incredible Hardships of the British Captives* (London, 1751), 32.

25. *Domestick Intelligence: or News Both from City and Country Impartially Related*, 14 February 1681.

26. Rodger, *The Wooden World*, 126.

27. [Daniel Defoe], *An Account of the Conduct and Proceedings of the Late John Gow Alias Smith* (London, 1725), 52–53.

NOTES TO CHAPTER 2

1. An article in the *Observator* reverses Johnson's logic: "But you must not believe these Privateers are Mann'd all with Sailors, they carry but one half or one third Sailors, and the rest are Landmen, who, in two or three years time, become Sailors; and thus the Privateers are made a Nursery for the Navy, which seldom or never wants Men." *Observator* 3, no. 52 (16 September 1704).

2. J. Cowley, *The Sailor's Companion, and Merchantman's Convoy* (Dublin, 1741), 24.

3. William Hacke, *A Collection of Original Voyages by Capt. William Hacke* (London, 1699), 6–7.

4. I do not mean to suggest that buccaneers *only* went after Spanish ships. However, the buccaneers were best known for their attacks on the Spaniards, thus they could be heroicized and tacitly approved by non-Spanish governments.

5. Charles Leslie, *A New History of Jamaica, from the Earliest Accounts, to the Taking of Porto Bello by Vice-Admiral Vernon* (London, 1740), 100.

6. Janice E. Thompson, *Mercenaries, Pirates, and Sovereigns: State-Building and Extraterritorial Violence in Early Modern Europe* (Princeton: Princeton University Press, 1994), esp. chap. 1. Every European country had its privateers. Indeed, the United States was among the last of the Western nations to outlaw privateering (in the middle of the nineteenth century).

7. From *The Collected Essays of Christopher Hill*, vol. 3, *People and Ideas in Seventeenth-Century England* (Amherst: University of Massachusetts Press, 1986), 161–87. Cited parenthetically in the text.

8. Hill assumes that Defoe wrote the *General History*. See also Johnson, "Of Captain Misson," in *General History*, 2:1–48.

9. Philip Gosse attempts (without success) a complete bibliography of the many editions of the *General History*. He writes in the preface, "In the following pages an attempt has been made to describe and fully collate the various editions and reprints that have appeared during the last two hundred years of the two works attributed to Captain Charles Johnson" (ix).

Defoe was not given attribution "until 1932, when Professor John Robert Moore recognized Defoe's hand, [and it] was made clear that Captain Johnson was but another mask of the indefatigable Daniel Defoe." Manuel Schonhorn, introduction to *A General History of the Pyrates* (Columbia: University of South Carolina Press, 1972), xxiii. See Philip Gosse, *A Bibliography of the Works of Capt. Charles Johnson* (London: Dulau and Company, 1927).

10. Exquemelin's volume was remarkably popular in seventeenth-century Europe.

First printed in Holland in 1677, it has a complicated publishing history. It was translated into Spanish in 1681, and then translated from Spanish into English, and first published in London in 1684. There were at least four London printings in that year, the first of which so outraged the rehabilitated former buccaneer Sir Henry Morgan that he sued the publisher for libel. In order to settle Morgan's lawsuit, the publisher added a preface to the subsequent printing that both defended the book's recounting of the Morgan story and interpolated high praise for Morgan's bravery. John Exquemelin, *Bucaniers of America: Or, A True Account of the Most Remarkable Assaults Committed of Late Years upon the Coasts of the West-Indies* (London, 1684). Cited parenthetically in the text.

11. Ritchie, *Captain Kidd and the War against the Pirates*, 22–23; Frank Sherry, *Raiders and Rebels* (New York: Hearst Marine Books, 1986), 61–62. Also note that the pirates of the Caribbean differed from the buccaneers. Some buccaneers became pirates, and posed enormous threats to northern European colonies in the Caribbean and up and down the eastern seaboard of the North American colonies. For lively descriptions, see Shelvocke, *A Voyage round the World,* esp. 12, 13, 15, 34, 36, 117, 120, 126–27.

12. Clinton V. Black, *Pirates of the West Indies* (Cambridge: Cambridge University Press, 1989), 10.

13. In the section on the sacking of Puerto Bello, for example, the English translation reads:

> But Captain *Morgan* was fully deceived in his judgment of this designe. For the Governour, who acted like a brave and courageous Souldier, refused not, in performance of his duty, to use his utmost endeavours to destroy whoever came near the Walls. The Religious Men and Women ceased not to cry unto him and beg of him by all the Saints of Heaven, he would deliver the Castle, and hereby spare both his and their own lives. But nothing could prevail with the obstinancy and fierceness that had possessed the Governour's mind. Thus many of the Religious men and Nuns were killed before they could fix the ladders. (1:96–97)

On the other hand, the Spanish version—*Piratas de la america* (Colonia Agrippina, 1681)—goes like this:

> Morgan engaged in this design; in the meantime the governor refused diligently to allow anyone near the wall, making himself a brave soldier. The religious people cried, and pleaded by all the saints of the heavens to give up the castle, in order to save themselves, and the poor nuns' lives; nothing could help them, by the obstinance of the said governor. Finally, with the loss of many religious men and nuns . . . the pirates entered, in many numbers, with great force. (My translation)

What is interesting to me is the way the Spanish governor is foregrounded in the English version and the nuns and monks are played down, whereas in the Spanish version, the nuns and monks are foregrounded while the governor—"brave and courageous" in the English version—is simply "obstinate" in the Spanish text. This seems to suggest that bravery will out, but Catholicism is always bad.

14. From the preface of an edition of *Bucaniers of America* abridged from the 4th ed. (London, 1684).

15. Exquemelin, *Bucaniers of America*, 2d ed. (London, 1684), preface.

16. Up to a point. By the 1660s and 1670s, policies were changing, and the interests of the English did not lie in being at constant war in the West Indies with the Spanish. Hence Morgan's rehabilitation. See, for example, Jenifer Marx, *Pirates and Privateeres of the Caribbean* (Malabar, FL: Krieger, 1992), 131–33.

17. Unsigned review from the *New York Herald*, 18 March 1915.

18. Editions of *Bucaniers of America* were printed every twenty years or so through the end of the eighteenth century. Editions came out less frequently during the nineteenth century, and in the twentieth century Exquemelin's name was forgotten, except by fans of the buccaneers. The latest edition is a facsimile from a small press. Interestingly, though there are fewer "official" editions of the *General History*, there are many books that plagiarize Johnson without credit. The *General History* may itself be as forgotten as Exquemelin's book, but the exploits and characters about whom Johnson writes are still in the public imagination.

19. Ritchie, *Captain Kidd and the War against the Pirates*, 1–27; Sherry, *Raiders and Rebels*, 22–51.

20. The political situation's effect on maritime employment can be noted in the general proclamations of James II, William and Mary, Anne, and George I. The proclamations include calls for impressment by the government, and demands for "able-bodied" seamen to present themselves are constant. See, for example, proclamations of 27 February 1689, 29 April 1689, 15 January 1690, 10 February 1691, 5 July 1690, 20 November 1690, many more through 1 February 1702, in British Library 21.h.3.

21. Rediker, *Between the Devil and the Deep Blue Sea*, 207–9, 212–15; *The Sailors Advocate*, 23.

22. I am discussing "privateers" only as I see the meaning shifting after the Restoration, with the establishment of the Whig and Tory political parties and the consolidation of the power of the East India Company. This is because piracy itself, as we think of it, represents the years 1695–1724, and this was also the great age of the "privateer" as described by Dampier, Shelvocke, Phelps, Cooke, and other famous privateer/authors.

23. Sometimes the government actively encouraged privateering. See, for example, William R., "Their Majesties Declaration for Encouragement of Officers, Seamen and Mariners, Employed in the Present Service" (London, 1689). Additionally, countries recognized each others' rights to plunder during times of war.

24. Cooke, *A Voyage to the South Sea*, A8r. See too Shelvocke and his "gentleman

adventurers" in *A Voyage round the World*, xxi–xxviii; or Bartholomew Sharpe, *The Voyages and Adventures of Capt. Barth. Sharp and Others* (London, 1684), 3; among others.

25. Sharpe, *Voyages and Adventures*, 8; Shelvocke, *A Voyage round the World*, 4, 10, 11, 12.

26. *A Full Account of the Actions of the Late Famous Pyrate, Capt. Kidd* (Dublin, 1701), 38.

27. Much of this discussion is based on the trial records and pamphlets published on Kidd, for example, *A Full Account of the Actions of the Late Famous Pyrate, Capt. Kidd*; Paul Lorrain, *The Ordinary of Newgate His Account of the Behaviour, Confessions of Captain William Kidd* (London, 1701); as well as Ritchie, *Captain Kidd and the War against the Pirates*, esp. 27–55; Dunbar Maury Hinrichs, *The Fateful Voyage of Captain Kidd* (New York: Bookman Associates, 1955); and *A Fair and True Discovery of the Robberies, Pyracies, and Other Notorious Actions, of That Famous English Pyrate, Capt. James Kelly* (London, 1700).

28. Kidd's letter of marque showed up two hundred years later in the London Public Record Office, where it still is. Ritchie, *Captain Kidd and the War against the Pirates*, 208. Kidd's letter of marque can be found at the PRO: HCA 1/15.108.

29. Captain Misson, in volume 2 of the *General History*, is a notable exception. He was the second son of a French aristocrat. Of course, Misson never existed either, being the product of Captain Johnson's imagination.

30. *The Whole Tryal, Examination and Condemnation of All the Pyrates, That Was Try'd and Condemn'd by the High Court of Admiralty* (London, 1725).

31. John Wilmot, *The Poems of John Wilmot Earl of Rochester*, ed. Keith Walker (Oxford: Basil Blackwell, 1984), 99.

32. Michel Serres, *Hermes: Literature, Science, Philosophy*, trans. Josué V. Harari and David F. Bell (Baltimore: John Hopkins University Press, 1982), esp. 65–82.

33. Greimas's square was introduced to me through Susan Green's essay "Semiotic Modalities of the Female Body in Aphra Behn's *The Dutch Lover*," in *Rereading Aphra Behn: History, Theory, and Criticism*, ed. Heidi Hutner (Charlottesville: University Press of Virginia, 1993), 121–47. See also N. Katherine Hayles, "Constrained Constructivism: Locating Inquiry in the Theater of Representation," *New Orleans Review* 18, no. 1 (spring 1991): 76–85. Ronald Schleifer, *A. J. Greimas and the Nature of Meaning: Linguistics, Semiotics, and Discourse Theory* (Lincoln: University of Nebraska Press, 1987), 25–33, has a useful explanation of the square.

NOTES TO CHAPTER 3

1. David Cordingly, *Under the Black Flag* (New York: Random House, 1996) is the only exception, and a fascinating book.

2. From an unpublished paper, which Professor Manuel Schonhorn was kind enough to allow me to read.

3. Redicker, *Between the Devil and the Deep Blue Sea*; Ritchie, *Captain Kidd and the War against the Pirates*; Baer, " 'The Complicated Plot of Piracy' "; idem, " 'Captain John Avery' and the Anatomy of a Mutiny," *Eighteenth Century Life*, February 1994. The three books about "female pirates" are Margaret S. Creighton and Lisa Norling, eds., *Iron Men, Wooden Women: Gender and Seafaring in the Atlantic World, 1700–1920* (Baltimore: Johns Hopkins University Press, 1996); Ulrike Klausmann, Marion Meinzerin, and Gabriel Kuhn, *Women Pirates and the Politics of the Jolly Roger*, trans. Tyler Austin and Nicholas Levis (Montreal: Black Rose Books, 1997); Jo Stanley, ed., *Bold in Her Breeches: Women Pirates across the Ages* (London: Pandora, 1995).

4. Hacke, *A Collection of Original Voyages*, 5.

5. There are hundreds of references for trials in the five decades after the Restoration in the British Library catalog, and the Huntington Library catalog, my two major sources for literary artifacts in this book. These trials range from short descriptions to detailed transcriptions that go on for several dozen pages. The majority of the piracy trials tend to be fairly detailed. The trials for sodomy, on the other hand, are far fewer in number, and tend to be descriptions of the proceedings against the accused sodomites.

6. See Lincoln Faller, *Crime and Defoe* (Cambridge: Cambridge University Press, 1993), 6, for a good discussion of the dying confessions of the criminals.

7. Also see the trial records listed in the bibliography; the *General History* lists trials in the biographies of the pirates, particularly the trials of Roberts and Bonnet in volume 1. Ritchie details the trial of the French crew (although some were English) entitled *The Proceedings of the Court of Admiralty, by a Special Commission, Being the Tryals of All the French Pirates at the Old-Baily* (London, 1700). As Ritchie points out, this is a very important trial because of the large number of pirates who were hanged on those days. See London PRO HCA l/15.18.

8. Ritchie, *Captain Kidd and the War against the Pirates*, 145–59; also see Thompson, *Mercenaries, Pirates, and Sovereigns*, 51.

9. For example, the notorious publisher Edmund Curll republished Castlehaven's trial as *The Case of Sodomy, in the Tryall of Mervin Lord Audley, Earl of Castlehaven, for Committing a Rape. And Sodomy with Two of His Servants, viz. (Laurence Fitz Patrick and Thomas Broadway) Who Was Try'd and Condemn'd by His Peers on the 25th of April, and Beheaded on Tower-Hill, May 14th, 1631* (London, 1708).

10. *The New Newgate Calendar; or, Malefactor's Bloody Register* (London, 1795).

11. See the files on Kidd's trial, particularly PRO HCA 1/15.3, 7, 13.

12. A few among several examples contemporary to Kidd's trial: *A Full Account of the Actions of the Late Famous Pyrate, Capt. Kidd*; Paul Lorrain, *The Ordinary of Newgate His Account of the Behaviour, Confessions of Captain William Kidd, and Other Pirates, That Were Executed at the Execution-Dock in Wapping, on Friday, May 23. 1701* (London, 1701); *A True Account of the Behaviour, Confession and Last Dying Speeches, of Captain William Kidd* (London, 1701).

13. This is based on my readings of not only pirate trials, but other popular trials that were published in pamphlet form between 1680 and 1720.

14. Cited parenthetically in the text.

15. See, for example, *The Tryals of Joseph Dawson* (London, 1696); *The Tryals of Major Stede Bonnet* (London, 1719); T. B. Howell, *A Complete Collection of State Trials* (London, 1812); and Captain Kidd's trial, which we have looked at.

16. From *The Arraignment, Tryal, and Condemnation, of Capt. John Quelch* (London, 1705), 5.

17. See Thompson, *Mercenaries, Pirates, and Sovereigns*, 46.

18. Daniel Defoe, *The Farther Adventures of Robinson Crusoe* (1720; New York: Jenson Society, 1905), 248. References to this text cited parenthetically.

19. See, among other trials, *Select Trials for Murder, Robbery, Burglary, Rapes, Sodomy, Coining, Forgery, Pyracy, and Other Offences and Misdemeanours . . . from the Year 1720* (London, 1764); *The Tryal and Conviction of Several Reputed Sodomites* (London, 1707); *A Full and True Account of the Discovery and Apprehending a Notorious Gang of Sodomites* (London, 1709).

20. *An Account of the Proceedings against Capt. Edward Rigby* (London, 1698). Cited parenthetically in the text.

21. *The Tryal and Conviction of Several Reputed Sodomites* (London, 1707).

22. *Select Trials for Murder, Robbery, Burglary, Rapes, Sodomy, Coining, Forgery, Pyracy, and Other Offences and Misdemeanours* (London, 1764).

23. Confessions of the condemned pirates were popular. Faller details the confessions in *Crime and Defoe* (6). Kidd's confession was so popular that at least two versions were published at his death.

24. Lennard Davis, *Factual Fictions* (New York: Columbia University Press, 1983), 126–27; Faller, *Crime and Defoe*, 6.

25. Lorrain, *The Ordinary of Newgate*.

26. *A True Account of the Behaviour, Confession and Last Dying Speeches, of Captain William Kidd*.

27. See particularly Foucault, *Discipline and Punish: The Birth of the Prison*, trans. Alan Sheridan (New York: Pantheon, 1977).

28. V. H. Bonner, *Pirate Laureate: The Life and Legends of Captain Kidd* (New Brunswick: Rutgers University Press, 1947). This book is a worthwhile attempt to find the "truth" of Kidd's story. Also see Hinrichs, *The Fateful Voyage of Captain Kidd*.

29. In addition to the ballads, which probably were written around the year of Kidd's execution (1701), there are pamphlets such as *Dialogue between the Ghost of Captain Kidd and the Napper in the Strand* (London, 1702); two different versions of his last words, the trial records, as I have noted, and John Corso, *The Case of John Corso, a Genoese Merchant* (London, 1701). In this interesting pamphlet, Corso attempts to get reparations for his losses from Kidd's piracy, even though Kidd has been hanged.

30. From *Capt. Kidd, a Noted Pirate, Who Was Hanged at Execution Dock, in England* (Boston: L. Deming, 1840). See Bonner, *Pirate Laureate: The Life and Legends of Captain Kidd* for a history of the Kidd ballads. The version quoted is only one of many versions, some of which have as many as thirty-five verses.

31. For example, in *The Tryals of Joseph Dawson*, Bab's Key is talked about as an important pirate hangout. Further, in proclamations that offered general pardons to the pirates, Kidd and Avery were the two exceptions. See PRO HCA 1/13.36.

32. [Charles Elms], *The Pirates Own Book, or Authentic Narratives of the Lives, Exploits, and Executions of the Most Celebrated Sea Robbers* (Portland: Francis Blake, 1855). Cited parenthetically in the text.

33. Frank R. Stockton, *Buccaneers and Pirates of Our Coasts* (New York: Macmillan, 1898). Cited parenthetically in the text.

34. *A Full Account of the Actions of the Late Famous Pyrate Capt. Kidd*, 38.

NOTES TO CHAPTER 4

1. See, for example, *The Life and Adventures of Capt. John Avery; the Famous English Pirate, (Rais'd from a Cabbin Boy, to a King) Now in Possession of Madagascar* (1709?), intr. Joel Baer (Los Angeles: William Andrews Clark Memorial Library, 1980), cited parenthetically in the text; and *The Famous Adventures of Captain John Avery of Plymouth: A Notorious Pirate* (Falkirk, 1809). I am indebted to Professor Baer's introduction for much of the factual information in this chapter.

2. See, for example, Johnson, 1:25–40; Dawson's "trial"; Charles Johnson's play *The Successful Pyrate* (London, 1714). For a full account of the legend, see Baer's recent essay on Avery, " 'Captain John Avery' and the Anatomy of a Mutiny."

3. [Daniel Defoe?], *The King of Pirates* (London, 1720), iii. Cited parenthetically in the text.

4. See Joel Baer, introduction to *The Life and Adventures of Capt. John Avery*, iii. Baer also points out that when the privateer Woodes Rogers published his travelogue, he "exploded" the myth of a pirate commonwealth, describing the poverty of the men still on Madagascar. Baer also argues that the myth of a strong pirate colony was so entrenched that "even the usually skeptical were eager to believe" in a fortified commonwealth.

5. *A Review of the State of the British Nation*, vol. 4 (facsimile, New York: AMS Press, 1965), 428.

6. See Baer, introduction to *The Life and Adventures of Capt. John Avery*; and Furbank and Owens, *The Canonisation of Daniel Defoe*, 106–7.

7. From Hans Turley, "Taming the Scourge of the Main: Charles Johnson's *The Successful Pyrate* and the Transgressive Hero" (presented at South Central Society for Eighteenth-Century Studies conference, Houston, February 1994).

8. See, for example, *The Tryals of Joseph Dawson*, and Johnson, 1:25–42.

9. See Defoe, *Atlas Maritimus* (London, 1728), 233–34.

10. See Johnson, *The Successful Pyrate* for the most extravagant version of this tale. In *Captain Singleton*, Singleton and Avery meet and discuss how to turn Madagascar into an outpost for the pirates. See also Baer, " 'Captain John Avery' and the Anatomy of a Mutiny."

11. Many books about Madagascar appeared in the early eighteenth century. Most of the privateers mentioned Madagascar, and many pamphlets decry the piracy in the area.

12. See *The Tryals of Joseph Dawson;* in addition to Baer, " 'Captain John Avery' and the Anatomy of a Mutiny."

13. For example, Johnson, *The Successful Pyrate; The Famous Adventures of Captain John Avery*, 12; see also later histories of pirates, such as Philip Gosse, *The Pirates' Who's Who* (London: Dulau and Company, 1924), 40–44; idem, *The History of Piracy* (1932; New York: Burt Franklin, 1968), 178–79.

14. See *The Famous Adventures of Captain John Avery*, 23; Gosse, *Pirates' Who's Who*, 43; Baer, " 'Captain John Avery' and the Anatomy of Mutiny."

NOTES TO CHAPTER 5

1. Gosse, *Pirates' Who's Who,* 7.

2. See Richetti, *Defoe's Narratives*, 64–65, 69–70, 76; see also idem, *Popular Fiction before Richardson* (Oxford: Clarendon, 1969). Faller in *Crime and Defoe* discusses piracy but only as it is another form of "crime," without noting the differences between criminals on land and maritime pirates that I discuss in chapter 1 (89–117, 192). Maximillian Novak discusses "Of Captain Misson" in his introduction to the Augustan Society reprint (Los Angeles: William Andrews Clark Memorial Library, 1961), i–v; he also discusses piracy briefly in *Realism, Myth, and History in Defoe's Fiction* (Lincoln: University of Nebraska Press, 1983), 13, 32, 33, 37, 73, 126, 159. See also Paula Backscheider, *Daniel Defoe: Ambition and Innovation* (Lexington: University Press of Kentucky, 1986), 159, 174. No one else makes a distinction between piracy and crime in general.

3. In 1724 two editions as well as another printing of each of these editions appeared. The second edition had substantial revisions. The third edition, which simply reprinted the second, came out in 1725, and a fourth was published in 1726. The *General History* was translated and published in Holland and Germany in 1725. Gosse's *Bibliography* details the book's printing history, but it is by no means complete. The second volume, which Gosse dates at 1726, is now dated at 1728, according to the British Library. See Gosse, *A Bibliography of the Works of Capt. Charles Johnson.*

4. For a good overview of the paucity of pirate historicity, see Larry Schweikart and B. R. Burg, "Stand By to Repel Historians: Modern Scholarship and Caribbean Pirates, 1650–1725," *Historian* 46, no. 2 (1984): 219–34. My own research has shown

that almost all popular histories from the latter years of the eighteenth century through the twentieth century are based on the *General History*, usually without attribution. Some works, such as Elms's *Pirates Own Book*, are plagiarized directly from it. Others, such as C. Whitehead, *Lives and Exploits of English Highwaymen, Pirates, and Robbers; Drawn from the Most Authentic Sources,* are "Revised and Continued to the Present Time" (London: Henry G. Bohn, 1842). See also *The Lives and Daring Deeds of the Most Celebrated Pirates and Buccaneers, of All Countries* (Philadelphia: Geo. G. Evans, [1860?]); Stockton, *Buccaneers and Pirates of Our Coasts; The Voyages and Adventures of Edward Teach* (Newcastle, 1800); and *The Famous Adventures of Captain John Avery,* among many others.

5. Besides the references to the *General History* in monographs and articles on Defoe already mentioned, I can find no other references from the past fifteen years to that work in literary studies.

6. This is not to say that critics ignore "history" and its relationship to fiction. Watt, McKeon, Davis, Armstrong, Ballaster, Faller, and most successfully Hunter all acknowledge the influence of late-seventeenth- and early-eighteenth-century "histories" on the "rise" or "origins" of the novel. Besides the problems inherent in the novel's "rise," or "origins," which I'll look at in more depth in the chapters on *Captain Singleton* and *Robinson Crusoe*, the history of the pirate has not been given its due as one of the literary tropes that help to define the novel. Further, the pirates in the *General History* have been taken at face value for many years. Gosse, for example, writes in the preface to his *Pirates' Who's Who*, "I believe that every man, or woman too . . . mentioned in this volume actually existed" (7). Ros Ballaster, *Seductive Forms: Women's Amatory Fiction from 1684 to 1740* (Oxford: Clarendon, 1992); Nancy Armstrong, *Desire and Domestic Fiction* (Oxford: Oxford University Press, 1987); Lennard J. Davis, *Factual Fictions*; Faller, *Crime and Defoe*; J. Paul Hunter, *Before Novels: The Cultural Contexts of Eighteenth-Century English Fiction* (New York: Norton, 1990); Michael McKeon, *The Origins of the English Novel* (Baltimore: Johns Hopkins University Press, 1987); Ian Watt, *The Rise of the Novel* (Berkeley: University of California Press, 1957).

7. A few examples out of many include *Blackbeard: A Page from the Colonial History of Philadelphia* (New York: Harper and Brothers, 1835); *The Sailor Boy* (New Haven, 1829); Henry Gringo, *Captain Brand, or the "Centipede"* (New York: Harper, 1864); *The Demon Ship* (Albany, 1831); *The Cabin Boy's Story* (New York, 1854). One of the few studies of early maritime fiction is Harold Francis Watson, *The Sailor in English Fiction and Drama: 1550–1800* (New York: Columbia University Press, 1931).

8. For example, Hunter traces the relevance of travel literature and didacticism for *Robinson Crusoe* (*The Reluctant Pilgrim*, 15–18, 35–46). In *Crime and Defoe*, Faller analyzes crime pamphlets to demonstrate their significance to Defoe's crime fiction (1–32). Richetti concentrates on the historiography of a few novels "to watch the narratives at their various tasks" to go beyond "static meaning" (*Defoe's Narratives*, 8). More recently, Sandra Sherman examines the theme of credit and how it "be-

comes a site for enacting the limits of discursive integrity" in *Finance and Fictionality in the Early Eighteenth Century: Accounting for Defoe* (Cambridge: Cambridge University Press, 1996), 13.

9. Foucault is, of course, the first source, for a new understanding of sexuality in *The History of Sexuality*, vol. 1, *An Introduction*, trans. Robert Hurley (New York: Random House, 1978), esp. 5–6, 114, 120–27. See also Armstrong, *Desire and Domestic Fiction*, which discusses the domestic novel, esp. 59–95; and Ballaster, *Seductive Forms*, which interrogates the novels of Behn, Manley, and Haywood, esp. 152–95.

10. See, for example, David F. Greenberg, *The Construction of Homosexuality* (Chicago: University of Chicago Press, 1988); G. S. Rousseau, "The Pursuit of Homosexuality in the Eighteenth Century: 'Utterly Confused Category' and/or Rich Repository?" in *'Tis Nature's Fault*, ed. Robert Purks Maccubin (Cambridge: Cambridge University Press, 1985); Kent Gerard and Gert Hekma, eds., *The Pursuit of Sodomy: Male Homosexuality in Renaissance and Enlightenment Europe* (New York: Harrington Park Press, 1989); Eve Kosofsky Sedgwick, *The Epistemology of the Closet* (Berkeley: University of California Press, 1990); Claude Summers, ed., *Homosexuality in Renaissance and Enlightenment England: Literary Representations in Historical Context* (New York: Harrington Park Press, 1992), among many others.

11. *Plain Reasons for the Growth of Sodomy in England: To Which Is Added, the Petit Maitre, an Odd Sort of Unpoetical Poem in the Trolly-Lolly Stile* (London, 1720). Cited parenthetically in the text.

12. See, for example, *The Tryal and Conviction of Several Reputed Sodomites; Account of the Proceedings against Capt. Edward Rigby; A Full and True Account of the Discovery and Apprehending a Notorious Gang of Sodomites.*

13. The *OED* defines "inhuman" as "not having the qualities proper or natural to a human being; esp. destitute of natural kindness or pity, brutal, unfeeling, cruel." "Unhuman," although defined as "inhuman," is also defined as "not pertaining to mankind." The sense I get from *Plain Reasons* is the latter.

14. Baer, " 'The Complicated Plot of Piracy,' " 7. Cited parenthetically in the text.

15. For more on the history of Madagascar, See F. D. Arnold-Forster, *The Madagascar Pirates* (New York: Lothrop, Lee and Shepard, 1957); Defoe, *Atlas Maritimus*, esp. 233–34; *Reasons for Reducing the Pyrates at Madagascar* (London, [1706 ?]); Ritchie, *Captain Kidd and the War against the Pirates*, esp. 82–84, 112–13, 120, 162, 216; Johnson, *General History*, vol. 1, esp. 25–42; Defoe, *The King of Pirates*, 28–64.

16. See Hill, "Radical Pirates?" 161–87. Although Rediker—with Baer, Cordingly, and Ritchie—is by far the most sophisticated of pirate historians, his is an overdetermined argument that, first, seamen are among the earliest proletariat; and second, their labor class values demarcate their reasons for turning pirate. The problem is that Rediker is so determined to prove his point, he is unwilling to discuss the way pirates become represented both as bloodthirsty fiends and how their

own cultural mores in addition to the economic value they place on their lives can be heroicized. See *Between the Devil and the Deep Blue Sea*, 254–87.

17. Christopher Hill, *The Century of Revolution* (1961; New York: Norton, 1982), 257.

18. Bonnet was tried in Charleston, South Carolina, in 1718. See *The Tryals of Major Stede Bonnet*.

19. *Plain Reasons for the Growth of Sodomy*, as we have seen, trivializes the sodomite. See also the "Trials" referred to earlier, as well as most famously, Tobias Smollett, *The Adventures of Roderick Random* (Oxford: Oxford University Press, 1979), and his description of Captain Whiffle, which manages to merge both sodomites and sailors in one of the funniest—if horribly homophobic—scenes in mid-eighteenth-century literature.

20. Gosse, *Pirates' Who's Who*, 52.

21. Marx, *Pirates and Privateers of the Caribbean*, 244. Cited parenthetically in the text. Black, *Pirates of the West Indies*, 90.

22. See Armstrong, *Desire and Domestic Fiction*, esp. 3–27.

23. For example, on 12 April 1718, the *Weekly-Journal* writes, "The Pirate Bonnet of 36 Guns and 300 Men is still a cruizing" (415). A pirate ship with thirty-six guns and three hundred men could be a terrifying sight to a trading schooner.

24. See Armstrong, *Desire and Domestic Fiction*, 59–95; Ballaster, *Seductive Forms*, esp. 100–113, 136–58.

25. Norman O. Brown, *Life against Death* (Middletown, CT: Wesleyan University Press, 1959), 69. Cited parenthetically in the text.

26. See proclamations at British Library: BL 21.h.3. Also King William gave a proclamation "For Preventing and Punishing Immorality and Prophaness" (A1r) in February 1697 in [Daniel Defoe], *An Account of the Societies for Reformation of Manners, in London and Westminster, and Other Parts of the Kingdom. With a Persuasive to Persons of All Ranks, to Be Zealous and Diligent in Promoting the Execution of the Laws against Prophaneness and Debauchery, for the Effecting a National Reformation. Published with the Approbation of a Considerable Number of the Lords Spiritual and Temporal* (London, 1699).

27. See Edward Ward, *The Wooden World Dissected*, 3d ed. (London, 1744), 41; in addition, see Rediker, *Between the Devil and the Deep Blue Sea*, 162.

28. Edward Ward, *The London-Spy Compleat*, 4th ed. (London, 1719), 41–42.

29. *The History of the Pirates Containing the Lives of These Noted Pirates* (Haverhill, MA, 1825), 133.

30. *The Lives and Daring Deeds of the Most Celebrated Pirates and Buccaneers.*

31. At the end of volume 2 of the *General History*, several of the pirates in the appendix are represented by "correspondents," writers who supposedly had firsthand experience with the pirates, and whom Johnson reproduces verbatim in the chapters. Schonhorn chooses to combine chapters from both volumes of the *General History* in order to give the appearance of chronology.

32. *Love Letters between a Certain Late Nobleman and the Famous Mr. Wilson* (1723), ed. Michael S. Kimmel (New York: Harrington Park Press, 1990).

33. See Gosse, *Pirates' Who's Who*, for example, 252–54.

NOTES TO CHAPTER 6

1. In the first edition of the *General History*, Roberts's story runs from page 161 through page 260. The biographies of other pirates are no more than half that length.

2. For other works that allude to pirate and privateer articles, see Shelvocke, *A Voyage round the World*, 34–36; Philip Ashton, *Ashton's Memorial* (London, 1726), 11–22; *An Account of the Conduct and Proceedings of the Late John Gow Alias Smith*, 53; "Articles of Agreement, Made This 10th Day of October in the Year of Our Lord 1695" (London, 1700).

3. See Randolph Trumbach, "Sodomitical Assaults, Gender Role, and Sexual Development in Eighteenth-Century London," in *The Pursuit of Sodomy*, ed. Gerard and Hekma, 407–32; and idem, "Sodomitical Subcultures, Sodomitical Roles, and the Gender Revolution of the Eighteenth Century: The Recent Historiography," in *'Tis Nature's Fault*, ed. Maccubin, 109–21.

4. See, among other sources, *Plain Reasons for the Growth of Sodomy*; Britannicus [Thomas Gordon], *The Conspirators; or, The Case of Catiline* (London, 1721); and *Love Letters between a Certain Late Nobleman and the Famous Mr. Wilson*.

5. "Brittanicus," *The Conspirators*, 24–25.

6. Marx, *Pirates and Privateers of the Caribbean*, 254; Sherry, *Raiders and Rebels*, 135.

7. Marx, *Pirates and Privateers of the Caribbean*, 251.

8. Trial transcript quoted in Stanley, ed. *Bold in Her Breeches*, 179. See PRO CO 137/14/XC18757.

9. Notable exceptions are Julie Wheelwright, in *Bold in Her Breeches*, ed. Stanley, 176–201, and several essays in Creighton and Norling, eds., *Iron Men, Wooden Women*.

10. See, for example, Watt, *The Rise of the Novel*, 241; Ballaster, *Seductive Forms*, 34–35, 164–65; and McKeon, *Origins of the English Novel*, 100.

11. Novak, introduction to the Augustan Society reprint of *Captain Misson*. Cited parenthetically in the text.

12. "Of Captain Misson" opens volume 2 of the *General History*. Misson's career is interrupted by the lives of Captain Bowen and Captain Kidd before it is picked up again in "Of Captain Tew, and His Crew."

13. Hill has made the most significant gestures toward rereading "Of Captain Misson" in his essay "Radical Pirates?". Novak edited the Augustan Reprint Society's facsimile of one half of Misson's story. Unfortunately, he does not include the second half—called "Of Captain Tew" in volume 2 of the *General History*—in

either his discussion in the introduction or the facsimile itself. "Of Captain Misson" has been overlooked by Richetti, Hunter, and Backscheider.

14. Hill, "Radical Pirates?"; and Rediker, *Between the Devil and the Deep Blue Sea.*

NOTES TO CHAPTER 7

1. Most notably Watt, *The Rise of the Novel,* 60–93; McKeon, too, ends his *Origins of the English Novel* with Defoe, Fielding, and Richardson. See also Pat Rogers, ed., *Defoe: The Critical Heritage* (London: Routledge, 1972) for an overview of Defoe criticism.

2. See critics such as Armstrong, *Desire and Domestic Fiction,* 16, 19, 106; McKeon, *Origins of the English Novel,* 315–37; Watt, *The Rise of the Novel,* 63–72, 76–83, 85–89. Davis, *Factual Fictions,* 161–75, makes compelling arguments based on an understanding of Foucault; Hunter, *The Reluctant Pilgrim,* 90–110, makes coherent, logical arguments about puritanism's effect on Defoe's writing.

3. Other works with pirate characters, settings, or descriptions by or attributed to Defoe include Charles Johnson [Daniel Defoe?], *A General History of the . . . Pyrates,* and *Atlas Maritimus, The King of Pirates, Robinson Crusoe* (London, 1719), *The Farther Adventures of Robinson Crusoe* (London, 1720), *The History and Remarkable Life of the Truly Honourable Col. Jacque Commonly Call'd Jack* (London, 1722), and *A New Voyage round the World* (London, 1724).

4. Goldberg, *Sodometries,* 20.

5. I base this on the status of *Singleton* in Defoe monographs by authors such as Faller, Novak, Backscheider, and Richetti. Faller, for example, in his book *Crime and Defoe,* is unable to do much with *Captain Singleton* because piracy and felony are different kinds of crime. Richetti in *Defoe's Narratives* and *Popular Fiction* does discuss piracy, but he does not define piracy as specifically as I do, and his discussion of *Captain Singleton* does not go as far as he could take it. In the few articles published on *Captain Singleton,* Singleton's journey across Africa is the most compelling aspect of the book. See, for example, Michael Seidel, "Defoe in Conrad's Africa," *Conradiana* 17, no. 2 (1985): 145–46; Pat Rogers, "Speaking within Compass: The Ground Covered in Two Works by Defoe," *Studies in the Literary Imagination* 15, no. 2 (fall 1982): 103–13.

6. These observations have been pointed out by Hunter, *The Reluctant Pilgrim,* ix–x; and by Nancy Armstrong and Leonard Tennenhouse, *The Imaginary Puritan: Literature, Intellectual Labor, and the Origins of Personal Life* (Berkeley: University of California Press, 1992), 189–91.

7. For more on these points, see Watt, *The Rise of the Novel,* 70–91; McKeon, *Origins of the English Novel,* 315–37; Armstrong and Tennenhouse, *The Imaginary Puritan,* 184–95; Rogers, *Defoe: The Critical Heritage,* 52–53 166–68.

8. Even Lincoln Faller, in his otherwise important corrective to the critical

misunderstanding of Defoe's other crimes novels (*Colonel Jack, Moll Flanders,* and *Roxana*), does not know quite what to do with *Captain Singleton*. Faller, *Crime and Defoe,* xii.

9. In addition to the works cited in note 3, only a few other articles focus on *Captain Singleton*: Timothy C. Blackburn, "The Coherence of Defoe's *Captain Singleton*," *Huntington Library Quarterly* 41 (1978) is the most notable of the essays, along with Manuel Schonhorn's article. Blackburn, who discusses Defoe's use of Locke's ideas, argues for the "coherence" of the book as a whole. However, he does not really suggest what "home" means to Singleton, and further, is puzzled, as are many of these writers, by the seemingly "strange" compact between Singleton and William at the end of the novel (119–36). Other works that focus on *Captain Singleton* include Laura Brown, *Ends of Empire: Women and Identity in Early Eighteenth-Century Literature* (Ithaca: Cornell University Press, 1993); Jonathan E. Hill, "Defoe's Singleton," *Papers of the Bibliographical Society of America* 84, no. 3 (September 1990): 286–96; Virgil Nemoianu, "Picaresque Retreat: From Xenophon's *Anabasis* to Defoe's *Singleton*," *Comparative Literature Studies* 23, no. 2 (summer 1986): 91–102; Manuel Schonhorn, "Defoe's *Captain Singleton*: A Reassessment with Observations," *Papers on Language and Literature* 7 (1971): 38–51; Gary J. Scrimgeour, "The Problem of Realism in Defoe's *Captain Singleton*," *Huntington Library Quarterly* 27 (1963): 21–37.

10. *The History and Remarkable Life of the Truly Honourable Col. Jacque Commonly Call'd Jack* (1722), ed. Samuel Holt Monk (Oxford: Oxford University Press, 1989), 308–9; *The Fortunes and Misfortunes of the Famous Moll Flanders* (1722), ed. Juliet Mitchell (London: Penguin English Library, 1978), 315.

11. Richetti, *Defoe's Narratives,* 88.

12. Rediker, *Between the Devil and the Deep Blue Sea,* 264–66, analyzes how the share system for pirates differs from that of ordinary seamen or privateers on more legitimate ships.

13. Faller makes distinctions between the "morally serious" criminal tract and the "frivolous" crime novels in *Turned to Account: The Forms and Functions of Criminal Biography in Late Seventeenth- and Early Eighteenth-Century England* (Cambridge: Cambridge University Press, 1987), 4–31. Both tracts and novels serve a function to dissuade citizens from criminal behavior. The only pirate books from the early eighteenth century that I have found are "morally serious." Even balladry serves a moral purpose, as Joel H. Baer argues in "Bold Captain Avery in the Privy Council: Early Variants of a Broadside Ballad from the Pepys Collection," *Folk Music Journal* 7, no. 1 (1995): 4–26.

14. In addition to their appearances as advertisements in early newspapers, proclamations can be found in the British Library (21.h.3) and in the London Public Record Office (HCA 1/15.11, 24, 25, 36).

15. [Daniel Defoe?], *A True Account of the Design, and Advantages of the South-Sea Trade* (London 1705), 20. Furbank and Owens neither attribute nor de-attribute

this pamphlet to Defoe. They point out that the arguments put forward here are similar to arguments made by Defoe in his *Review*. See *The Canonisation of Daniel Defoe*, 108. However, in *Defoe De-Attributions*, Furbank and Owens consider that an attribution to Defoe is "in a certain amount of doubt" (49).

16. *A Review of the State of the British Nation*, vol. 4, 428.

17. Watt, *The Rise of the Novel*, 74–92; Hunter, *The Reluctant Pilgrim*, particularly the introduction.

18. In a well-known passage at the end of *Robinson Crusoe* when Crusoe returns to England, he tells the reader,

> first of all I marry'd, and that not either to my disadvantage or dissatisfaction, and had three children, two sons and one daughter: but my wife dying, and my nephew coming home with good success from a voyage to Spain, my inclination to go abroad, and his importunity, prevailed and engaged me to go in his ship, as a private trader to the East Indies.

Robinson Crusoe, ed. Angus Ross (London: Penguin Books, 1965), 298.

19. Richetti, *Defoe's Narratives*, 93.

NOTES TO CHAPTER 8

1. Hunter, *The Reluctant Pilgrim*, x; Watt, *The Rise of the Novel*, 60–92. Backscheider, Novak, and Richetti, among others, all tend to focus on the island, just as Singleton's journey across Africa becomes the focus of that novel for most criticism.

2. Richetti, *Defoe's Narratives*, 21.

3. From Karl Marx, "Towards a Critique of Hegel's Philosophy of Right," in *Karl Marx: Selected Writings*, ed. David McLellan (Oxford: Oxford University Press, 1977), 64.

4. For a discussion of Defoe's pen-for-hire reputation, see Backscheider, *Daniel Defoe: His Life*, 139–94. Gildon satirizes Defoe's reputation as a pen-for-hire.

5. See Henry Clinton Hutchins, Robinson Crusoe *and Its Printing* (New York: Columbia University Press, 1925), 52–128. The popularity of the *Farther Adventures* has been seriously underestimated over the years; critical evaluation has not taken into account the number of editions that were published throughout the eighteenth century.

6. For a good discussion of Defoe's prefaces, see Faller, *Crime and Defoe*, 76–109.

7. See Armstrong and Tennenhouse, *The Imaginary Puritan*, 185–90.

8. Charles Gildon, *The Life and Surprizing Adventure of Mr. D----- De F--* (London, 1719), 25. Cited parenthetically in the text.

9. Armstrong, in *Desire and Domestic Fiction*, notes that the Edgeworths "began to endorse the reading of fiction that made social conformity seem necessary, if not

entirely desirable." She goes on to point out that *Robinson Crusoe* was used to teach young *girls* the need to stay at home, and in fact, learn to be "domestic" through the "female" character of Crusoe (16). Note, too, it is *Robinson Crusoe* that Armstrong talks about, not the *Farther Adventures* or the *Serious Reflections*.

10. Hunter argues that "objectivity of tone and style characterizes the tradition as a whole. An important aspect of this objectivity is the absence of any informing idea or theme: chronology, replaced by topicality when the narrative is interrupted to describe a particular place, is the only organizing force in the books, thematic considerations being inappropriate to the 'pose' or conventions of the form." *The Reluctant Pilgrim*, 16.

11. Privateers and sailors feared falling into Spanish hands more than being marooned or being captured by Indians. Spaniards are often portrayed as an example of how *not* to treat indigenous people, not only by Defoe in *Robinson Crusoe*, but in almost all English travel literature of the period. Dryden is a notable exception to this portrayal of the Spaniards in his tragedies *The Indian Queen* (1663) and *The Indian Emperour, or, The Conquest of Mexico by the Spanish, Being the Sequel of the Indian Queen* (1665).

12. "Liberty of Conscience" was an important political concept both at the turn of the eighteenth century and again around 1715. In addition to *The Shortest-Way with the Dissenters* (London, 1702), which resulted in a stay in the stocks, see the dialogue between Defoe and opponents to the dissenters from 1713 to 1715 and Backscheider, *Daniel Defoe: His Life*, esp. 87, 94, 100, 103, 130, 133–34.

13. See Crusoe's list of inhabitants, *Farther Adventures*, 94.

14. See Christopher Flint, "Orphaning the Family," *English Literary History* 55, no. 2 (summer 1988): 381–419; Timothy Blackburn, "Friday's Religion," *Eighteenth Century Studies* 18, no. 3 (spring 1985): 360–82; Richard Braverman, "Crusoe's Legacy," *Studies in the Novel* 18, no. 1 (spring 1986): 1–28 for recent work on the relationship between Friday and Crusoe.

15. Humphrey Richardson, *The Secret Life of Robinson Crusoe* (Covina, CA: Collectors Publications, 1967), 9. I thank Professor Alexander Pettit for alerting me to this reference.

16. Richardson, *Secret Life*, 176. By the end of the novel, the two are rescued and return to England. The first thing they do is "make contact with two ladies out of London who were waiting on the quay" for the ship to come in. However, "the two men proved so awkward, so uncouth, so demanding that the women were obliged to summon the police . . . . When the police arrived, manacled the two rascals, and led them off to jail. A new life was beginning for them" (188).

17. J. M. Coetzee, *Foe* (New York: Penguin, 1986); Maurice Tournier, *Friday*, trans. Norman Denny (Baltimore: Johns Hopkins University Press, 1967), 166.

18. Georges Bataille, *Eroticism: Death and Sensuality*, trans. Mary Dalwood (1962; San Francisco: City Light Books, 1986), 23, 35.

19. Crusoe's opinion of the Great Wall of China is particularly choice:

I say, I stood still an hour to look at [the Great Wall] on every side, near and far off; I mean, that was within my view; and the guide of our caravan, who had been extolling it for the wonder of the world, was mighty eager to hear my opinion of it. I told him it was a most excellent thing to keep off the Tartars, which he happened not to understand as I meant it, and so took it for a compliment. (*Farther Adventures*, 270–71)

20. Isobel Grundy, in "Farther Adventures of Robinson Crusoe," *Scriblerian* 14, no. 2 (1982): 122–24, uses the title and references the *Serious Reflections* to discuss *China Moon* by Maxine Hong Kingston. Fakrul Alam, "Religious and Linguistic Colonialism in Defoe's Fiction," *North Dakota Quarterly* 55, no. 3 (1987), 116–23, discusses "religion" in the Crusoe novels, but without any of the historical context I am trying to provide. Otherwise, in books about Defoe such as Backscheider's, Novak's, or Hunter's, the *Serious Reflections* is noted as one of Defoe's works, but never commented on except as subordinate to *Robinson Crusoe*.

21. Davis notes this in *Factual Fictions*. For Davis, however, the point is Defoe's ability to construct a "reality" based on accretion of detail, thus creating a new kind of "novel" that imitates "reality" in ways that frighten Gildon (152–75). "Defoe's works seem still plainly to bear the marks," Davis argues, "of their intimate connection with the news/novels discourse" (155).

22. Brown, *Life against Death*, 19.

Bibliography

An Account of the Proceedings against Capt. Edward Rigby, at the Sessions of Gaol Delivery, Held at Justice-Hall in the Old Bailey, on Wednesday, the Seventh Day of December 1698. For Intending to Commit the Abominable Sin of Sodomy on the Body of One William Minton. London, 1698.

Adventures of Pirates and Sea-Rovers. New York: Harper and Brothers, 1908.

Alam, Fakrul. "Religious and Linguistic Colonialism in Defoe's Fiction." *North Dakota Quarterly* 55, no. 3 (1987): 116–23.

Armstrong, Nancy. *Desire and Domestic Fiction: A Political History of the Novel.* Oxford: Oxford University Press, 1987.

Armstrong, Nancy and Leonard Tennenhouse. "The American Origins of the English Novel." *American Literary History* 4, no. 3 (fall 1992): 386–410.

———. *The Imaginary Puritan: Literature, Intellectual Labor, and the Origins of Personal Life.* Berkeley: University of California Press, 1992.

Arnold-Forster, F. D. *The Madagascar Pirates.* New York: Lothrop, Lee and Shepard, 1957.

The Arraignment, Tryal, and Condemnation, of Capt. John Quelch, and Others of His Company &c. for Sundry Piracies, Robberies, and Murder, Committed upon the Subjects of the King of Portugal, Her Majesty's Allie, on the Coast of Brasil, &c. London, 1705.

"Articles of Agreement, Made This 10th Day of October in the Year of Our Lord 1695. Between the Right Honourable Richard Earl of Bellomont of the One Part, and Robert Livingston, Esq; and Capt. William Kid of the Other Part." London, 1700.

Ashton, Philip. *Ashton's Memorial: or, An Authentick Account of The Strange Adventures and Signal Deliverances of Mr. Philip Ashton; Who, after He Had Made His Escape from the Pirates, Liv'd Alone on a Desolate Island for about 16 Months, &c. With a Short Account of Mr. Nicholas Merritt, Who Was Taken at the Same Time. To Which Is Added, A Sermon on Dan. iii. 17 by John Barnard, V.D.M.* London, 1726.

Backscheider, Paula. *Daniel Defoe: Ambition and Innovation.* Lexington: University Press of Kentucky, 1986.

———. *Daniel Defoe: His Life.* Baltimore: Johns Hopkins University Press, 1989.

Baer, Joel H. "Bold Captain Avery in the Privy Council: Early Variants of a Broadside Ballad from the Pepys Collection." *Folk Music* 7 no. 1 (1995).

———. " 'Captain John Avery' and the Anatomy of a Mutiny." *Eighteenth Century Life*, February 1994.

———. " 'The Complicated Plot of Piracy': Aspects of English Criminal Law and the Image of the Pirate in Defoe." *Eighteenth Century Culture* 14. Madison: University of Wisconsin Press, 1985: 3–16. First published in *Eighteenth Century Culture* 23, no. 1 (winter 1982).

Ballaster, Ros. *Seductive Forms: Women's Amatory Fiction from 1684 to 1740.* Oxford: Clarendon, 1992.

Barbarian Cruelty; or, An Accurate and Impartial Narrative of the Unparallel'd Sufferings and Almost Incredible Hardships of the British Captives, Belonging to the Inspector Privateer, Capt. Richard Veale, Commander, during Their Slavery under the Arbitrary and Despotic Government of Muley Abdallah, Emperor of Fez and Morocco, from January 1745–46, to Their Happy Ransom and Deliverance from Their Painful Captivities, Compleated in December 1750, by the Bounty and Benevolence of His Present Majesty King George. London, 1751.

Barker, B[enjamin]. *Blackbeard; or, the Pirate of the Roanoke.* Boston, 1847.

Barlow, Edward. *Barlow's Journal of His Life at Sea in King's Ships, East and West Indiamen and Other Merchantmen from 1659 to 1703.* Transcribed by Basil Lubbock. London: Hurst and Blackett, 1934.

Bataille, Georges. *Eroticism: Death and Sensuality.* Trans. Mary Dalwood. San Francisco: City Light Books, 1986.

Betagh, William. *A Voyage round the World. Being an Account of a Remarkable Enterprize, Begun in the Year 1719, Chiefly to Cruise on the Spaniards in the Great South Ocean. Relating the True historical Facts of That Whole Affair: Testifyd by Many Imployd Therein; and Confirmed by Authorities from the Owners. By William Betagh, Captain of Marines in That Expedition.* London, 1728.

Black, Clinton V. *Pirates of the West Indies.* Cambridge: Cambridge University Press, 1989.

Black, Jeremy. *The English Press in the Eighteenth Century.* London: Croom Helm, 1987.

Blackbeard: A Page from the Colonial History of Philadelphia. New York: Harper and Brothers, 1835.

Blackburn, Timothy C. "The Coherence of Defoe's *Captain Singleton*." *Huntington Library Quarterly* 41 (1978).

———. "Friday's Religion: Its Nature and Importance in *Robinson Crusoe*." *Eighteenth Century Studies* 18, no. 3 (spring 1985): 360–82.

Blackburn, William. " 'Mirror in the Sea': *Treasure Island* and the Internalization of Juvenile Romance." *Children's Literature Quarterly* 8, no. 3 (fall 1983): 7–12.

Blackstone, William. *Commentaries on the Laws of England* (London: 1769). Intro. Thomas A. Green. Chicago: University of Chicago Press, 1979.

Blood, Thomas. *The Narrative of Col. Tho. Blood, Concerning the Design Reported to Be Lately Laid against the Life and Honour of His Grace George Duke of Buckingham Wherein Colonel Blood Is Charged to Have Conspired with Maurice Hickey, Philip de Mar, and Several Others, to Suborn the Testimony of Samuel Ryther and Philemon Coddan to Swear Buggery against the Said Duke. Together with a Copy of the Information Exhibited in the Crown-Office against the Said Colonel Blood, Hickely, Le Mar, and the Rest.* London, 1680.

Bonner, V. H. *Pirate Laureate: The Life and Legends of Captain Kidd.* New Brunswick: Rutgers University Press, 1947.

Bradley, Robert T. *The Lure of Peru.* London: Macmillan, 1989.

Braverman, Richard. "Crusoe's Legacy." *Studies in the Novel* 18, no. 1 (spring 1986): 1–28.

Britannicus [Thomas Gordon]. *The Conspirators; or, The Case of Catiline, As Collected from the Best Historians, Impartially Examin'd; with Respect to His Declared and Covert Abettors; and the Artifices Used to Skreen the Conspirators from Punishment.* London, 1721.

Brown, Laura. *Ends of Empire: Women and Identity in Early Eighteenth-Century Literature.* Ithaca: Cornell University Press, 1993.

Brown, Norman O. *Life against Death.* Middletown, CT: Wesleyan University Press, 1959.

Burg, B. R. *Sodomy and the Pirate Tradition.* New York: New York University Press, 1982.

The Cabin Boy's Story. New York, 1854.

Capt. Kidd, a Noted Pirate, Who Was Hanged at Execution Dock, in England. Boston: L. Deming, 1840.

The Case of Capt. Tho. Green, Commander of the Ship Worcester, and His Crew, Tried and Condemned for Pyracy and Murther, in the High Court Admiralty of Scotland. London, 1705.

The Case of Sodomy, in the Tryall of Mervin Lord Audley, Earl of Castlehaven, for Committing a Rape. And Sodomy with Two of His Servants, viz. (Laurence Fitz Patrick and Thomas Broadway) Who Was Try'd and Condemn'd by His Peers on the 25th of April, and Beheaded on Tower-Hill, May 14th, 1631. London, 1708.

Clastres, Pierre. *Archeology of Violence.* Trans. Jeanine Herman. New York: Semiotext(e), 1994.

———. *Society against the State.* Trans. Robert Hurley in collaboration with Abe Stein. Oxford: Basil Blackwell, 1977.

Coetzee, J. M. *Foe.* New York: Penguin, 1986.

Colman, Benjamin. *It is a Fearful Thing to Fall into the Hands of the Living God. A Sermon Preached to Some Miserable Pirates July 10, 1726. On the Lord's Day, before Their Execution. By Benjamin Colman, Pastor of a Church in Boston. To Which Is Added Some Account of Said Pirates.* Boston, 1726.

Cooke, Edward. *A Voyage to the South Sea, and round the World, Perform'd in the*

Years 1708, 1709, 1710, and 1711. Containing a Journal of All Memorable Transactions during the Said Voyage . . . by Capt. Edward Cooke. London, 1712.

Cordingly, David. *Under the Black Flag: Romance and Reality of Life among the Pirates.* New York: Random House, 1996.

Corso, John. *The Case of John Corso, a Genoese Merchant.* London, 1701.

Cowley, J. *The Sailor's Companion, and Merchantman's Convoy.* Dublin, 1741.

Creighton, Margaret S., and Lisa Norling, eds. *Iron Men, Wooden Women: Gender and Seafaring in the Atlantic World, 1700–1920.* Baltimore: Johns Hopkins University Press, 1996.

Crusoniana; or Truth versus Fiction, Elucidated in a History of the Islands of Juan Fernandez. Manchester, 1843.

Dampier, William. *A New Voyage round the World.* 2d ed. London, 1697.

Davis, Lennard J. *Factual Fictions: The Origins of the English Novel.* New York: Columbia University Press, 1983.

———. " 'Known Unknown' Locations: The Ideology of Novelistic Landscape in *Robinson Crusoe.*" *Sociocriticism* 4–5 (1986–87): 87–113.

Dean, John. *A True and Genuine Narrative of the Whole Affair Relating to the Ship Sussex, as Sent to the Directors of the Honourable East India Company.* London, 1728.

[Defoe, Daniel]. *An Account of the Conduct and Proceedings of the Late John Gow Alias Smith, Captain of the Late Pirates, Executed for Murther and Piracy Commited on Board the George Galley, Afterwards Call'd the Revenge; with a Relation of All the Horrid Murthers They Committed in Cold Blood: As Also of Their Being Taken at the Islands of Orkney, and Sent up Prisoners to London.* London, 1725.

[———]. *An Account of the Societies for Reformation of Manners, in London and Westminster, and Other Parts of the Kingdom. With a Persuasive to Persons of All Ranks, to Be Zealous and Diligent in Promoting the Execution of the Laws against Prophaneness and Debauchery, for the Effecting a National Reformation. Published with the Approbation of a Considerable Number of the Lords Spiritual and Temporal.* London, 1699.

[———]. *A Collection of Miscellany Letters, Selected out of Mist's Weekly Journal.* Vol. 4. London, 1727.

[———]. *The King of Pirates: Being an Account of the Famous Enterprises of Captain Avery, the Mock King of Madagascar, with His Rambles and Piracies; Wherein All the Sham Accounts Formerly Publish'd of Him, Are Detected.* London, 1720.

[———?]. *A True Account of the Design, and Advantages of the South-Sea Trade.* London, 1705.

[———]. *Unparallel'd Cruelty; or The Tryal of Capt. Jeane of Bristol.* London, 1726.

Defoe, Daniel. *Atlas Maritimus and Commercialis; or, A General View of the World, So Far as Relates to Trade and Navigation: Describing All the Coasts, Ports, Harbours, and Noted Rivers, according to the Latest Discoveries and Most Exact Observations.* London, 1728

————. *The Farther Adventures of Robinson Crusoe* (1719). New York: Jenson Society, 1905.

————. *The Fortunes and Misfortunes of the Famous Moll Flanders* (1722). Ed. Juliet Mitchell. London: Penguin English Library, 1978.

————. *The History and Remarkable Life of the Truly Honourable Col. Jacque Commonly Call'd Jack* (1722). Ed. Samuel Holt Monk. Oxford: Oxford University Press, 1989.

————. *The Life, Adventures, and Pyracies, of the Famous Captain Singleton* (1720). Ed. Shiv K. Kumar. Oxford: Oxford University Press, 1990.

————. *The Life and Strange Surprising Adventures of Robinson Crusoe, of York, Mariner* (1719). Ed. Angus Ross. London: Penguin Books, 1963.

————. *A New Voyage round the World* (1724). New York: Jenson Society, 1905.

————. *A Review of the State of the British Nation*. Vol. 4. Facsimile, New York: AMS Press, 1965.

————. *Roxana, the Fortunate Mistress* (1724). Ed. David Blewett. London: Penguin English Library, 1982.

————. *The Serious Reflections of Robinson Crusoe* (1720). New York: Jenson Society, 1905.

————. *The Shortest-Way with the Dissenters: Or Proposals for the Establishment of the Church*. London, 1702.

The Demon Ship, or The Pirate of the Mediterranean. Albany, 1831.

de Pointi, M. *Monsier de Pointi's Expedition to Cartagena: Being a Particular Relation, I. Of the Taking and Plundering of That City, by the French, in the Year 1697. II. Of Their Meeting with Admiral Nevil, in Their Return, and the Course They Steer'd to Get Clear of Him. III. Of Their Passing by Commodore Norris, at Newfoundland. IV. Of Their Encounter with Capt. Harlow, at Their Going into Brest. English'd from the Original Publish'd at Paris by Monsier de Pointis Himself. And Illustrated with a Large Draught of the City of Cartagena, Its Harbour and Forts.* London, 1699.

Dialogue between the Ghost of Captain Kidd and the Napper in the Strand. London, 1702.

A Discourse of the Laws Relating to Pirates and Piracies, and the Marine Affairs of Great Britain. London, 1726.

The Domestick Intelligence: Or News Both from City and Country Impartially Related. 14 February 1681.

Drury, Robert [Daniel Defoe?]. *Madagascar; or Robert Drury's Journal*. London, 1729.

Dryden, John. *The Indian Emperour* (1665). In *The Works of John Dryden*, vol. 9, ed. Edward Niles Hooker and H. T. Swedenberg, Jr. Berkeley: University of California Press, 1956.

————. *The Indian Queen* (1663). In *The Works of John Dryden*, vol. 8, ed. Edward

Niles Hooker and H. T. Swedenberg, Jr. Berkeley: University of California Press, 1956.

An Elegy on the Much Lamented Death of Captain Thomas Green; Who Was Executed with Others of His Crew, under the Pretence of Being a Piracy &c. in Scotland, April the 11th 1705. London, 1705.

[Elms, Charles]. *The Pirates Own Book, or Authentic Narratives of the Lives, Exploits, and Executions of the Most Celebrated Sea Robbers with Historical Sketches of the Joassamee, Spanish, Ladrone, West India, Malay, and Algerine Pirates.* Portland: Francis Blake, 1855.

Epstein, Julia, and Kristina Straub. "Introduction: The Guarded Body." In *Body Guards: The Cultural Politics of Gender Ambiguity*, ed. Julia Epstein and Kristina Straub. New York: Routledge, 1991.

Exquemelin, John. *Bucaniers of America: Or, A True Account of the Most Remarkable Assaults Committed of Late Years upon the Coasts of the West-Indies, by the Bucaniers of Jamaica and Tortuga, Both English and French. Wherein Are Contained Most Especially, the Unparallel'd Exploits of Sir Henry Morgan, Our English Jamaican Hero, Who Sack'd Puerto Velo, burnt Panama &c.* London, 1684.

———. *The Bucaniers of America.* 4th ed., abridged. London, 1684.

———. *The Buccaneers of America.* Ed. William Swan Stallybrass. Glorieta, NM: Rio Grande Press, 1992.

———. *Piratas de la america, y luz a la defensa de las costas de Indias Occidentales.* Colonia Agrippina, 1681.

A Fair and True Discovery of the Robberies, Pyracies, and Other Notorious Actions, of That Famous English Pyrate, Capt. James Kelly, Who Was Executed on Fryday the 13th of July 1700. With an Account of His Joyning with Capt. Kidd, and Other Remarkable Pyrates in Several Parts of the World: With All the Most Material Passages of His Life, to the Time of His Death. Written with His Own Hand, during his Confinement in Newgate; and Delivered to His Wife, the Day of His Execution: Published by Her Order and Desire. London, 1700.

Faller, Lincoln. *Crime and Defoe.* Cambridge: Cambridge University Press, 1993.

———. *Turned to Account: The Forms and Functions of Criminal Biography in Late Seventeenth- and Early Eighteenth-Century England.* Cambridge: Cambridge University Press, 1987.

The Famous Adventures of Captain John Avery of Plymouth: A Notorious Pirate. Falkirk, 1809.

Fea, Allan. *The Real Captain Cleveland.* London: Martin Secker, 1912.

Fenner, Phyllis R., ed. *Pirates, Pirates, Pirates: Stories of Cutlasses and Corsairs, Buried Treasures and Buccaneers, Ships and Swashbucklers.* New York: Franklin Watts, 1951.

Flint, Christopher. "Orphaning the Family: The Role of Kinship in *Robinson Crusoe*." *English Literary History* 55, no. 2 (summer 1988): 381–419.

Fortescue, F. *Robinson Crusoe; or, The Island of Juan Fernandez, an Operatic Drama, in Three Acts*. Boston, 1822.

Foucault, Michel. *Discipline and Punish: The Birth of the Prison*. Trans. Alan Sheridan. New York: Pantheon, 1977.

——. *The History of Sexuality*. Vol. 1, *An Introduction*. Trans. Robert Hurley. New York: Random House, 1978.

A Full Account of the Actions of the Late Famous Pyrate, Capt. Kidd. With the Proceedings against Him, and a Vindication of the Right Honourable Richard Earl of Bellomont . . . from the Unjust Reflections Cast upon Tehm [sic]. By a Person of Quality. Dublin, 1701.

A Full and True Account of the Discovery and Apprehending a Notorious Gang of Sodomites. London, 1709.

Funnell, William. *A Voyage round the World Containing an Account of Captain Dampier's Expedition into the South-Seas in the Ship St George, in the Years 1703 and 1704. With His Various Adventures, Engagements, &c. And a Particular and Exact Description of Several Islands in the Atlantick Ocean, the Brazilian Coast, the Passage round Cape Horn, and the Coasts of Chili, Peru, and Mexico. Together with the Author's Voyage from Amapalla on the West-Coast of Mexico, to East-India. His Passing by Three Unknown Islands, and thro' a New-discover'd Streight Near the Coast of New-Guinea; His Arrival at Amboyna: With a Large Description of That and Other Spice Islands; as Also of Batavia, the Cape of Good Hope, &c. By William Funnel, Mate to Captain Dampier*. London, 1707.

Furbank, P. N. and W. R. Owens. *The Canonisation of Daniel Defoe*. New Haven: Yale University Press, 1988.

——. *Defoe De-Attributions: A Critique of J. R. Moore's Checklist*. London: Hambledon Press, 1994.

Gerard, Kent, and Gert Hekma, eds. *The Pursuit of Sodomy: Male Homosexuality in Renaissance and Enlightenment Europe*. New York: Harrington Park Press, 1989.

Gildon, Charles. *The Life and Surprizing Adventure of Mr. D----- De F--, Who Has Liv'd above Fifty Years by Himself, in the Kingdoms of North and South Britain . . . with Remarks Serious and Comical upon the Life of Crusoe*. London, 1719.

Glisserman, Martin. "*Robinson Crusoe*: The Vicissitudes of Greed—Cannibalism and Capitalism." *American Imago* 47, nos. 3–4 (fall–winter 1990): 197–231.

Goldberg, Jonathan. *Sodometries: Renaissance Texts, Modern Sensibilities*. Stanford: Stanford University Press, 1992.

Gosse, Philip. *A Bibliography of the Works of Capt. Charles Johnson*. London: Dulau and Company, 1927.

——. *The History of Pirates*. 1932; New York: Burt Franklin, 1968.

——. *The Pirates' Who's Who*. London: Dulau and Company, 1924.

Green, Susan. "Semiotic Modalities of the Female Body in Aphra Behn's *The Dutch Lover*." In *Rereading Aphra Behn: History, Theory, and Criticism*, ed. Heidi Hutner. Charlottesville: University Press of Virginia, 1993.

Greenberg, David F. *The Construction of Homosexuality.* Chicago: University of Chicago Press, 1988.

Gringo, Henry [H. A. Wise, U.S.N.]. *Captain Brande, or The "Centipede."* New York: Harper, 1864.

Grundy, Isobel. "Farther Adventures of Robinson Crusoe." *Scriblerian and the KitCats* 14, no. 2 (1982): 122–24.

Hacke, William. *A Collection of Original Voyages by Capt. William Hacke.* London, 1699.

Harris, Michael. *London Newspapers in the Age of Walpole: A Study of the Origins of the Modern English Press.* Cranbury, NJ: Associated University Press, 1987.

Hayles, N. Katherine. "Constrained Constructivism: Locating Scientific Inquiry in the Theater of Representation." *New Orleans Review* 18, no. 1 (spring 1991): 76–85.

Hill, Christopher. *The Century of Revolution: 1603–1714.* 1961; New York: Norton, 1982.

———. "Radical Pirates?" In *The Collected Essays of Christopher Hill.* Vol. 3, *People and Ideas in Seventeenth-Century England.* Amherst: University of Massachusetts Press, 1986.

Hill, Jonathan E. "Defoe's Singleton." *Papers of the Bibliographical Society of America* 84, no. 3 (September 1990): 286–96.

Hinrichs, Dunbar Maury. *The Fateful Voyage of Captain Kidd.* New York: Bookman Associates, 1955.

The History of the Pirates Containing the Lives of These Noted Pirates . . . and the Expedition of Commander Porter. Haverhill, MA, 1825.

Howell, T. B. *A Complete Collection of State Trials and Proceedings for High Treason and Other Crimes and Misdemeanors from the Earliest Period to the Present Time, with Notes and other Illustrations Compiled by T. B. Howell.* London, 1812.

Hunter, J. Paul. *Before Novels: The Cultural Contexts of Eighteenth-Century English Fiction.* New York: Norton, 1990.

———. *The Reluctant Pilgrim: Defoe's Emblematic Method and Quest for Form in Robinson Crusoe.* Baltimore: Johns Hopkins University Press, 1966.

Hutchins, Henry Clinton. Robinson Crusoe *and its Printing, 1719–1731.* New York: Columbia University Press, 1925.

James, Isaac. *Providence Displayed: or, The Remarkable Adventures of Alexander Selkirk, of Largo, in Scotland; Who Lived Four Years and Four Months by Himself, on the Island of Juan Fernandez; from Whence He Returned with Capt. Woodes Rogers, of Bristol, and on Whose Adventures Was Founded the Celebrated Novel of Robinson Crusoe. With a Description of the Island, and an Account of Several Other Persons Left There, Particularly William, a Mosquito Indian, and Capt. Davis's Men: Including Brief Memoirs of the Famous Capt. Wm. Dampier. To Which Is Added a Supplement, Containing the History of Peter Serrano, Ephraim How, and Others, Left in Similar Situations.* Bristol, 1800.

Johnson, Charles [pseud.]. *Captain Misson.* Edited with an introduction by Maximillian Novak. Augustan Reprint Society, series no. 87. Los Angeles: William Andrews Clark Memorial Library, 1961.

———. *A General History of the Lives and Adventures of the Most Famous Highwaymen, Murderers, Street Robbers, &c. To Which Is Added, A Genuine Account of the Voyages and Plunders of the Most Notorious Pyrates.* London, 1734.

———. *A General History of the Pyrates.* 2d ed. London, 1724.

———. *A General History of the Pyrates.* Ed. Manuel Schonhorn. Columbia: University of South Carolina Press, 1972.

———. *A General History of the Robberies and Murders of the Most Notorious Pyrates.* London, 1724.

———. *Historie der engelsche zee-roovers.* Amsterdam, 1725.

———. *The History of the Pyrates.* Vol. 2. London, 1728.

———. *Lives and Exploits of English Highwaymen, Pirates, & Robbers; Drawn from the Most Authentic Sources.* Revised and Continued to the Present Time, by C. Whitehead, Esq. London: Henry G. Bohn, 1842.

Johnson, Charles. *The Successful Pyrate.* London: 1714.

Klausmann, Ulrike, Marion Meinzerin, and Gabriel Kuhn. *Women Pirates and the Politics of the Jolly Roger.* Trans. Tyler Austin and Nicholas Levis. Montreal: Black Rose Books, 1997.

The Last Speeches and Dying Words of Captain Thomas Green, Commander of the Ship Worcester, and of Capt. John Madder Chief Mate of the Said Ship, Who Were Executed near Leith, April 11th, 1705. London, [1705?].

Lee, Robert E. *Blackbeard the Pirate: A Reappraisal of His Life and Times.* Winston-Salem, NC: John F. Blair, 1974.

Leslie, Charles. *A New History of Jamaica, from the Earliest Accounts, to the Taking of Porto Bello by Vice-Admiral Vernon.* London, 1740.

A Letter from Scotland to a Friend in London: Containing a Particular Narrative of the Whole Proceedings against the Worcester and Her Crew, from Her First Arrival in Leith-Road, to the 20th of April 1705. In Which the Secret Intrigues, and Bloody Designs of the Prosecutors Are Detected and Expos'd. Also an Account of the Sudden Death of the Principal Evidence of the Day Sentence Was Past; the Prisoners Behaviour after Condemnation, and Their Manner of Execution; with Observations and Reflections upon the Whole. London, 1705.

The Life and Adventures of Capt. John Avery, the Famous English Pirate, (Rais'd from a Cabbin Boy, to a King) Now in Possession of Madagascar. [1709?]. Intr. Joel Baer. Los Angeles: William Andrews Clark Memorial Library, 1980.

The Lives and Daring Deeds of the Most Celebrated Pirates and Buccaneers, of All Countries. Philadelphia: Geo. G. Evans, [1860?].

Lorrain, Paul. *The Ordinary of Newgate His Account of the Behaviour, Confessions of Captain William Kidd, and Other Pirates, That Were Executed at the Execution-Dock in Wapping, on Friday, May 23. 1701.* London, 1701.

Love Letters between a Certain Late Nobleman and the Famous Mr. Wilson (1723). Ed. Michael S. Kimmel. New York: Harrington Park Press, 1990.

de Luffan, Raveneau. *A Journal of a Voyage Made into the South Sea, by the Buccaniers or Freebooters of America; from the Year 1684–1689. Written by the Sier Raveneau de Luffan to Which Is Added the Youage of the Sieur De Montauban, Captain of the Freebooters on the Coast of Guiney, in the Year 1695.* London, 1695.

Marx, Jenifer. *Pirates and Privateers of the Caribbean.* Malabar, FL: Krieger, 1992.

Marx, Karl. "Towards a Critique of Hegel's *Philosophy of Right.*" In *Karl Marx: Selected Writings.* Ed. David McLelllan. Oxford: Oxford University Press, 1977.

McKeon, Michael. *The Origins of the English Novel.* Baltimore: Johns Hopkins University Press, 1987.

Moore, John Robert. *Defoe in the Pillory and Other Studies.* Bloomington: Indiana University Press, 1939.

Nemoianu, Virgil. "Picaresque Retreat: From Xenophon's *Anabasis* to Defoe's *Singleton.*" *Comparative Literature Studies* 23, no. 2 (summer 1986): 91–102.

The New Newgate Calendar; or, Malefactor's Bloody Register. London, 1795.

Norris, Gerald. *West Country Pirates and Buccaneers.* Dorset: Dovecote Press, 1990.

Novak, Maximillian E. *Realism, Myth, and History in Defoe's Fiction.* Lincoln: University of Nebraska Press, 1983.

———. "The Unmentionable and the Ineffable in Defoe's Fiction." *Studies in the Literary Imagination* 15, no. 2 (1992): 85–102.

Parker, Lucretia. *Piratical Barbarity, or The Female Captive. Comprising the Particulars of the Capture of the English Sloop Eliza-Ann, on Her Passage from St. Johns to Antigua, and the Horrid Massacre of the Unfortunate Crew by the Pirates, March 12, 1825 and of the Unparalleled Sufferings of Miss Lucretia Parker, a Passenger on Board Said Sloop—Who after Being Retained a Prisoner Eleven Days by the Pirates, Was Miraculously Delivered from Their Cruel Hands.* New York, [1825?].

Paulson, William. *The Noise of Culture: Literary Texts in a World of Information.* Ithaca: Cornell University Press, 1988.

Pellham, Edward. *Gods Power and Providence: Shewed, in the Miraculous Preservation and Deliverance of Eight Englishmen. Faithfully Reported by Edward Pellham.* London, 1621.

Phelps, Thomas. *A True Account of the Captivity of Thomas Phelps at Machaness in Barbary and of His Strange Escape in Company of Edmund Baxter and Others, as Also of the Burning Two of the Greatest Pirate-Ships belonging to That Kingdom, in the River of Mamora; upon the Thirteenth day of June 1685.* London, 1685.

Plain Reasons for the Growth of Sodomy in England: To Which Is Added, the Petit Maitre, An Odd Sort of Unpoetical Poem in the Trolly-Lolly Stile. London, 1720.

Planche, J. R. *The Pirate: A Musical Drama in Three Acts.* Based on the novel by Walter Scott. London, 1816.

Plunder and Bribery Further Discover'd, in a Memorial Humbly Offer'd to the British Parliament. London, 1712.

Pocock, I. *Robinson Crusoe; or, The Bold Buccaniers: A Romantic Drama, in Two Acts by I. Pocock, Esq.* London, [1830?].

The Prime Minister and King. With Political Remarks, by way of Caution to All Crowned Heads and Evil Ministers. London, 1720.

The Proceedings of the Court of Admiralty, by a special Commission, Being the Tryals of All the French Pirates at the Old-Baily, on Monday, Tuesday, Thursday and Friday Being the 21st, 22d, 24th, 25th Days of October, 1700, and in the 12th Year of His Majesty's Reign. London, 1700.

Reasons for Reducing the Pyrates at Madagascar: And Proposals Humbly Offered to the Honourable House of Commons, for effecting the same. London, [1706?].

Redicker, Marcus. *Between the Devil and the Deep Blue Sea.* Cambridge: Cambridge University Press, 1987.

———. "Liberty beneath the Jolly Roger: The Lives of Anne Bonny and Mary Read, Pirates." In *Iron Men, Wooden Women,* ed. Margaret S. Creighton and Lisa Norling. Baltimore: Johns Hopkins University Press, 1996.

Richardson, Humphrey. *The Secret Life of Robinson Crusoe.* Covina, CA: Collectors Publications, 1967.

Richetti, John J. *Defoe's Narratives.* Oxford: Clarendon, 1975.

———. *Popular Fiction before Richardson.* Oxford: Clarendon, 1969.

Ritchie, Robert C. *Captain Kidd and the War against the Pirates.* Cambridge: Harvard University Press, 1987.

———. "Pirates and Buccaneers." In *The Age of William III and Mary II: Power, Politics, and Patronage, 1688–1702,* ed. Robert P. Maccubbin and Martha Hamilton-Phillips. Williamsburg: College of William and Mary, 1989.

———. "Samuel Burgess." In *New Approaches to the History of Colonial and Revolutionary New York,* ed. Conrad Wright and William Pencok. Charlottesville: University of Virginia Press, 1988.

Rodger, N. A. M. *The Wooden World.* London: Fontana Press, 1986.

Rogers, Pat, ed. *Defoe: The Critical Heritage.* London: Routledge, 1972.

———. "Speaking within Compass: The Ground Covered in Two Works by Defoe." *Studies in the Literary Imagination* 15, no. 2 (fall 1982): 103–13.

Rogers, Woodes. *A Cruising Voyage round the World: First to the South-Seas, Thence to the East-Indies, and Homewards by the Cape of Good Hope. Begun in 1708, and Finish'd in 1711. Containing a Journal of All the Remarkable Transactions; Particularly, of the Taking of Puna and Guiaquil, of the Acapulco Ship, and Other Prizes; an Account of Alexander Selkirk's Living Alone Four Years and Four Months in an Island; and a Brief Description of Several Countries in Our Course Noted for Trade, Especially in the South-Sea. By Captain Woodes Rogers, Commander in Chief on this Expedition, with the Ships Duke and Dutchess of Bristol.* London, 1712.

Rousseau, G. S. "The Pursuit of Homosexuality in the Eighteenth Century: 'Utterly Confused Category' and/or Rich Repository?" In *'Tis Nature's Fault,* ed. Robert Purks Maccubbin. Cambridge: Cambridge University Press, 1985.

R. W. *The Sailors Advocate Containing a Pamphlet, Printed in the Year 1707, Entitled, An Enquiry into the Causes of Our Naval Miscarriages.* London, 1728.

The Sailor Boy. New Haven, 1829.

The Sailor Boy's Songster. [184?].

Schleifer, Ronald. *A. J. Greimas and the Nature of Meaning: Linguistics, Semiotics, and Discourse Theory.* Lincoln: University of Nebraska Press, 1987.

Schonhorn, Manuel. "Defoe's *Captain Singleton*: A Reassessment with Observations." *Papers on Language and Literature* 7 (1971): 38–51.

———. *Defoe's Politics: Parliament, Power, Kingship, and* Robinson Crusoe. Cambridge: Cambridge University Press, 1991.

Schweikart, Larry, and B. R. Burg. "Stand By to Repel Historians: Modern Scholarship and Caribbean Pirates, 1650–1725." *Historian* 46, no. 2 (1984): 219–34.

Scrimgeour, Gary J. "The Problem of Realism in Defoe's *Captain Singleton.*" *Huntington Library Quarterly* 27 (1963): 21–37.

Secord, Arthur Wellesley. *Studies in the Narrative Method of Defoe.* Urbana: University of Illinois Press, 1924.

Sedgwick, Eve Kosofsky. *The Epistemology of the Closet.* Berkeley: University of California Press, 1990.

Segrais, M. *The Beautiful Pyrate; or The Constant Lovers in Five Novels Translated from the French of M. Segrais, Author of Zayde, and the Princess of Cleves.* London, 1725.

Seidel, Michael. "Defoe in Conrad's Africa." *Conradiana: A Journal of Joseph Conrad Studies* 17, no. 2 (1985): 145–46.

Select Trials for Murder, Robbery, Burglary, Rapes, Sodomy, Coining, Forgery, Pyracy, and Other Offences and Misdemeanours, at the Sessions House in the Old-Bailey, to Which Are Added Genuine Accounts of the Lives, Exploits, Behaviour, Confessions, and Dying-Speeches, of the Most Notorious Convicts, from the Year 1741 to the Present Year, 1764, Inclusive; Which Complete the Trials from the Year 1720. Vol. 1. London, 1764.

Serres, Michel. *Hermes: Literature, Science, Philosophy.* Ed. Josué V. Harari and David F. Bell. Baltimore: Johns Hopkins University Press, 1982.

Sharpe, Bartholomew. *The Voyages and Adventures of Capt. Barth. Sharp and Others in the South Sea: Being a Journal of the Same. Also Capt. Van Horn with His Buccanieres Surprizing of la Vera Cruz to Which Is Added the True Relation of Sir Henry Morgan His Expedition against the Spaniards in the West Indies, and His Taking Panama. Together with the President of Panama's Account of the Same Expedition: Translated out of Spanish. And Col Beston's Adjustment of the Peace between the Spaniards and English in the West Indies.* London, 1684.

Shelvocke, George. *A Voyage round the World by the Way of the Great South Sea. Perform'd in the Years 1719, 20, 21, 22, in the Speedwell of London, of 24 Guns and 100 Men, (under His Majesty's Commission to Cruize on the Spaniards in the Late War with the Spanish Crown) till She Was Cast Away on the Island of Juan*

Fernandes, in May 1720; and Afterwards Continu'd in the Recovery, the Jesus Maria and Sacra Familia, &c. By. Capt. George Shelvocke, Commander of the Speedwell, Recovery, &c. in This Expedition. London, 1726.

Sherman, Sandra. *Finance and Fictionality in the Early Eighteenth Century: Accounting for Defoe.* Cambridge: Cambridge University Press, 1996.

Sherry, Frank. *Raiders and Rebels.* New York: Hearst Marine Books, 1986.

A Short Account of the Situations and Incidents Exhibited in the Pantomime of Robinson Crusoe, at the Theatre Royal, Drury Lane, Taken from the Original Story. London, 1797.

Sill, Geoffrey M. *Defoe and the Idea of Fiction.* Newark: University of Delaware Press, 1983.

Smollett, Tobias. *The Adventures of Roderick Random.* Ed. Paul-Gabriel Bouce. Oxford: Oxford University Press, 1979.

Stanley, Jo, ed. *Bold in Her Breeches: Women Pirates across the Ages.* London: Pandora, 1995.

Stevenson, Robert Louis. *Treasure Island.* London: Cassell and Company, 1883.

Stockton, Frank R. *Buccaneers and Pirates of Our Coasts.* New York: Macmillan, 1898.

Summers, Claude, ed. *Homosexuality in Renaissance and Enlightenment England: Literary Representations in Historical Context.* New York: Harrington Park Press, 1992.

Thompson, Janice E. *Mercenaries, Pirates, and Sovereigns: State-Building and Extraterritorial Violence in Early Modern Europe.* Princeton: Princeton University Press, 1994.

Tournier, Maurice. *Friday.* Trans. Norman Denny. Baltimore: Johns Hopkins University Press, 1967.

Trial of Captain Thomas Vaughan for High Treason in the High Seas. London, 1696.

The True Account of the Behaviour and Confession of the Criminals, Condemned on Thursday the 15th. Day of April, 1686 . . . Executed at Tyburn, and the Other Five Repriev'd. London, 1686.

A True Account of the Behaviour, Confession and Last Dying Speeches, of Captain William Kidd, and the Rest of the Pirates, That Were Executed at Execution Dock in Wapping, on Friday the 23d of May. 1701. London, 1701.

A True Account of a Fight between Captain John Leech, Commander of the Ship Ann of London, of 14 Guns, and 19 Men, from Jamaica, and a French Privateer of 24 Guns, and Some Petteraroes: As It Came in a Letter to his Owners from Plymouth, Dated the Second of This Instant January, 1689. London, 1689–90.

The True Account of the Proceedings at the Tryal Held at the Marshalseas, on Friday, the 17th. of the Instant February, 1680, by Vertue of a Special Commission Granted by the King, out of the Admiralty, for Trying of Captain Crompton Guyther, and 7 of His Men, viz. William Coles, Joseph Bullivant, Joh. Baxter, Francis Wansell, Francis Martyn, John Gibson, and William Jones, for Piracy by Them Committed on a Ship Belonging to the Dutch, on the 3d. of December last, Who Were All Taken and Pinioned Together, and Brought before the King and Council, Who Committed Them to the Marshalseas. London, 1681.

A True Account of the Voyage of the Nottingham Galley. London, 1711.

A True Relation of a Most Horrid Conspiracy and Running Away with the Ship Adventure Having on Board Forty Thousand Pieces of Eight, and Other Goods to a Great Value. Together with the Cruel and Barbarous Leaving and Turning Ashore upon the Island Naias, in the East-Indies, the Captain, and Three Merchants Which Were Passengers, and Sixteen Honest and Able Seamen, Eight Whereof Miserably Perished by Hunger and Hardship, and But Four of the Remainder Yet Come to England. London, 1700.

Trumbach, Randolph. "Sodomitical Assaults, Gender Role, and Sexual Development in Eighteenth-Century London." In *The Pursuit of Sodomy: Male Homosexuality in Renaissance and Enlightenment Europe*, eds. Kent Gerard and Gert Hekma. New York: Harrington Park Press, 1989.

———. "Sodomitical Subcultures, Sodomitical Roles, and the Gender Revolution of the Eighteenth Century: The Recent Historiography." In *'Tis Nature's Fault*, ed. R. P. Maccubbin. Cambridge: Cambridge University Press, 1987.

The Tryal and Conviction of Several Reputed Sodomites, before the Right Honourable the Lord Mayor and Recorder of London. London, 1707.

The Tryal, Examination and Condemnation, of Captain Green of the Worcester, and his whole Ships Crew, for the Murther of Captain Dummond, and all his Scots Ships Crew, near Malabar; Before the high Court of Admiralty in Scotland on the 14th of March 1705. London, 1705.

The Tryal of Capt. Thomas Green and his Crew, Before the Judge of the High Court of Admiralty of Scotland; And the Assessors appointed by the Lords of Privy Council. At the Instance of Mr. Alexander Higgins Advocate, Procurator-Fiscal to the said Court, for Piracy, Robbery, and Murder. Edinburgh, 1705.

The Tryals of Joseph Dawson, Edward Forseith, William May, William Bishop, James Lewis, and John Sparkes for Several Piracies and Robberies by Them Committed, in the Company of Every the Grand Pirate, Near the Coasts of the East-Indies; and Several Other Places on the Seas. Giving an Account of Their Villainous Robberies and Barbarities. At the Admiralty Sessions, Begun at the Old-Baily on the 29th of October, 1696. and Ended on the 6th. of November. London, 1696.

The Tryals of Major Stede Bonnet, and Other Pirates . . . Who Were All Condemn'd for Piracy, as Also the Tryals of Thomas Nichols, Rowland Sharp, Jonathan Clarke, and Thomas Gerrat, for Piracy, Who Were Acquitted. London, 1719.

Turley, Hans. "Taming the Scourge of the Main: Charles Johnson's *The Successful Pyrate* and the Transgressive Hero." Paper presented at South Central Society for Eighteenth-Century Studies, Houston, February 1994.

United Kingdom. Public Record Office. High Court of the Admiralty (13/1; 15/1).

Unparallel'd Cruelty; or The Tryal of Capt. Jeane of Bristol. London, 1726.

Visiak, E. H. *Buccaneer Ballads*. London: Elkin Matthews, 1910.

The Voyages and Adventures of Edward Teach, Commonly Called Black Beard, the Notorious Pirate. Newcastle, 1800.

Ward, Edward. *The London-Spy Compleat, in Eighteen Parts. The First Volume of the Author's Writings*. 4th ed. London, 1719.

———. *The Rambling Rakes: Or, London Libertines*. London, 1700.

———. *The Wooden World Dissected, in the Character of a Ship of War*. 3d ed. London, 1744.

Watson, Harold Francis. *The Sailor in English Fiction and Drama: 1550–1800*. New York: Columbia University Press, 1931.

Watt, Ian. *The Rise of the Novel*. Berkeley: University of California Press, 1957

White, Hayden V. *Metahistory: The Historical Imagination in Nineteenth-Century Europe*. Baltimore: Johns Hopkins University Press, 1975.

The Whole Tryal, Examination, and Condemnation of all the Pirates, That was Try'd and Condemn'd by the High Court of Admiralty, at the Session-House in the Old Bailey; on Wednesday and Thursday, the 26. and 27. of this instant May, 1725. For several Inhumane Murders and Notorious Pyracies, by them committed on the High Seas. London, 1725.

Wiegman, Robyn. "Economics and the Body: Gendered Sites in *Robinson Crusoe* and *Roxana*." *Criticism* 31, no. 1 (1989): 33–51.

William R. [William I]. "Their Majesties Declaration for Encouragement of Officers, Seamen and Mariners, Employed in the Present Service." London, 1689.

Wilmot, John. *The Poems of John Wilmot, Earl of Rochester*. Ed. Keith Walker. Oxford: Basil Blackwell, 1984.

Zahedieh, Nuala. "The Merchants of Port Royal, Jamaica, and the Spanish Contraband Trade, 1655–1692." *William and Mary Quarterly* 43 (October 1986): 570–93.

Index

About the Author

After working at ABC News for almost a decade, Hans Turley moved from New York to Seattle, went back to school, and received his Ph.D. from the University of Washington in 1994. He has received several predoctoral and postdoctoral fellowships from such libraries as the Huntington in California, and the Ransom Center at the University of Texas at Austin. He has published articles and reviews in such journals as *Radical Teacher, Eighteenth-Century Studies,* and *Studies in the Novel.* He is coeditor of the journal *The Eighteenth-Century: Theory and Interpretation.*

After two years as a tenure-track assistant professor at Texas Tech University, Turley moved to the University of Connecticut at Storrs in 1998 as a tenure-track assistant professor. He teaches the Restoration and eighteenth-century British literature, as well as classes in short fiction and gay and lesbian studies. He is particularly interested in the novel. He is beginning research on a long project that looks at the fiction and primary texts surrounding the 1688 abdication of James II. Turley lives in Willimantic, Connecticut, with his partner and their dog.